Utopia and Organization

A selection of previous *Sociological Review* Monographs

The Sociology of Monsters[†]
ed. John Law

Sport, Leisure and Social Relations[†]
eds John Horne, David Jary and Alan Tomlinson

Gender and Bureaucracy*
eds Mike Savage and Anne Witz

The Sociology of Death: theory, culture, practice*
ed. David Clark

The Cultures of Computing
ed. Susan Leigh Star

Theorizing Museums*
ed. Sharon Macdonald and Gordon Fyfe

Consumption Mattters*
eds Stephen Edgell, Kevin Hetherington and Alan Warde

Ideas of Difference*
eds Kevin Hetherington and Rolland Munro

The Laws of the Markets*
ed. Michael Callon

Actor Network Theory and After*
eds John Law and John Hassard

Whose Europe? The turn towards democracy*
eds Dennis Smith and Sue Wright

Renewing Class Analysis*
eds Rosemary Cromptom, Fiona Devine, Mike Savage and John Scott

Reading Bourdieu on Society and Culture
ed. Bridget Fowler

The Consumption of Mass
ed. Nick Lee and Rolland Munro

The Age of Anxiety: Conspiracy Theory and the Human Sciences
eds Jane Parish and Martin Parker

[†]Available from The Sociological Review Office, Keele University, Keele, Staffs ST5 5BG.
*Available from Marston Book Services, PO Box 270, Abingdon, Oxon OX14 4YW.

The Sociological Review Monographs

Since 1958 *The Sociological Review* has established a tradition of publishing Monographs on issues of general sociological interest. The Monograph is an edited book length collection of research papers which is published and distributed in association with Blackwell Publishers. We are keen to receive innovative collections of work in sociology and related disciplines with a particular emphasis on exploring empirical materials and theoretical frameworks which are currently under-developed. If you wish to discuss ideas for a Monograph then please contact the Monographs Editor, Martin Parker, at *The Sociological Review*, Keele University, Newcastle-under-Lyme, North Staffordshire, ST5 5BG, Email m.parker@mngt.keele.ac.uk

Utopia and Organization

Edited by Martin Parker

Blackwell Publishing/The Sociological Review

Copyright © The Editorial Board of the Sociological Review 2002

First published in 2002

Blackwell Publishing
108 Cowley Road, Oxford OX4 1JF, UK

and
350 Main Street
Malden, MA 02148, USA

British Library Cataloguing in Publication Data

A CIP catalogue record for this book is available from the British Library

Library of Congress Cataloging-in-Publication Data applied for

ISBN 1-4051-0072-9

This book is printed on acid-free paper.

Contents

Utopia and the organizational imagination: outopia

Martin Parker

Things fall apart; the centre cannot hold;
Mere anarchy is loosed upon the world,
The blood-dimmed tide is loosed, and everywhere
The ceremony of innocence is drowned;
The best lack all conviction, while the worst
Are full of passionate intensity.

WB Yeats 'The Second Coming' (1921)

As I am writing this, people are dying in the ruins of the World Trade Centre. It is difficult to imagine a more symbolic representation of hierarchical corporate capitalism and its tragic global consequences. The New York skyline has, in countless films, become the epitome of modernity. It is the backdrop to tales of the modern and its skyscrapers are iconic symbols of power and wealth. Originally the term 'skyscraper' was used to describe the highest sail on a ship. Such height was an attempt to touch the sky and catch the wind to places not yet visited. A glittering and breath-taking dream of aspiration that lifted vision from the ground. But the dream always looked better from a distance. Within the concrete canyons of Manhattan, height is not visible but the chaotic clamour of wealth and poverty is. The vertical clarity of longing seems a long way from the streets. But now a new image is forever superimposed over the countless reproductions of this glimmering city. Two jet liners, again icons of technological possibility. Screaming, blood and death. Utopia has collapsed, and we are left with flags and armies and crusades once more. This seems the worst of times to be writing about dreams and aspiration.

But what might that mean? Beginning a book on utopia with the idea that utopianism has ended seems positively perverse, yet celebrating glorious dreams in the face of actual nightmares seems insensitive. Surely only the inhabitants of ivory towers could continue to write whilst the ruins of other towers lie smouldering? To make matters worse, and as many of the chapters in this book argue, perhaps utopia is the problem anyway. It is precisely because our gods, kings, presidents and scientists have dreamed of order and purity that we have often tried to organize the world according to a grand plan, whether it be Versailles or trains that run on time. The tragedy that endlessly follows from such hubris should surely teach us that such dreams are dangerous. Raising our dreams this high makes them highly vulnerable. So it is not utopias that we need but pragmatism, modesty and realism. Small stories to replace the grand narratives that only ever end up with yet another final solution. Or, taking a managerialist spin, we need a more sensible third way of thinking about connecting means and ends. If we have visions and missions, then let them be expressed in vision and mission statements and given clear benchmarks. There is no point in asking for the moon on a stick, but we can produce cheap sticks through a sensible division of labour and sell them with effective market segmentation strategies. Leave the moon for dreamers.

There have been a massive number of attempts to think about the literary, historical and political meaning of utopias[1], but this book seeks to do something rather different. As my remarks above hinted, utopia can also be thought of as an organizational matter. That is to say, utopias are statements of alternative organization, attempts to put forward plans which remedy the perceived shortcomings of a particular present age. The essays collected here are by writers who are interested in organizations and organizing in the broadest of terms. In some sense then, this is a book about the sociology of organizing, and it is this that I want to stress in response to the doubts and provocations which I expressed to begin with. Organizing, in the sense that I want to suggest here, is the attempt to collect and divide people and things according to some kind of pattern. It is the process that constitutes the social, that constructs differences and similarities across space and time. Sometimes, but by no means always, this results in quasi-objects called organizations. These objects – universities, corporations, states, the World Trade Organisation – have structural properties that pattern organizing processes in fairly specific ways. They are not structures, in the sense that buildings are[2], but rather slower processes with more specific mechanisms for organizing space and time.

I am not attempting to resolve the meanderings of sociology's structure and agency debate here, simply to open up a generous understanding of the word 'organization'. My point in doing this is to suggest that there are many ways of organizing, and hence many different kinds of organization that might be produced. If you like, this is to insist on recognizing the sheer diversity of ways that human beings have organized themselves. Some of these different forms of organization can be treated as variables, almost in the way that organizational contingency theorists from the 1960s onwards have suggested their curiously a-political 'best fit' between organizational structures and environmental conditions. This means that different forms of hierarchy, legitimacy, codification of rules, processes of selection and socialization, distribution of resources, spatial and temporal arrangements can result in organizations as different as a monastic order or a city state, a feminist co-operative or a multi-national corporation[3]. Organizing can be done in many different ways.

Nowadays, however, it seems that there are an increasing number of people who believe that most of these alternatives should be consigned to the dustbin of history. The sciences of management, the proclamations of management gurus and the policies of more or less liberal pro-market politicians are consolidating into a kind of consensus. Not all of these people are speaking in the same way for the same reasons, but the end result is a general faith in what might be called market managerialism (Frank, 2000; Parker, 2002). Canonical to this faith are the activities of managers, the intellectual enterprise of the business school and the social activity of management. This is combined with the proposition that there is one best way to do exchange, a very specific interpretation of something called 'the market'⁴. Whether the topic at hand is healthcare, education, production, consumption or globalization, it is assumed that 'the market' forms a kind of horizon within which all organizations must operate. Management is the process by which the hidden hands of this market can be understood, and managers are its palm readers.

In summary then, organizing can be done in many ways, but at the moment is being narrowed to one best way. As Marie Louise Berneri wrote immediately after the Second World War:

> Our age is an age of compromises, of half-measures, of the lesser evil. Visionaries are derided or despised, and 'practical men' rule our lives. (1971:1)

But does this mean that utopianism has ended? Berneri thought not, but that was fifty years ago. Nowadays it seem that the 'practical men' have an even tighter grip on our organizational imaginations. A market managerial way of thinking would normally be described as realistic rather than utopian, and this is hence to define utopia in a very specific way – which Jacques, in this volume, calls 'crypto-utopian'. If utopian means 'impractical' or 'unrealistic' then it is, by definition, the opposite of sensible managerial strategies to organize the world. And, of course, who would want to be impractical and unrealistic? Only someone who wanted to withdraw from the world, and who wished to have no influence over the matters that concern everyday folk. But let me twist this a bit, as Jacques does, and slowly introduce the awkward matter of politics into this discussion. As I argued above, market managerialism is but one organizational alternative amongst many, yet it has become hegemonic. Many authors might argue that this hegemony has been achieved because of its superiority to other organizational forms, the work of Francis Fukuyama being probably the most widely known and generalized example (1992). Hence, as Grey and Garsten's chapter illustrates, the popularity of the metaphor of slow moving dinosaurs being replaced by agile and smarter forms, such as market liberalism, globalization and democracy. In other words, alternatives died out because they didn't work. There is a neat story of progress at work here, one that can be told in terms of a certain kind of inevitability. Whether framed as evolutionary adaptation, complexity and systems theory, free market liberalization, third way managerialism or the onward march of the human spirit, the point is that utopian alternatives are actually dystopian because they don't (and can't) work. According to these accounts, the judgement of history is one of inductive practicality. If it hasn't worked so far, it won't work in the future.

But let us note a few things here, and in so doing comment on the organization of the concepts that frame this negative view of utopia. The first point is a fairly obvious question of what gets termed utopian. For many years futurologists (academic and guru) have sold volumes of speculation on a huge scale. Authors like Peter Drucker, Daniel Bell, Alvin Toffler, Tom Peters, Charles Handy, Peter Senge and even Bill Gates have all written within a genre of book length fantasy which proposes that people will be happier, richer and smarter if the world is organized in such-and-such a way. Often they might claim that they are merely extrapolating present trends, that they have their noses to the wind and so on but, whatever their tenuous connections with some kind of empirical research, these books are still essentially speculative. In this sense, it is quite possible to treat the various epochal labels that have been deployed in this genre – post-industrialism, post-capitalism, information society, leisure society, postmodernism[5] and so on – as being modestly unimaginative versions of utopia. As Reedy shows in his chapter, instead of *The Republic*, *The City of the Sun* or *The New Atlantis*, we have a teetering pile of glossy books celebrating markets, managers and technology. It is an odd trick of marketing and conceptual confusion that allows these books not to be labelled utopian, but what is even more remarkable is that they are taken to be descriptively grounded and prescriptively important. These are utopias that matter.

Policy makers, politicians, managers and academics do not spend hours and pages discussing how to realize More's original *Utopia*, Andrea's *Christianopolis* or De Foigny's *New Discovery of Terra Incognita Australis*. Yet they do invest very substantial amounts of time and money on more contemporary dreams of a brave new world. The point I am making here is that the decision about what gets labelled utopian, and what is practical speculation, is a rather fragile one. It is one that reflects a prior division between the realm of the practical and the realm of the dreamer. This division closes off alternatives, not by no longer performing utopian thought, but by defining most forms of utopianism as not being part of reasonable alternatives. So a pro-market managerialism which is utopian in form gets naturalized and justified at the same time that discussions of other ways of thinking about organizing are closeted as curios. As Mannheim taught us (see Ackroyd, this volume) this is the way that ideology operates. Ideology tells us that this is the way that the world is, and the way it should be and will be. Radical alternatives do not need to be suppressed or burnt in the streets, merely labelled as utopian. That in itself is enough to consign them to the quiet graves of the library shelves, to be periodically rediscovered by historians and literary critics.

Another way of telling this account, and perhaps of explaining the source of this ideology trick, is to examine who wins in the market managerial utopias. Plato celebrated the philosophers, Bacon the scientists and Morris the craft worker. Contemporary managerial utopias celebrate a different set of winners – the heroic leader, the entrepreneur, the excellent company, the portfolio worker. These characters manage to surf the waves of change, understand global markets and find self-actualization (Lightfoot and Lilley, this volume). The losers are those people and places that don't embrace change. Market protectionism, state interference, the friction caused by the values held by certain communities or occupations, bureaucratic proceduralism and so on are presented as obstacles to winning. If the losers are mentioned at all, people working in shit jobs in export processing zones for shit wages (for example), they are framed as under-developed and insufficiently modernised. After all, descriptions of working poverty, massive inequality, environmental degradation and a militarized new world order cannot be reasonably considered to be utopian. Market managerial utopias can only be constructed if such matters are either ignored or held to be temporary inconveniences. These are certainly selective, fantastic and imaginary accounts, but not categorized as such.

So it could be argued that utopianism has not ended, but it is mostly no longer called utopianism and has an increasingly conservative character. These are utopias which take the dominant ideas from the most favoured parts of the first world and then generalize them through airport bookstalls across the globe. At the moment, generalized market managerial common-sense seems inevitable, logical and complete. However, this is not to say that it is uncontested. There are also many fantastically dystopian visions of what the present age is, and what it might become. Sometimes these are expressed in the careful language of intellectuals, McDonaldization or the Foucauldian version of the panopticon for example (Ritzer, 2000; Foucault, 1991), sometimes through science fiction and fantasy (Smith *et al.* 2001; Lightfoot and Lilley, this volume) or even popular versions of conspiracy theory (Parish and Parker, 2001). The point here though is that these are largely negative visions. They are pictures of the present, sometimes masquerading as the near future, that continue in the tradition of *Brave New World* and *1984*. Rather than inspiring visions, these are cautionary tales. They are accounts of what we must not become, or why we should regret what we have done so far. By definition, dystopias do not propose anything but horror and scepticism. If the reader embraces the horror, they *might* be energized to do something to avoid it (possibly even something utopian), but that consequence is not provided for in the dystopia itself.

So, as Yeats puts it in my epigraph, it seems that at the present time 'the best lack all conviction, while the worst are full of passionate intensity'. He was writing after the poppy fields of the Western Front had been fertilized with the blood of young men, and the age of innocence had become a matter of nostalgia. It is surely no accident that the rise of the dystopian novel can be dated from around then too (Parker 2002). Nowadays we still have plenty of dystopias, and mountains of conservative utopias, but where are the radical utopias? Where are the attempts to put forward alternatives to Berneri's present age of 'practical men'? It is actually rather difficult to imagine what such a work might look like, suspended as we are between cynicism and managerialism. The very idea of attempting to construct an utopia is beset with difficulties, not least that of being accused of being utopian. Yet, as is obvious, it has not always been so, and the present lack of faith in alternatives is the exception rather than the rule. For centuries, the literary utopian vision has been a powerful form of social critique. From Thomas More's original *Utopia*, through Samuel Butler's *Erewhon* and William Morris's *News From Nowhere*, to more recent feminist science fictions like those of Ursula LeGuin and Marge Piercy, alternative forms of social order have been articulated to cast a critical eye on the oppressions and inanities of the present. Many of these earlier works were constructed as fictions, fables or fantasies precisely in order to avoid the political and authorial problems that might follow from criticizing forms of power too directly.

Yet, in a less explicit way, social theory has had a strongly utopian streak too. From Fourier, Saint-Simon and Comte onwards, functionalist, evolutionary and behaviourist positions, as well as the critical deployments of Marxism, feminism, anti-imperialism and environmentalism, have implicitly relied on a vision of a better world, a more transparent society within which 'knowledge' banishes ignorance, cruelty, mysticism, disorganization and words like 'democracy', 'communication', 'sovereignty', 'autonomy' and so on actually come to refer to principles in practice (Kumar, 1991:31; Knights and Willmott, this volume). The common confusion over the word 'ideal' in Weber's 'ideal type' crystallizes this movement rather nicely. So much radical social science still implicitly or explicitly trades on assumptions about the world being otherwise than it is, but it too has been increasingly colonized by the language of practical managerialism and professional academic practice. To take these in turn, the administration of both research and teaching has become increasingly oriented to deliverables and objectives. State policy makers, in the name of employers, determine what should be researched (enterprise, consumption, the e-conomy) and also what kind of transferable skills and learning objectives should be conveyed and performed within defined programmes of study. Within such administered horizons, radical utopian intent must inevitably wither in favour of small steps and small wins. It is difficult to think hard about the future when the problems of practicality, methodology, subject benchmarks and work-related competencies bind researchers and teachers so tightly to a managerial present. At the same time, a substantial apparatus of dissemination through certain kinds of journals and books increasingly defines the nature of the successful academic career. Whilst it may be possible to study utopias, and get any resulting texts published in learned journals, it is difficult to practice utopianism. Learning the mundane tricks of the academic profession almost always involves bracketing such dreams for other parts of the day and night, a form of separation (or inauthenticity) that Fournier discusses towards the end of her contribution to this book.

But, as I suggested earlier, there is another impediment to the realization of radical utopianism at the present time. If managerialists see utopianism as a pointless form of idealism, then a generation of intellectuals brought up in the shadow of the linguistic turn see utopia as a road to hell, however often it is paved with good intentions. Or, rather, as a symptom of the megalomaniac desire to produce order and control through blueprints of progress. This, I think, is the dominant theme for many of the authors in this book. From the second half of the 20th century onwards, a new social theoretical orthodoxy of heterodoxy has emerged which wraps together masculinity, imperialism, science, heterosexuality, humanism, nationalism, capitalism and a range of associated terms and attaches them to a story of hubris. These dominant ideologies or discourses[6] are then, through a dizzying variety of subaltern engagements, exposed for their simultaneous partiality and arrogance. In so doing, the entanglements of the particular allow for a re-telling of other histories, and for new voices (human, and non-human) to enter the academy. On the detailed level, as the chapters by Knights and Willmott, and Law and Mol show, this is undoubtedly all to the good. There is no point in pretending that the world is coherent, complete, transparent, controllable and so on, when this is obviously not the case. However, I feel that the general morality tale that then might follow has some more questionable consequences. For those persuaded by this spirit of the age, what ties the list of epistemological arrogances together is their belief in grand solutions, in the totalizing nature of their visions for organizing the world. It is because of these kind of over-extended assumptions that we end up with the death camps, nuclear weapons and the gulag archipelago. Or now, with a further militarized version of the *Pax Americana* which is unfolding across the globe.

So it is the very faith in social engineering (whether in railways or other work places) through the technologies of power, which produces consequences which are globally dystopian. This attitude, often crudely summarized as 'postmodernism', is now argued to have dealt a final blow to these grand narratives of progress and emancipation. We are said to have lost faith in utopianism, in the perfectibility of the human species. For Giddens, utopianism becomes awkwardly attached to realism, and from Lyotard to Bauman, it seems that it is this very quest for utopia that leads us to subscribe to forms of social organization that end up being deeply oppressive. So, for Burrell and Dale in this volume, the attempt to control nature as if it were a garden excludes or constrains that which is deemed to be wild, that which always spills over and confuses all our attempts at order. There is much to be commended in these arguments, and in a more careful and humble understanding of human being in the world as a commonplace utopia (Munro, this volume). Yet the move from specific engagements with forms of ideology, or the insistence on the locatability of all social practices, can easily end up as a general dismissal of any notion of progress, and hence another nail in the coffin of radical utopianism. Perhaps this is for the best, and we should (with Voltaire's Candide, and Rolland Munro) just cultivate our own gardens, and not insist on tidying up everybody else's.

It seems that radical utopianism is beset on all sides. The managerialists would suggest that it is unrealistic, and incapable of formulating sensible connections between practical means and achievable ends. The only utopias that they will accept are those that market themselves with the breathless hyperbole of global capitalism. The intellectuals would suggest that radical utopianism is dangerous, because utopias turn into places where people use any means and legitimise them with glorious ends. In the end, force of one kind or another takes the place of reason. And, if those two were not enough, the state of the world leads many to believe that passionate cynicism or even principled withdrawal are more coherent responses. Dystopias are cooler than utopias right now, and questions of style have a way of becoming questions of substance. The disaster movie destruction of the World Trade Centre, the lonely wailing of mothers for children killed by missiles, or the quieter starvation of millions, do not establish easy conditions for radical utopian thought.

Utopia, the latin neologism coined by Thomas More in 1516, seems to have been intended to have two possible meanings (Turner, 1965). The first, *outopia*, means 'not-place'. Utopia is nowhere. In the face of the present, this seems the best way to leave matters. There is not much else to say, since passionate conviction seems to carry such high costs, and no leap of logic justifies it sufficiently. I will now let the authors speak for themselves, framed as they are by the context in which I have set them. The second part of this essay, and the second meaning of More's neologism, will be found at the end of this book[7].

Notes

1 See, for a good short introduction, Kumar, 1991 and for a collection, Carey, 1999.
2 Though – since glass flows, bricks crumble and jet planes destroy – even buildings can be considered to be processes too in a longer term sense.
3 They can also result in quasi-organizations like families, friendship networks, communities or cultures but this chapter is primarily focussed on formal organization, so I don't propose to develop this issue any further here.
4 Again, a form of organization in which processes are constrained by general rules. For more on the socially constructed and historically specific nature of markets, see Callon (1998) and Fournier in this volume.
5 Though this last one also has some more interesting connotations too, see Parker (1992), and the discussion later in the chapter.
6 The latter being a more popular term at the moment.
7 A book organized, as the perceptive reader will note, as a movement from pessimism to optimism. My apologies to all my authors for framing their work in such a wilfully utopian manner, and against the avowed intentions and understandings of most of their essays. My sincere thanks to them too, for writing such splendid essays.

References

Berneri, M. (1971) *Journey Through Utopia*. New York: Schocken.
Callon, M. (ed.) (1998) *The Laws of the Markets*. Oxford: Blackwell.
Carey, J. (ed.) (1999) *The Faber Book of Utopias*. London: Faber & Faber.
Foucault, M. (1991) *Discipline and Punish*. London: Penguin.
Fukuyama, F. (1992) *The End of History and the Last Man*. London: Penguin.
Kumar, K. (1991) *Utopianism*. Milton Keynes: Open University Press.
Parker, M. (1992) 'Post-modern Organizations or Postmodern Organization Theory?' *Organization Studies*, 13/1: 1–17.
Parish, J. and Parker, M. (eds) (2001) *The Age of Anxiety: Conspiracy Theory and the Human Sciences*. Oxford: Blackwell.
Parker, M. (2002) *Against Management*. Cambridge: Polity.
Ritzer, G. (2000) *The McDonaldization of Society*. Thousand Oaks, CA: Pine Forge.
Smith, W., Higgins, M., Parker, M. and Lightfoot, G. (eds) (2001) *Science Fiction and Organization*. London: Routledge.
Turner, P. (1965) 'Introduction', in More, T *Utopia*. London: Penguin.

Organized and disorganized utopias: an essay on presumption

Christopher Grey and Christina Garsten

Introduction

In this chapter we give attention to a broad sweep of utopian thought, considering the place of organization and disorganization within such thought. We intend organization to capture both its normal meaning within organization theory, that is, the organization of work; and its generic meaning of social organization, which brings us into the realms of political and social theory. Since utopias are typically social and political philosophies about how the world should best be arranged, it is unsurprising that organization has a key place within them. We have subtitled the piece as 'an essay on presumption' because the core of our stance on utopianism is that it frequently entails presumptions of knowledge, about the world and about what is best for other people, which are not just distasteful in principle but also, often, horrific in their consequences.

We trace a story of modern utopian thinking which distinguishes between organized and disorganized utopias. Like any other framework, this one can hardly capture, and presumably distorts, the complexity and variety of what it purports to classify. But it does have the merit of identifying at least one axis – organization and disorganization – which runs through utopian thought and links this to various kinds of political and social arrangement. For utopias have typically imagined a society which is either perfectly organized or one which eschews organization in favour of a perfect disorganization where freedom from regulation reigns. We do not suggest that this axis is the only one of relevance and, in particular, we draw distinctions between utopias, whether organized or disorganized, which are based upon differing political principles, for example those of state socialism or the free market.

We give particular attention to the place of work within utopian thinking. For whilst organization figures as a guiding thread in terms of utopian political thinking, the arrangement of productive activity is so central to almost any conceivable polity that utopian thinkers have tended to treat it extensively. In disorganized utopias the key issue is: how will any work get done at all and how, since it is a collective activity, can it be co-ordinated? In organized utopias the key issue is: how can work be arranged so as to be precisely and efficiently correlated with societal aims? Given the scope of these concerns, we will perhaps be forgiven for wandering between rather different levels of analysis and across domains of political history and theory as well as sociology and organizational theory. Indeed, it is central to our stance on organizational theory that it is always inseparable from political rationalities, and that the traditional understanding of organization theory as a purely technical discipline is one which is indefensibly narrow (cf MacIntyre, 1981). Moreover, we take it to be important to locate contemporary discussions about organization within a historical frame of reference.

We begin with a brief account of what we understand utopia to be: namely, a blueprint for a desired world which is nevertheless located in present day concerns. We then discuss the ways in which organization and work feature in utopian thought, taking the examples of Fourier and Saint-Simon. The next section considers the politics of utopianism primarily in terms of its link with totalitarianism, which we judge to be a consequence of the presumption of utopians to know what the world is and should be. This totalitarianism provided an impetus for the development of the anti-utopianism of Popper and Hayek, which are the subject of the next section, and which we interpret as having fed, ironically, into a market utopianism that has recently taken on a radical new form. This we understand to be the utopia (or utopias) of disorganized capitalism and central to it are new understandings of work. Having outlined that utopia we return in a conclusion to the theme of presumption, to argue that the new market utopians of global capitalism can be criticized in similar terms to those we employed in our discussion of the totalitarian outcomes of more familiar forms of utopian thinking.

Utopia and reality

Utopias are commonly understood as transcending reality, time and place and have often been described as unrealistic for this reason (eg Williams, 1965:176). Nothing could be further from the truth. Utopias are intimately tied to the historical and social milieu in which they arise. In one sense, which appears both significant and trivial, we could say that the very possibility of formulating a utopia, so called, only emerges once Thomas More had made this coinage in the 16th century. In another sense, we could say that the content of utopias reflects very specific preoccupations: either positing a utopia in radical opposition to, or by extrapolation from, the here and now. Karl Mannheim, in his classic analysis *Ideology and Utopia* makes exactly this point:

> Change in substance and form of the utopia does not take place in a realm which is independent of social life. It could be shown rather, especially in modern historical developments, that the successive forms of utopia, in their beginnings are intimately bound up with given historical stages of development, and in each of these with particular social strata. (Mannheim, 1936/1960:185)

Moreover, for Mannheim utopias refer to imagined or wished for versions of the human condition which are envisaged as actually happening in the world. No matter how 'impractical' they may be, utopias are thereby to be distinguished from religious conceptions of paradise or other unworldly constructs.

The significance of understanding utopias as being, in these various senses, related to reality is twofold. On the one hand, it means that they can be analysed sociologically and politically (rather than, for example, theologically). On the other hand, it means that we should never forget how intimately utopian thinking is related to human experience and, often, suffering as well as to human imagination. If, as Marx polemically claimed, the aim of philosophy is to change the world, then utopianism can lay fair claim to philosophical success albeit often in ways which were unintended and sometimes horrific, of which more later.

Utopia, work and organization

It is a longstanding feature of philosophical anthropology to distinguish between *homo faber* and *animal laborans* (Arendt, 1958:136). Whereas as the latter merely lives in the world, the former 'works upon' the world. For Arendt, as for Marx and many others, working upon the world is taken to be a defining feature of the human condition. We have already indicated that the organization of work is an important issue for utopians, yet it is understood in two rather different ways. In this section we explore these by comparing the 18th-century utopian thinking of Fourier and Saint-Simon, who can be thought of as representing these two enduring approaches to work and, consequently, two traditions of envisaging organization within utopia.

For Fourier, work had a double edge to it:

> Freedom from worry is a form of happiness experienced by the animals. But it is also a human right, although it can only be enjoyed in Civilization by the very rich. Far from being careless of the morrow, nine-tenths of civilized men are worried about the present day because they are obliged to devote themselves to loathsome work that is forced upon them. And so on Sunday they go to cafes and places of amusement to enjoy a few moments of the sort of carefreeness that is vainly sought by so many rich men who are themselves pursued by anxiety (cited in Beecher and Bienvenu, 1971:142).

It was Fourier's emphasis on passional fulfilment, on the flowering of the passions, as Man's destiny, that made his utopia unusual. He believed the great task of social thought to be to show how work and the desire for pleasure could be reconciled. Whereas some 18th century utopians had been content to remain rather vague about work, Fourier insisted on a meticulous discussion of the subject. In his version of the basic social and economic unit of utopia, the Phalanx, the proper relationship between the passions and work would be established. This relationship, as Fourier saw it, was reciprocal: the appeasement of man's desires depended on the products of labour; but work, in turn, could be nothing but 'eternal torture', unless it was performed at the urging of the passions (Beecher and Bienvenu, 1971:42–43).

Charles Fourier agreed with his contemporary and fellow 'utopian socialist', Henri de Saint-Simon, that work occupied a low place in European society's scale of values, but insisted that if men had little love for work, it was with good reason. Work was a man's destiny, but so too were happiness, comfort, and rich passionate fulfilment. While he agreed that work was a central social problem, he would not join the chorus of classical economists, bourgeois moralists, and socialist theorists, who were praising work and attempting to restore the value of work as a religious or social duty and value in itself (Beecher and Bienvenu, 1971:27–28). Compared to many of his contemporaries, Fourier was seen to be a romantic reactionary, a prophet with a vision at odds with the practical world (which is to say, even other utopians accused him of utopianism). But his thinking represents one branch of what was to become a significant schism in utopian thought – namely that of libertarian anarchism (Carter, 1971:21).

The other branch can be seen as represented in the work of Saint-Simon, and the contrast is apparent not least in the latter's appreciation of the practicalities of industry. For Saint-Simon, *les industriels* are to be compared positively with the bureaucrats who are parasites. *Les industriels*, unlike later socialist analysis, encompassed not just workers but also, and perhaps particularly, entrepreneurs and business leaders. In formulations that find a curious contemporary echo, at least in the Anglo-Saxon world, Saint-Simon suggests that the sole test of the desirability of a law is whether it is useful or harmful to industry. His utopian vision is one of order and efficiency rather than either democracy or passion. In a sense he could be called the first managerial utopian, by virtue of his preoccupation with means rather than ends. Certainly he placed rationality centre stage, believing that utopia could be achieved without compulsion since human rationality would itself lead inexorably to his desired state of affairs. This stress on an organized, rational world marks Saint-Simon out as very much of his time, the late 18th and early 19th century. A disciple of Auguste Comte, the 'founder' of positivism, he exemplifies one highly significant trend in Enlightenment social philosophy and expresses one kind of modernist utopia. The Saint-Simonians, who were competing with Fourier for a following, advocated authoritarian psychological and vocational theories, and they contended that their industrial psychology was superior to Fourier's precisely because it was based on the rational principles of hierarchy and authority.

Underlying these different apprehensions of work we can see distinct formulations of human nature. In one tradition, work appears as a passion and a psychological necessity. Work is part of what makes us human, and fulfilling work is part of what makes us fulfilled humans. Given these assumptions, the utopian task is to structure a society which allows work to be meaningful and expressive of passions. In the second tradition, work is something which, whilst central to human existence in that it is necessary, is viewed with antipathy by individual human beings. At the very least, instead of people working together harmoniously if left to their own desires, the Saint-Simonian tradition implies the need to corral human effort so as to ensure the efficient discharge of work.

These assumptions about human nature are not, of course, confined to work. At root they reflect conflicting views about whether human beings can live together without regulation or whether, if so left, they will tend to abuse each others' rights and act in an anti-social manner. Perhaps even more fundamentally, they reflect different views on whether human beings are or are not naturally good and whether they are or are not naturally selfish. In political philosophy this distinction is normally expressed in terms of the difference between Rousseau, who regarded the state of nature as one of harmony and mutual respect, and Hobbes (and, in less dramatic vein, Locke) who saw the state of nature as at least having the tendency to degenerate to a condition of a war of all against all. In a mutated form we find a similar polarity in much management thinking captured, for example, by McGregor's distinction between theory X and theory Y management. In the former, work is something which will be avoided in the absence of coercive management, in the latter, something which will be embraced if people have fulfilling work and a degree of self-management.

At the extreme, these distinctions flow to the propositions either that work will only get done if it is organized and managed or that work will best get done if people have freedom to self-organize and manage. Thus work and the bundle of assumptions about human nature which go with work mutate, in utopian thought, into a distinction between organized and disorganized utopias. In the former, work must be systematically organized; in the latter all will be well if people are left to their own devices. Needless to say, such assumptions have implications also for a range of issues about the extent of democracy and the nature of the State.

From hope to horror: Utopianism and 20th-century politics

Although the utopians we have discussed so far are usually designated as some species of socialist, they (along with others such as Robert Owen, William Morris and, in the 20th Century, Simone Weil) depict a form of socialism which is at odds with Marxism. Marx himself was dismissive of 'utopian' socialism and Engels' *Socialism: Utopian and Scientific*, along with the historic split between Marx and Bakunin, Marxism and Anarchism, at the Basel Congress of 1872, initiated a separation between two versions of socialism. The former supposedly was based upon no more than wishful thinking, the latter upon a 'scientific' analysis of economics and class relations. We might consider these versions to be disorganized and organized utopias. At one level, the division is that, within Anarchism and the non-Marxist varieties of socialism, the State either does not figure or only most minimally so. Yet even in Marxism it was understood that the State would wither away after the revolution, and the distinction initially is much more to do with the Marxist version of Party organization and discipline and the primacy of scientific analysis of society. As Marxism mutated into Stalinism in the Soviet Union, both statism and party discipline became a point of distinction from Anarchism and other versions of socialism (see Reedy, this volume). But we might additionally argue that the appeal to science made by Marxism carried with it the presumption of authority and a claim to know the truth about the world. It implies both an organization of society and an organization of knowledge.

The bloody apotheosis of these ideational and ideological disputes came during the 1936–39 Spanish Civil War when the CNT anarchists and POUM socialists sought to construct a society based upon localized collective ownership, gender equality, and democratic workplace and military organization. These attempts to operationalize a kind of disorganized utopia in, approximately, the anarchist tradition have been widely described, famously by George Orwell in *Homage to Catalonia* and less famously but perhaps more authentically in Franz Borkenau's *Spanish Cockpit* and Gaston Laval's *Collectives in the Spanish Revolution* (Woodcock, 1977:244ff). It is well known what became of these experiments. Denied arms and, finally, disbanded, arrested, tortured and murdered by the Communists, they ended in black and red blood leaking into the scorched hillsides and plains of the Aragon. And whilst the Communist rationale for this was in part the need for discipline and, note well, *organization* in the fight against Franco, Fascism shortly prevailed in Spain where it endured for almost 50 years.

We might regard this episode as, despite sporadic revivals, a kind of terminal moment for utopias of disorganized socialism. And it marked another kind of death, too. Marxist socialism had arrogated to itself a vision of scientifically inspired social progress and the logic of historical development, embodied in the Soviet Union. In a sense, the dream of progressive rationalism which started with the French Revolution ended with the betrayal in Spain, although there were to be a series of codas in Budapest and Prague in the post-war period. Given these events and, for more recent commentators, the collapse of the Soviet Union, a number of social theorists, such as Daniel Bell (1960), Francis Fukuyama (1989), and Russell Jacoby (1999), have argued, albeit from different standpoints, that utopianism is dead.

Daniel Bell's *The End of Ideology* offered sharp formulations of the exhaustion of old 19th-century ideologies as having being undermined by the horrors of Soviet communism and the success of liberal capitalism. Fukuyama, while sharing Bell's view on the victory of welfare or liberal capitalism over radical ideology, expressed nostalgia for the history of big ideas and robust ideologies, and regretted what he saw as the end of radicalism and ideology. For Europe, a 'growing "Common Marketization"' defines the future, he declared (cited in Jacoby, 1999:9). In *The End of Utopia*, Jacoby declares the death of utopianism to be born out of the exhaustion of political alternatives. A paralysing lack of vision for the future has beset the liberal left to the point where intellectuals and critics can no longer envisage a different society, only a modified one, in which the market, once derided as degrading, is now dubbed rational and humane.

But non-socialist organized utopias have hardly fared better. The dream of a rational and organized society was held not just by Stalinists but was part of a persistent faith within western societies from the Enlightenment onwards. As with Saint-Simon, the vision of a managed society in which efficiency, order and rationality prevailed is one which unites Victorian patriarchs and 20th century social democrats, welfarists, corporatists and technocrats. The charnel-house terminal point of this version of utopia is to be found in the slave labour and death camps of Auschwitz, Dachau, Treblinka, Bergen-Belsen and Ravensbruck – the whole roll call of horror that has indelibly stained and falsified European pretensions to civilization. For, according to Bauman's (1989) compelling analysis, the holocaust, in its industrialized, bureaucratized genocide, was not the antithesis of or an aberration from modern civilization but rather an expression of that very civilization. Although it would be both grotesque and facile to ignore the differences of method and intention between fascism and social democracy, it would, equally, be complacent to ignore their points of commonality. In a passage which clearly links the two, Bauman suggests:

> . . . that the bureaucratic culture which prompts us to view society as an object of administration, as a collection of so many 'problems' to be solved, as 'nature' to be 'controlled', 'mastered' and 'improved' or 'remade', as a legitimate target for social engineering, and in general a garden to be designed and kept in the planned shape by force . . . was the very atmosphere in which the idea of the Holocaust could be conceived . . . developed and brought to its conclusion. (Bauman, 1989:18)

This is how utopias end, then. In blood and betrayal, repression, degradation, mutilation, torture and mass murder: 'the evil tidings of what man's presumption made of man in Auschwitz' (Levi, 1958/1979:61). The word presumption is an informative one here – and we have chosen to use it throughout this chapter – for it is presumption which goes to the heart of the intolerance that characterizes utopianism. As one of the most distinguished political theorists of totalitarianism has observed:

> There has been evident for many centuries in Europe a line of thought on the organization of human society which has many points of resemblance to 'totalitarianism'. This is the type of theorizing about politics usually called Utopianism. (Schapiro, 1972:85)

And so we return to the point that utopianism represents more than otherworldly dreaming. In its organized variants, utopianism creates blueprints for society that – cause would be too strong a word – allow or give licence to real, in this world, horror and suffering. With this very much in mind, we can find from the mid-20th century onwards a set of reactions against organized utopianism, and it is surely by no means coincidental that many of these emerged from Central Europe which had been the cockpit of totalitarianism.

The 'Plan to resist all planning'

The Austrian born philosopher Karl Popper fled Vienna to escape the threat of Fascism. In a series of publications – *The Open Society and its Enemies* (1945), *The Poverty of Historicism* (1957) and *Conjectures and Refutations* (1963) – he developed a version of epistemological provisionalism, the view that we can never say, finally, that we know the truth. This is consistent with his social philosophy in which he criticizes historicism, the doctrine that history develops according to laws which allow prediction. Taken together, these arguments strike a blow at 'scientific socialism' and at fascism, but no less at social democratic social engineering. Popper rejects the possibility of devising arrangements which will have predictable impacts on social relations, although that is not say that small-scale or, as he calls it, 'piecemeal social engineering' should not and can not be attempted. Provisionalism and anti-historicism make out a powerful case against the blueprints and totalitarian tendencies – against the presumption of knowledge – which are the hallmark of organized utopianism. For utopianism, whatever its good intentions may be, 'produces hell' (Popper in Miller, 1983:41). It requires claims to knowledge that we cannot have and a capacity to manage social relations that we can never possess. Popper, in other words, insisted that the idea of utopia is dangerous and violent, and that utopians would crush their opponents.

In an intriguing series of parallels, Friederich von Hayek also left Vienna shortly before the Fascists arrived and, briefly, was Popper's colleague at the London School of Economics. An economist who is now most associated with the monetarism that informed the New Right in the 1980s, he also published, in 1944 – a year before Popper's *The Open Society* – *The Road to Serfdom*. Here and elsewhere Hayek, like Popper, argues against planning on the basis that it inevitably leads to totalitarianism. For Hayek, communism and fascism are merely variants of the same totalitarianism, whilst democratic socialism relies upon general utopian ideals that bring an end to individual liberty. He does not, however, reject utopian thinking in and of itself, which he regards as fundamental to the task of the social scientist. Indeed he devotes considerable space to the elaboration of his version of utopia (Hayek, 1960). Here utopia is conceived of in terms of a spontaneous order ('catallaxy') developing organically and taking the social form of the free market.

We might call this a utopia of disorganized capitalism and to do so is to make a crucial point. Hodgson (1999:6) argues that although utopianism has often been equated with various versions of socialism and collectivism, it is no less applicable to that vision of the free market which neglects the cultural, institutional and social construction of the market. The utopia of the pure free market posits a self-regulating entity operating through autonomous individuals and according to unvarying natural laws and providing optimal solutions not just to economic distribution but also, for example in the work of Nozick (1974), to political and social decision making. The appeal of this version of utopian thinking has been profound, so much so that it often takes on the appearance not of utopia in its pejorative sense but of simple realism: you can't buck the market.

Like many other versions of utopia, the free market rests upon claims about rationality. Partly, in ways analogous but politically diametrically opposite to utopian socialists, this is a matter of a faith in individual, as opposed to systemic, rationality. But also:

> Ironically, Hayek's utopian project was an appeal to reason to limit the scope of rationalist thought. It involved, as Michael Oakeshott wittily remarked, 'a plan to resist all planning' (Hodgson, 1999:8)

As with organized and disorganized socialist utopias, but with more worldly success, market utopias provide a certain kind of blueprint ('a plan to resist all planning') which its proponents aim to bring into existence. In so doing, as to some extent has occurred, utopia can be represented as reality, just as it was in those societies which sought to operationalize socialist utopias. And, as with those societies, the process of creating utopia has created many casualties and much suffering. The free market has its own death camps, more usually called the third world. Proponents of free market utopia would abjure that description and, if they recognized it as meaningful at all, might well argue that once the whole world has been brought into the global market much of the suffering and inequality it engenders will disappear. But this seems to be structurally similar to the argument that once world socialism is achieved then the labour camps will disappear and the state will wither away – and equally 'utopian'.

The New World Order and the new world of work

Although Hayek formulated his free market utopia in the middle of the 20th century, the practical political impact of this type of thinking came later. For, whilst contained within market economies, much of the middle to late 20th century was dominated not by disorganized but by organized capitalism. This distinction, drawn by Lash and Urry (1987), is an instructive one. Organized capitalism is characterized, *inter alia*, by the concentration and centralization of capital, bureaucratization and the growth of an expert managerial class, regional economies built around cities and nations and active state management of economy and society. Disorganized capitalism sees a global rather a nationally focussed economy, with a deconcentration of capital, fragmented and flexible organizational forms, erosion of class as a meaningful identifier and a declining role for the State. We might say that the organized capitalism is redolent of Saint-Simon's organized, managerial utopia and disorganized capitalism more reminiscent of Hayek's disorganized market utopia. Or, to use a different terminology, it is the distinction between the visible and invisible hand.

Organized capitalism is entirely bound up with planning – organizations seeking to exert monopoly control and to design rational bureaucratic structures, state organizations seeking to manage, regulate and intervene in economy and society. But this version of organization and of statecraft has been dealt several hefty blows in the last twenty years: precisely those blows that lead to the observation of disorganized capitalism. These include the gradual dismantling of national regulations and trade barriers, a related retreat from welfarism and corporatism, and the establishment of flexible and entrepreneurial – or post-bureaucratic – organizations as the template for organizational design. In *Pessimism*, Bailey (1988:73–76) describes the healing capacities of the free market, neo-liberal utopia, in which the paradise of the fully liberated, deregulated market competition finds the shortest and cheapest way to riches and happiness:

> Basically society is seen as a natural order in which satisfactory social institutions arise unintentionally. Interference, conscious design via planning and 'politicization' of social provision are all seen as dangerous disruptions of a spontaneous social order. (Bailey: 1988:75)

Given this naturalism, it is unsurprising that market utopias currently have the appearance of realism since this realism is both a condition (they informed its development) and a consequence (they are informed by its development) of something like a global free market. Moreover, the appearance of realism is bolstered by the lack of grandiosity of some versions of current market utopias: they are rather myopic, manageable little utopias in bounded, limited places. While the Disney corporation may have invented the idea of the 'branded city', the gated community at once a homage to American dreams and an escape from the very same society, 'branded places' are now being established throughout the Western world. Theme parks, shopping malls, cruise ships, and towns imitate the Disney concept to offer part-time experiences of market utopia. In Naomi Klein's words (2001:157), 'there is something undeniably seductive about these branded worlds', having to do with 'the genuine thrill of utopianism, or the illusion of it, at any rate'.

While these little utopias provide their own versions of order and harmony, we do not find in them what was offered by the more grandiose versions of utopia; large-scale, designed, and organized social systems. They are merely islands in a sea of disorganized market capitalism, offering a sense of concrete place and authenticity in hyberglobality. However, this should not disguise the fact that there is also a 'big picture' for the utopia of disorganized capitalism. Although deriving from a logic of the spontaneous market, there is a considerable political effort involved in constructing this market (which parallels the point made earlier that it is this inconsistency that allows us to say that market utopias are just that). Institutions such as the World Trade Organization and the European Union play an active role both in the framing of rules and the articulation of legitimation for the utopian vision they are pursuing.

In recent times, this has attracted direct attention from the burgeoning anti-globalization movement (see Fournier, this volume). A case in point is the grassroots movement Attac (l'Association pour la taxation des transactions financières pour l'aidre aux citoyens), a fast-growing organization propagating 'humane globalization' as their ideal version of future society. The Attac Founder Ignacio Ramonet has claimed that the globalization of capital has created among people a sense of insecurity. The hyperglobal market now surpasses the nation-state as a basic instance for democracy, and has given rise to a new form of statehood. This state is a supernational one, with its own structures, spheres of power, and frames of action. The cluster of the IMF, OECD, WTO, and the World Bank plays a significant role in governing this new supranational nation-state and praises the virtues of the market. This is, furthermore, a state with no society (Clinell, 2000:11–12).

It is clear, to return to our opening theme, that, as with other utopias, work occupies a central place in that of disorganized capitalism. To be sure, it would seriously overstate the case to claim that organized and industrial capitalism are necessarily finished, or even in overall decline, and that new forms of work are in the ascendant (Warhurst & Thompson, 1998; Bradley *et al.*, 2000). But that is not the point. Utopian thinking does not describe reality but, as we noted earlier, expresses a vision of reality which reacts against or extrapolates from certain features of the present. The utopias associated with disorganized capitalism are important because they are influential, not because they are unchallenged and certainly not because they are accurate descriptions of the present.

The new utopia is distinctive in that it speaks of alternative work organizations and a different breed of workers. Interestingly, in doing so, it takes over some of the language of disorganized socialism in its rejection of the state and embrace of self-management – albeit with very different aims and effects. Perhaps a key issue is that of human nature assumptions, which we discussed in relation to the main traditions of philosophical and utopian thought earlier in this chapter. For the new market utopians, there is a blending of these traditions so that whilst the market posits the existence of autonomous self-interested individuals, the descriptions of work point towards an image of fulfilled and committed labour. A number of recent volumes have announced the end of work and employment as we in the West have known them since the creation of the welfare state (Beck, 2001). In Naomi Klein's view:

'a sense of impermanence is blowing through the labor force, destabilizing everyone from office temps to high-tech independent contractors to restaurant and retail clerks. Factory jobs are being outsourced, garment jobs are morphing into homework, and in every industry, temporary contracts are replacing full, secure employment. In a growing number of instances, even CEOs are opting for shorter stints at one corporation after another, breezing in and out of different corner offices and purging half the employees as they come and go' (Klein, 2000:231).

This would seem to capture much of the spirit of contemporary visions of the future world of work. In such visions, responsibility for the creation and allocation of work, as well as for making work into an empowering enterprise, will have shifted from the welfare state towards the individual. Organizational hierarchies will have been abolished, individuals instead navigating along networks of connections and information. While some would argue that developments in this direction are signs of disintegration, others would have it the other way, viewing instead the emergence of a new dynamic, capitalist order. In 'the new organizational era', as Arthur and Rousseau (1996) have it, the shape of work – how people organize themselves and each other – is shifting, and 'shifting' becomes the reality of work. They offer 'a new lexicon' for a new career paradigm, with new meanings for old concepts, and new concepts that encompass novel meanings. Their lexicon is intended to shift our understanding of concepts like 'organization', 'employment', 'occupation', 'work', 'learning', 'civility', and 'self'. For example:

> *Organization:* Old meaning: a legal entity defining authority relations and property rights. New meaning: organizing through networks, value chains, and so on – a more dynamic, process-centred usage.

> *Employment:* Old meaning: the action of employing a person; alternatively, a state of being employed, or a person's regular occupation or business. New meaning: a temporary state, or the current manifestation of long-term employability.

According to Arthur and Rousseau, this new organizational era offers as well a new relation between order and chaos; something of an ordered chaotic existence. As the authors have it, chaos has itself become respectable. It has shifted from denoting an undesirable condition to being the principal factor behind what is seen as an orderly universe (Wheatley, 1994). Here again, the disorganized character of contemporary capitalism is evident, but with an inverted role being given to chaos, as a source of vitality and movement, and hence for the making of order.

Similar versions of the role and character of work and workers in market utopias are widespread. Together, they form something of a semantic cluster of keywords such as empowerment, employability, flexibility, networking, enterprise culture, lifelong learning, knowledge work, and the like. Such keywords embody a new rationality and morality and are engines of the potential creation of new kinds of work organizations and subjectivities. Again, these visions of work that empower individuals, of flexible and entrepreneurial workers, appear not only optimistic, but also quite realistic in nature in that their proponents can and do claim that this is the direction in which the workplace is currently moving. However, we may agree with Miller and Rose (1995:460) that while attempts to transform the nature of work and the identity of the worker through large-scale programmes are eternally optimistic, they are also eternally judged to have failed, and the reasons for this failure utilized as the basis for further attempts to reform work. In this sense, as in others, contemporary utopian thinking is indeed utopian, for its realization is always endlessly deferred.

Conclusion: the presumption of the new Utopians

In this chapter we have attempted to show the intimate linkages of work, organization and politics in utopian thought. In envisaging the good society, utopian thinking tends to fall towards a dream of complete organization or complete disorganization and to configure work in this light. But to do so is typically to engage in presumptions to knowledge and to superiority of vision which, when enacted, entail the over-riding of individuals and of competing viewpoints. In organized utopias this is very evident when it leads to the liquidation of actual or imagined opponents, or to their subsumption as functionaries or automatons into the grand design of the utopian blueprint. In the disorganized utopias of anarchists and some socialists this is not true to the extent that they tend to give priority to discussion, consensus and involvement. That may mean that some individuals do not get what they want, but it does not mean that their right to exist is removed (thus the local collectivization in Republican Spain disgruntled small landowners, whereas their counterparts in the Stalinist Soviet Union, the Kulaks, were murdered).

The dubious achievement of the utopia of the global free market is to combine disorganization with presumption. This presumption seems to be two-fold. On the one hand, in a rather familiar way, it is to be found in the manner in which international agencies, without even the tenuous legitimacy of election, presume to order the world in the name of their vision of globality. Increasingly they construct a world in which labour rights and welfare provision are over-ridden in favour of the anarchic fight for profits between trans-national corporations. Countries which refuse to comply are punished by relocations to those which do and, in the process, the individuals within those countries face extreme poverty and even death. Their counterparts in less resistant countries have the reward of sweatshop working conditions and subsistence wages. In richer countries the suffering caused may be less extreme. Nonetheless, the threat of re-location of free-floating capital is constantly used to justify ever more intensive working conditions and the erosion of social welfare. Contemporary capitalism may indeed be disorganized, but that disorganization is an achievement of a very organized set of institutions which, when challenged as in Seattle, Toronto, Gothenburg and Genoa, for example, respond with barricades, plastic bullets and tear gas administered by ranks of faceless men with visors, armour, riot shields and batons.

We spoke earlier of the link between utopian thinking and totalitarianism and, further, argued that market ideology is a form of utopianism. Is it, too, a form of totalitarianism? It is important to be careful not to be too sweeping here but in one sense we think the answer is yes. Hannah Arendt, in her analysis of totalitarianism, remarks that the striking thing 'about Nazism and Stalinism is the robot-like behaviour of both victims and executioners, both evidently feeling that they had no choice . . . but merely obeying forces greater than human wills' (Canovan, 1974:18). Just as Bauman links such totalitarianism to other, apparently more benign, forms of social organization, so too can it be linked to market utopias. For these, too, tell us that there are forces greater than human will and individual action: their presumption is to tell us that in the face of market forces there is no choice.

But the new utopians are presumptious in another way, too. In their idealized models of flexible knowledge-work, for all that these are more benign images than the sweatshop, they seek to engineer an insidious new form of subjectivity. The manipulations of corporate culturism, the ever-increasing demands for 24/7 working, the individualization of responsibility, the erosion of community and its replacement with consumerism, all contribute to what Richard Sennett has evocatively called 'the corrosion of character' (Sennett, 1998). We made the point at the outset that utopias are rooted in reaction to or extrapolation from the present. The new utopians of the global market do not even pretend to set their societies in the distant future, or in distant places, but in a global capitalism in which poverty, environmental destruction, child labour, and war are still very much present and themselves commodified in the global media market. The future of 'branded places' looks very much like the affluent enclaves of today, only more secluded, ordered, and pleasant. The future of work looks very much like the heroic and breathlessly described world of the software firms and ad agencies of MBA case studies. The new utopians are deeply embedded in the socio-political structures of their time and place, and are busy enacting their vision of the future as we write. They posit an absence of alternatives (what Jacques calls 'crypto-utopianism', this volume) and, in so doing, presume to tell us what the world will be and to punish – economically, psychologically and corporally – those who disagree by daring to imagine something different. And where dissent is not punished (for example when it comes from those such as ourselves who work in unusually privileged conditions) it is dismissed – as utopian.

Such a move – to call others utopian – is, according to our analysis, an expression of presumptiousness. That is, by using utopian in its traditional, pejorative sense of unrealistic, an attempt is made to enforce a particular version of what is real – to insist that there is no choice. Our stance is exactly opposite to this. We believe that it is vital always to recognize that there are choices and alternatives, both politically and individually, and that the world could be different to how it is. This is not at all to be utopian for, in saying that the world could be different, we do not have the presumption to tell others how the world should be.

Bibliography

Arendt, H. (1958) *The Human Condition*. Chicago: University of Chicago Press.
Arthur, M.B. and Rousseau, D.M. (1996) 'Introduction: The Boundaryless career as a new employment principle', in M.B. Arthur and D.M. Rousseau (eds) *The Boundaryless Career*, pp. 3–20. Oxford: Oxford University Press.
Bailey, J. (1988) *Pessimism*. London: Routledge.

Bauman, Z. (1983) *Modernity and the Holocaust.* Cambridge: Polity.

Beck, U. (2001) *The New World of Work.* Cambridge: Polity.

Beecher, J. and Bienvenu, R. (eds) (1971) *The Utopian Vision of Charles Fourier.* Boston: Beacon Press.

Bell, D. (1960) *The End of Ideology.* New York: Free Press.

Bradley, H. *et al.* (2000) *Myths at Work.* Cambridge: Polity.

Canovan, M. (1974) *The Political Thought of Hannah Arendt.* London: Dent.

Carter, A. (1973) *The Political Theory of Anarchism.* London: Routledge, Kegan & Paul.

Clinell, B. (2000) *Attac.* Stockholm: Agora.

Frankl, B. (1987) *The Post-Industrial Utopians.* Cambridge: Polity Press.

Fukuyama, F., The End of History?. *The National Interest*, 16 (Summer).

Hayek von, F. (1960) *The Constitution of Liberty.* London: Routledge Kegan Paul.

Hodgson, G. (1999) *Economics and Utopia.* London: Routledge.

Jacoby, R. (1999) *The End of Utopia.* New York: Basic Books.

Klein, N. (2000) *No Logo.* London: Harper Collins.

Lash, S. and Urry, J. (1987) *Disorganized Capitalism.* Cambridge: Polity.

Levi, P. (1979) *If This is a Man.* London: Penguin, (orig. 1958).

MacIntyre, A. (1981) *After Virtue.* London: Duckworth.

Mannheim, K. (1960) *Ideology and Utopia.* London: Routledge Kegan Paul.

Miller, D. (ed.) (1983) *A Pocket Popper.* London: Fontana.

Miller, P. and Rose, N. (1995) 'Production, identity and democracy', *Theory and Society* 24: 427–467.

Nozick, R. (1974) *Anarchy, State and Utopia.* Oxford: Blackwell.

Popper, K. (1945) *The Defence of Rationalism* in Miller D. (ed.) (1983) *The Pocket Popper.* London: Fontana.

Schapiro, L. (1972) *Totalitarianism.* London: Macmillan/Pall Mall Press.

Sennett, R. (1998) The Corrosion of Character: The Personal Consequences of Work in the New Capitalism. New York: W.W. Norton.

Warhurst, C. and Thompson, P. (1998) 'Hands, Hearts and Minds: Changing Work and Workers at the End of the Century', in P. Thompson and C. Warhurst (eds) *Workplaces of the Future*, pp. 1–24, London: Macmillan.

Williams, R. (1965) *The Long Revolution.* London: Penguin.

Woodcock, G. (ed.) (1977) *The Anarchist Reader.* London: Fontana.

What is a crypto-utopia and why does it matter?

Roy Stager Jacques

The entire world continues to dream of New York, even as New York dominates and exploits it. (Jean Baudrillard, *America*.)

The purpose of this chapter is to introduce the concept of the crypto-utopia, a neologism introduced in order to link certain strands of recent post-analytic thought to the present topic. Understanding this concept will be relatively easy for the average reader of a book such as this. Understanding the implications of such a concept is more difficult. Hardest of all will be the activity of linking this knowledge to action that influences the relations of power which are the object of analysis. This chapter ends with a plea for producers of knowledge to expand the definition of engagement to include both the production of new knowledge *and* the activities necessary to nurture the relationship between such knowledge and change in the world.

Please note as you read, I am an American. If there is one thing I learned working abroad, it is that I must speak as an American; when I write 'we,' I most often mean 'we Americans'. As in my book *Manufacturing the Employee* (Jacques, 1996), my intention is to critique America as an American. This is relevant to the world not because we are exemplars, not because (as we widely believe) we have a special Covenant with the Almighty, but because the world outside America is largely 'collateral damage' as we act in the world. This point is less important to note when we are distressing the rest of the world to meet our needs, for then it is obvious. It is more important to note when the rest of the world is helping us to propagate our discursive agenda, whether it is in the export of 'management' (see Jacques, 1996) or in helping us in a 'War on Terror.'

I believe the disjuncture between academia and meaningful action, which is the subject of the final section in this chapter, has relevance to readers of many countries. I can see from my experience in New Zealand that this is so. I can also see from that experience that the specific forms of the problem and the potential means of addressing it vary with national context. I can only leave it to the reader to assess the relevance of my points for him or herself.

Prologue (Please be patient, this *does* lead to a point)

September 11, 2001

Four American jets have just been highjacked. Two have been driven into New York City's World Trade Centre; a third has crashed, leaving the Pentagon in flames and the fourth has 'merely' destroyed its occupants. Already it is clear that the death toll attached to this tragedy will be a four or even five-figure number. Against the overpowering magnitude of the very material suffering caused today, any intellectualizing, especially critical discursive analysis, seems fatuous, something suited only to some one-scene Pangloss in a Fellini sketch of academe in Fascist Italy. And yet . . . And yet, one has to ask, in this orgy of network news analysis, where is the insight of Edward Said? Of Salman Rushdie? Are these oversights mere coincidence?

Within days – in fact, within these first hours – discursive tracks are being very carefully laid through the sociopolitical jungle. This 'information highway' will metastasize as if magically. It will seem such a feature of the natural landscape that to call it otherwise will be to risk dismissal as a fool. Yet determining who will travel these paths and the route they will follow, will determine the material fate of thousands, millions, of people. I do not question that something terrible has happened. I am questioning HOW this tragedy is being constructed as terrible. After all, to be frank, the Kobe earthquake was shocking, but fortunately it was off the evening news after a few days (*life must go on*). They must have recovered OK; we can still get new Playstations and Hondas. After all, they survived Hiroshima and Nagasaki (*that's different; it was wartime*). The machete deaths of three-quarters of a million Hutus and Tutsis was unfortunate, of course, but not so much that it could replace Sweeps Week in teleprogramming (*what can I do?*). Twenty thousand deaths from flooding in Bangla Desh is saddening, but really, there are so many of those little brown people; rounding up or down 20,000 from a billion is probably within the margin of demographic error. Statistically, the number of deaths are not significantly different from zero (*and why don't they just move to higher ground?*). The ongoing tragedy of AIDS in Africa is disturbing – we certainly hope it doesn't spread to any endangered species. But behind the PC statements of concern, it's comforting to know that we might as well have our steaks and chips; the good Reverend Malthus must have had a point (*racing improves the breed*). Oh, and how many Kurds have died horribly as a direct result of the U.S. encouraging them to rise against Saddam, then leaving them to stand alone on the field of battle (*What's a Kurd?*)? In the 1989 movie *Sex, lies and videotape*, we laugh at Andie MacDowell in the opening scene as she discusses her anxiety about the world garbage situation with her therapist. It's silly to have real anxiety about things we only see on TV.

But what has happened today, in God's New York, is not just a tragedy, not just macabre entertainment. It is EVIL. I know so because I have been told this by the sitting President; by his political opponent the ex-First Lady; by 'responsible' (that is to say, similarly-minded) world leaders such as Mr. Blair, by network news anchors and by ex-President William Jefferson Clinton, a man with a documented propensity for using the precise definition of a word. This EVIL has attacked GOOD. America is not just for Americans anymore; it is 'a beacon of freedom to the world.' The very fact that all people from all countries are welcome here is the very thing that infuriates 'those people,' madmen who fly planes into buildings. America is good, not because it is a pork barrel within which 5% of the world gets to consume more or less ten times our per-capita share of the world's resources. No. Our consumption is necessary – FOR YOU! Always live better than your clients. America is a symbol for the rest of the world, a sign that your miserable lives can be redeemed if enough of your GDP is ploughed into making t-shirts for Disney so that your children might wear t-shirts from Disney, your grandchildren might visit Disneyworld and your great-grandchildren might open a Disneyworld in your grayscale little back-water nation. You happy-go-lucky day labourers have no idea how hard it is to be a pawn of capitalist consumerism. Tomorrow, because Wall Street is compassionate, we will close in memory of the dead. But the next day, we must have two desserts at lunch so that all of you can know that *some day*, you might do so as well. To do otherwise would be irresponsible. You must understand this. In America, there are no poor people, only people who have not yet become rich.

Yes, EVIL has attacked GOOD. Our role now, as Americans, is to defend for the entire world, the belief that GOOD inevitably wins over EVIL. This has been suggested by our President. It is currently a quite bipartisan notion. If we fail in this, we fail for all humanity. EVIL will win the war it has declared on GOOD.

Yes, the President, the military, both political parties and the (American) press, have been very explicit in warning that 'this is an act of war.' Technically, I might quibble that an act of war can be made only by an entity capable of conducting a war. Countries start wars; people commit crimes. What I am decorated for doing under my country's flag in war, I am imprisoned or executed for doing under my own volition in crime. How big a group of people one must have in order to become a country is admittedly unclear (but let us leave that for the analytical philosophers to work on, if they ever work out the question about their own epistemological validity). More to the point: if four teams of six people, even with a backup support network, have executed this crime, it is just that, a CRIME. I suppose it is also a CONSPIRACY. But to establish the act as an act of war while leaving *fill in the blank* as the actor, is a discursive game. Today, September 11ᵗʰ, 2001, we are in the presence of a tragedy. That cannot be changed by words. According to American law, we are in the presence of a crime as well. But, to understand the present event as an ACT OF WAR in which EVIL has, to its INEVITABLE DETRIMENT, declared war on GOOD, is to play an important role in a discursive game that will have an important influence on, at minimum:

- Millions of Palestinians
- All Arab nations (except the 'good' Saudis who are not ontologically Arab because they let us have their oil)
- Defence expenditures, especially of the US, but of many other nations
- All organizations whose work will be restricted in order to fund defence expenditures
- Americans, who will very likely live through this tragedy without becoming any more aware how our actions in the world can hurt people so badly they will give their lives in attacks such as this one.
- You get the idea . . .

September 12, 2001

The discursive bulldozers have cleared the rough path of the information highway and crews have already begun decorating the roadway. In today's national mourning service, a central reading was from the book of Apocalypse (flaming sword, hand of God, final victory over evil. Subtle). By more or less general agreement, yesterday's Event will now be called the Attack on America (that brings another 21 countries in as the aggrieved, from Canada to Chile). A coordinated effort has begun to put American flags on all cars and businesses and to tie red, white and blue ribbons on any surface that will hold still long enough. (What will we do if EVIL turns out to come from a country whose flag is red, white and blue? That's a logical connection. Discursive operators have different modes of connection). The television reports are already shifting to footage – probably Gulf-War vintage – describing the awesome power of the weaponry GOOD will yield against EVIL.

Do I sound flippant? I am not; I am sad. Now I remember for the first time in years why I felt so totally alienated during the Gulf War of 1991. I do not condone what the terrorists have done. I do believe the attack was an 'Attack on America' (both the idea of America and the international acts of America). I believe we should stand together as a nation and I would likely support punitive actions against the perpetrators. My fear, however, is that we are not defining yesterday's event as tragic retribution experienced by us as a concrete, self-interested group. We are defining it as a symbolic act done to us as the world's representatives of Goodness. In doing so, I fear that:

- **We will minimize anything that might be learned about the conditions that brought us to this position.** While we are asking 'who did this?' It might be more useful for us to ask 'why are ordinary Palestinians dancing in the streets with joy at the news?'
- **We will maximize the possibility of acting without due concern.** Even our past president was not beyond shooting a few Patriot missiles whenever his domestic career was in jeopardy. This is the current President's chance to show the world that he is his own man by doing exactly what his father did ten years ago in Iraq. Just last week, a major national news magazine was

criticizing the Secretary of Defence for lackluster performance. Time to 'get those numbers up', General Powell. Messy details like the World Court and international diplomacy can be dispensed with if we have genuine Armageddon and not merely a criminal conspiracy. International diplomacy of the highest order is being done discursively.

- **We will lose the chance to ask questions from which we might better learn to deal with the impossibilities of the world we are creating.** Many have compared the scene of the past two days to Pearl Harbour. What about Hiroshima? Dresden? Hanoi? Baghdad? Even if a white life *is* worth several hundred yellow ones, when is it permissible in military matters to engage civilians in combat? We claim to be fighting on principle? Can we better define the principle that permits Hiroshima and does not permit destroying the World Trade Centre?

- **We will know no more tomorrow than today what can be done to prevent such disasters.** America readily stiffens prison sentences to prevent crimes despite ample sociological evidence that penalties are a weak deterrent and incarceration is training *for* sociopathic and criminal behaviour (in this, we are exemplary, but far from unique). Similarly, it is not unthinkable that because of this event Americans will invest billions in space weaponry and other military toys which leave us no more able to deal with an event such as this. It is a danger that we will be promoting policies throughout the world that make events such as these more likely, but which either happen outside prime time viewing or at least keep gasoline cheap – preferably both.

Those with family psychotherapy backgrounds (either as vendors or consumers) may recognize an analogy here. In 'dysfunctional family systems' it is common to define the world in terms of simplistic right/wrong relationships, failure to recognize that individuals can be flawed and imperfect without being 'evil,' and a willingness to do harm to those close to you in the name of principles which must go unexamined. As with small systems, so with large. One must face complexity self-critically, without expecting simplistic solutions, if one is to learn and grow. But before one can burst the bubble of magical thinking in which we are unblemished heroes and exemplars, we must show that there IS a bubble. For the ideal of Good America attacked by Evil is not Utopian, it is Crypto Utopian.

America (the discursive concept and the socio-political entity) must be accountable for the above, but the above attitudes and beliefs are not unique to America. In New Zealand, one might draw many comparisons to the idea that 'we' (white people) have been good to 'our Maori' and that Maori 'special interests' are Evil. One might question how the discursive prominence of Gallipoli and 'sport' form a quasi-religion influencing a gamut of issues from gender scripts to willingness to die in foreign wars for G7 nations' interests. My guess is that Mr. Blair's ability to commit British resources to the good fight against old colonial enemies in the defense of free-flowing crude oil draws on the crypto-utopian. I would ask you, the reader, to judge the connection to your own situation.

–Topias, Crypto– and other

America. . . . is a utopia which has behaved from the very beginning as though it were already achieved. (Jean Baudrillard, *America*)

The audience for this volume will have prior familiarity with the concept of *eu*topias, and perhaps dystopias and heterotopias. In this chapter, I would like to use the neologism *crypto-utopia* to connect some streams of recent critical social thought. I define as crypto-utopian, any forms of thought and practice which treats perception, value and/or belief as hard reality. Religious zealots who treat 'the' Word of (their) God as indisputable truth are engaging in crypto-utopian practice, elevating their biases while depriving differing beliefs, not just of legitimacy, but of the *possibility* of legitimacy. The priesthood of empiricism is similarly crypto-utopian in confusing objectivity as a social construct ('agreement among experts') with Objectivity as a hard reality. And let us not fail to look within the Critical community. Those of us whose worldview treats class as the central reality rather than as a construct, those of us who are in the process of codifying Foucauldian writing into a New Testament of discursive platitudes ('look; it's panoptic!') are creating crypto-utopian communities as well. In order to contrast crypto-utopian thinking with the other -topias, let us briefly scan the bestiary.

The *utopia* (eu-topia) is familiar enough to all of us. From Plato's Republic, to the City on the Hill of the Massachusetts Bay Puritans, to Marx's Scientific Socialism, we have found realities presented to us as ideals toward which to strive. Even when they move from Earth to Heaven, utopias are idealistic in that they ask us to judge the reality of the immediate world with reference to the imagined reality of a hypothetical one. In its traditional function, then, the utopia functions as a sort of road map to a hopefully better place. The dark side of utopia is the *dystopia*. Although we can find antecedents in Swift, Dante and even the book of Revelation, the dystopic vision is especially at home in the scree of late industrial modernity. The fact that 'Kafkaesque' and 'Orwellian' have become recognizable adjectives attests to the towering stature of these dystopic visions. 'Here we go round the prickly pear, early in the morning.'[1]

If we retain the cynicism of the dystopia, but remove the weight of despair, we create the context from which the *heterotopia* emerges. Perhaps the animal-headed, human-bodied deities of many traditional belief systems were hetero-topic in a sense. So, of course was the painting of Hieronymus Bosch. But such labeling is anachronistic. Culturally, heterotopic vision is firmly tied to the unravelling of Western modernity. Heterotopic thought relinquishes the ideal of synoptic perfection and floats in a polydimensional reality, a world where all the pieces do not and, necessarily, *can* not, fit into the same puzzle. Magritte, of course, must be mentioned as an icon of the heterotopia. People who stand in mid air; clouds where walls should be and walls where window glass should be – the world of Magritte's paintings is not merely nonexistent; it is impossible. It violates the laws of time, space and physics. It is not surprising that Foucault was fascinated by heterotopic thinking.[2] Heterotopia in representational art and the *bricolage* of Foucault's Paris clique are two emergences of the same phenomenon. In the painting of Magritte or the politics of Foucault, we see a retreat from trying to build a New World Order, a forsaking of Grand Unified Theories. Like Chance in Jerzy Kosinski's *Being There*, we must leave the running of the world to mysterious forces and learn to just tend our garden.

Between dystopian and heterotopic thought there runs the same difference of assumptions about the possibility of meaningful action that we see between Marxists (etc). And Postmodernists (etc). Dystopia is basically a negative reflection of the ideal society. The dystopia operates under the same rules of logic, of time and space that rule in utopia. Like the image of Christian Hell, the dystopia is presented as a tool for negating the negation and achieving the ideal state. In this sense, it serves the same purpose as utopian thinking. One is the carrot, the other the stick. Heterotopic thought arises with the belief that the scattered fragments cannot be put into a coherent whole. The Great Song returns no more and we are left listening to pebbles rattling under the receding wave.[3]

> *Brief digression: And where do we put phenomena like the Fantastic Realism of Borges, Marquez and Allende? While technically heterotopic according to my definitions, these visions are less exemplary of the typology I am discussing than they are illustrative of the need to understand the narrow sociohistorical relevance of my typology. Even in the playful heterotopias of Magritte, there is a despair at the loss of connection to a Grand Narrative that we find absent from, for instance, Fantastic Realism, comfortable in the utter normalcy of its heterotopicity. In Marquez there is grief, but such grief is situational, not ontological. For that matter, even within my culture there is a generation emerging – those too young to remember a world without music videos or video games – which appears to be capable of creating heterotopic visions which lack wistfulness for a return to the illusion of unity. The peace sign and the wiccan pentangle co-exist happily in the music video without a need for symbolic reconciliation. But I am not of that generation, nor can I understand Fantastic Realism from the inside. I will try not to make the foolish mistake endemic to the old, of trying to analyse everything within the limited framework of my increasingly outdated comprehension.*

Crypto-Utopia

There is one quality shared by all three concepts mentioned thus far. Whatever their differences, the eu, dys and hetero forms of topiary are presented as idealized visions. What of the idealized vision of the world which is presented as a hard reality? If we include such thought in our discussion, we see that this is the dominant -topia of Modernity, the Crypto-utopia. Consider this example:

'Restoring' 'Democracy' in Kuwait

*In his sole domestically popular act as an American President, George the First (Bush, that is) rallied most of the world's advanced military firepower to restore the American people's god-given right to an unlimited supply of cheap oil. At some level, the average American knew the Gulf War was about gasoline, but we could not mobilize on this basis. Ostensibly, this was not a pragmatic war; it was a moral one – Americans need victories to be moral victories. We fought because Saddam was Evil. We fought because we are the virtuous defenders of 'the free world.' As yellow ribbons[4] proliferated on every tree in the country, we fought to 'support our troops.' We even fought to absurdly 'restore' democracy to a country that had, until that point, neither possessed nor sought it. The one thing we did **not** fight for was oil.*

'Well,' one might object, 'leaders have long known that mobilizing the masses is easier when they have a cause, be it God, Country or Family. Read *Mein Kampf*.' Indeed, but there is an important difference. George the First did not write a *Mein Kampf*, and this absence is significant. However objectionable we may find Hitler's values to be, he stated them *as* values. *Mein Kampf* is a utopian treatise, one that, like *Das Kapital*, combines a view of the ideal world with a Beidecker for getting there. But for Bush, it was not incidental that he was a faceless bureaucrat; it was essential to the operation of the discursive processes producing him as the apparent leader. He did not stand for subject-centred values or even for the values of a group. George led the forces that stood for Truth, Goodness, Justice, Democracy – universal values. It was not George's war, nor even ours, but God's. That Americans could be mobilized to stand behind a signifier like 'restoring democracy' was idealistic in the extreme, but this idealism operated within a shell of apparent realism. Americans were not acknowledging any values at all; we were just 'doing what was right.' This is the most dangerous form of idealism.

The crypto-utopia, then, is a form of idealized vision of the world that pretends not to be a vision at all. I find it ironic that although Americans are a wildly idealistic culture, the value idealized is pragmatism. This has implications which extend globally, partially because America is a global empire, but more deeply, because 'America' as a discursive phenomenon is a product of industrial capitalism which is prominent in post-industrial capitalist relations globally (Jacques, 1996). The dominant utopia of Modernity is not the dystopic or heterotopic. These are epiphenomena, cultural side-shows. The medium of our dominant discourses is the crypto-utopian assumption that we are Realists, that we operate without visions. The paradox (and danger) of Modernity and the paradox of the 'American Dream' are one: the dream that we are not dreamers; the ideology that we are not ideological; *the blind faith that Reality is empirical.* As Midgeley (1985:1) wrote in her critique of what I would call crypto-utopian scientific attitudes toward the 'theory' of evolution:

The theory of evolution is not just an inert piece of theoretical science. It is, and cannot help being, also a powerful folk-tale about human origins. Any such narrative must have symbolic force. We are probably the first culture not to make that its main function. Most stories about human origins must have been devised purely with a view to symbolic and poetic fittingness . . . Scientists, when they find themselves caught up in these webs of symbolism, sometimes complain, calling for a sanitary cordon to keep them away from science. But this seems to be both psychologically and logically impossible.

Dreaming of New York

In his book *America*, Baudrillard (1989:28) shows an acute awareness of this paradox. The italicized phrase below could be taken as the very definition of a crypto-utopia.

> This [*America*] is the only country which gives you the opportunity to be so brutally naive: things, faces, skies, and deserts are expected to be simply what they are. This is the land of the 'just as it is.' America. . . . is *a utopia which has behaved from the very beginning as though it were already achieved.* (italics added).

Baudrillard misses one subtle point. When he writes that America has behaved 'from the very beginning' as though its utopia were already achieved, he misses a distinction between the good old fashioned utopianism of neo-Medieval New England and the emerging crypto-utopianism of New Amsterdam. This is important. He writes of New York city:

> It is a world completely rotten with wealth, power, senility, indifference, puritanism and mental hygiene, poverty and waste, technological futility and aimless violence, and yet I cannot help but feel it has about it something of the dawning of the universe. Perhaps because the entire world continues to dream of New York, even as new York dominates and exploits it. (1989:23).

The use of 'puritanism' above is inappropriate. The Massachusetts Bay Colony Puritan Utopia was an explicit one. It was transparent. The Puritan dream which produced New England and the Quaker dream which produced Pennsylvania were straightforward utopias in the spirit of *Pilgrim's Progress*, or *The Leviathan*. The utopia was a *belief*, a vision, an abstraction constituting a yardstick against which society could be evaluated.

Somewhere between the New (and presumably improved) England of Perfectionist Roundheads and the New York observed by Baudrillard, American utopianism undergoes a qualitative change. It becomes circular; it goes underground. The business of America is no longer conformity to an abstraction. The 'dream' comes to be held by those who claim not to dream. It becomes embedded within activity judged, not against an external standard, but as activity *qua* activity. It is good because it is activity; it is good because it is good. The purpose of activity is activity. The goal of achievement is achievement. 'The business of America is business'.[5] Calvinist salvation is no longer achieved through *good* works, but through the *quantity* of work, whatever its quality. This crypto-utopian transformation is materially connected to commerce. Unlike its surrounding colonies, New York was not founded as the consequence of any explicit ideological vision. From its inception, it was opportunistically occupied with the pursuit of wealth. Furthermore, New York only came to the cultural fore in the U.S. after the mid-19th century, when it was an appropriate cultural capital for a nation dominated by corporate interests (this is analysed at length in Jacques, 1996).

The Neo-medieval vision of the Reformation has never died in America, but it has become ever more marginal, almost from its inception. By the 19th century, we find this simple utopianism only in isolated communities walled off from the general *busyness* of dominant American culture – Robert Owens' followers at New Harmony, the Amanas, the Oneidas, the Shakers. As time passes, their descendants have become ever more marginal: the communal movements of the 1960s, the Branch Davidians who attained notoriety at their Waco *auto da fe*, the anti-government Militia groups, survivalists and apocalyptic eschatologists. Utopians are those *outside* the vision. The new American Dream, manufactured c.1870–1920 (see Jacques, 1996) is solidly crypto-Utopian. It became embedded in an ideology of materialism, one that neither ascends from earth to heaven, or descends from heaven to earth. This materialism that moves *over* the earth, seeking no heaven higher than that of *'getting ahead.'* For the Puritan, material prosperity was a sign that one may be of the Elect, but the purpose of being among the elect was to achieve a spiritual prosperity in comparison to which material success was inconsequential. For the Crypto-utopian, material prosperity constitutes both membership in the Elect *and* the reward itself. It does not matter if the path toward the Dream has become circular because the path itself has become the reward. Baudrillard is not quite correct in stating that America 'is a utopia which has behaved from the very beginning as though it were already achieved,' but this observation is appropriate to the present crypto-utopian America.

Utilizing the idea of the Crypto-Utopia

The idea of the crypto-utopia does not represent a new concept (does anything?). I use this neologism to relate several strands of social thought to the topic of the present book. Despite enormous divergences, all the lost children of Nietzsche have contributed to a growing awareness of the radically constructed nature of meaning in the world. Nietzscheans, Saussureans, existentialists, social constructionists, poststructuralists, postmodernists and others face a common problem. All must recognize our own beliefs *as* beliefs, while facing a dominant discourse whose beliefs are 'believed' to be fact, hard Reality, uninterpreted data, value-free Truth.

Brief digression: The response I always get from crypto-utopians is that I am caricaturing them, that this is not their belief. Yes, it is and no, I am not.

However much crypto-utopian subjects acknowledge the incompleteness, ambiguity and error in their data, they do not relinquish the idea of an underlying hard reality. It is only a few days since I last heard a colleague on the Critical Management Studies listserve e-berating 'ideological' Critical theorists for not using critical thinking as an objective analytical tool – as he imagines he does. For such folks, data is still treated as containing Truth. Any difference between Hard reality and the data is attributed to the imperfection of methods and incompleteness of the empirical project – to distortion. The underlying belief that this distortion can, in principle, be cleared up with enough monkeys and enough typewriters is an idealistic belief that cannot be questioned as ideological without incurring the wrath of the believers. This belief – that the empirical machine will one day vomit forth Truth – is crypto-utopian however much one acknowledges that 'further research is necessary.'

The metaphor of utopia might help us connect to these fertile streams of recent thought. My hope would be that such linkages might be of some use in facing two practical problems of constructionist thought. The first is that of proselytizing. My experience with anti-essentialism has been that one can, with a reasonable degree of diligence and a modicum of intelligence, easily see the poverty of essentialist thought and its inability to demonstrate its own validity despite three centuries of dominance. It is much harder to demonstrate this to the dominant majority who cling to the objectivity of matter, the existence of common sense and belief in a human 'nature' – a majority who will not venture beyond Good and Evil into a world where reality is an ethical responsibility rather than a natural force. Every new means of representing constructionist ideas is a new tool for the work of proselytising. In this spirit, I suggest the concept of the crypto-utopia.

The second problem is one of action. Unless we can link concepts like that of crypto-utopia to ways of changing power relationships within social reality, our efforts are purely onanistic (there's a seed metaphor coming in a couple of pages). It is fashionable within certain circles to cite Thesis XI, but having done so is not to have acted; it is merely to have integrated the *idea* of action into potentially idle conversations. It is much more difficult to discern how one might engage with relationships of power in the organizational world in a manner that has an effect on these relationships. My experience of being a 'critical' scholar was that as soon as one ventures into *verboten* intellectual territory (which, by the way, is virtually the entire world of knowledge lying outside very narrow dogmatic limits), one is branded a 'radical' scholar and, by that very labelling, sealed off from participation in meaningful relationships of power. Admittedly, this was within the American university system and within schools of management, but even at New Zealand's University of Otago, where I did not feel marginalized within my school, I felt equally disconnected from meaningful social action. The hermetically sealed bubble which contains the 500 or so critical organizational scholars with whom I am familiar is a frequently pleasant and stimulating place, but the price of entry to this intellectual country-club prison seems to be forfeiture of links to organizations outside academia.

Epilogue, October 11, 2001

The philosophers have only *interpreted* the world, in various ways; the point, however, is to *change* it. (Karl Marx, *Theses on Feuerbach*, Thesis XI)

The difference between creativity and innovation is the difference between thinking about getting things done in the world and getting things done. (Michael E. Gerber, *The E-Myth Revisited: Why Most Small Businesses Don't Work and What to Do About It.*)

It is a month since 'America's New War' has been declared by CNN and Congress. Among many things worthy of note in the last thirty days, I have been impressed with the postings to a critical management theory listserve to which I am subscribed. Some postings have resonated with my feelings and beliefs. Many have horrified me. A couple have actually caused me to reflect deeply. But what impresses me the most as an observer now watching from outside academia is the all but universal belief within this group that engaging in e-diatribes constitutes a form of engagement with the issues, a form of praxis. This is an example of the assumption that critical thought and proselytizing is useful because it changes the perceptions of those with whom we are engaged in this activity and that change puts people into the world who act differently than they would otherwise have done. I have wrestled with this legitimator for about fifteen years and have come to believe it is so only to an exceedingly limited extent. Those who disagree might ask why poets and dissident intellectuals are jailed in other parts of the world while they are free to speak in the US and, for the most part, throughout the G7 nations' world. I fear the answer has less to do with 'Western' liberties and more to do with the irrelevancy of these enunciative modalities. Nobody cares. Let the professors profess; it adds a note of perceived tolerance to the social landscape while endangering nothing of value. My present choice to run a business rather than continue as a professor stems largely from my sense of utter disconnection from the relations of power governing the business relationships I spent the better part of two decades studying.

To a great extent, the professorate as a whole participates in a broader marginalization endemic to a society of media spectacle. In America, some commented that this was well-documented in Barry Levinson's 1997 movie *Wag the Dog*, in which a very Clintonesque US President manufactures a Gulf War scenario in order to deflect attention from an administration scandal. A few commentators now see this movie as a blueprint for the mobilization of sentiment that is the necessary ally to the mobilization of weaponry as the US goes off to Afghanistan to hunt down – well, something. Those who see only this far, however, miss an additional important layer of meaning. A short time after *Wag the Dog* played in theatres, one of President Clinton's scandals (who can keep track?) blew up in the newspapers. A major Hollywood director was seen going into the White House, presumably to consult on the situation. Shortly thereafter, media attention was directed toward Patriot missiles being launched against what was allegedly the nest of Osama Bin Laden. At the time, to most Americans, this person was Osama Bin Who? The necessity of waging war on him was hardly a national priority. It was widely commented at the time that events were closely following the script of the movie. Life imitating art, blah, blah, blah. But to me, here's the interesting point: *nothing further happened!*

Knowledge, as Michel Foucault repeatedly asserted, is not power. Knowledge is *produced by* power; it is *used by* power. It is not, in itself, remotely powerful. When we, as academics, assume that because we are changing the store of knowledge our students and readers take into the world we are therefore changing the world, we vastly overstate our degree of engagement. Occasionally, our message will reach people who can determine for themselves how to link the knowledge to power and in that sense we will have the occasional effect. But if this is the limit of our engagement, we are like the Biblical farmer sowing seeds indiscriminately on all types of ground and failing to nurture the plants. Sure, the occasional pine grows straight out of a crack on a cliff face, but that is not the way to bet. Remember the reward Onan earned for his poor seed husbandry?

I have sometimes responded to those who found my studies esoteric by comparing the social sciences to a physical science process. The theoretical physicist is impenetrable to all but a few dozen initiates, but he or she provides material which is worked on by the electronics engineer, the design engineer, the sales person and, before we know it, the microwave oven has appeared in our daily lives based on the esoteric 'magic' (as it appears to most of us) of particle physics and thermodynamics. Where this analogy breaks down in the social sciences is that the linkages are nonexistent or hopelessly in the pocket of vested interests. Yes, this is worst in the US, but it is not unique to the US. Schools of business (commerce) may have somewhat stronger connections than, say anthropology or sociology, but these connections are more vested in the *status quo*, so where the problem or marginalization of the discipline is less, the problem of marginalization of critical ideas is greater and the prospect is generally poor.

As harsh as the above may sound, I remain deeply indebted to Critical scholarship. Only last week, I told a fellow tenant in the mall where I do business that the one thing that had most practically prepared me for success in representing the Tenants' Association to the landlord was my background in feminist theory, which permitted me to appreciate how her more indirect and nurturing strategy was more effective than the head-butting approach of my predecessor. Kurt Lewin was almost right. Nothing is as practical as a good (feminist, poststructuralist) theory.

Ah, but how do we move from epistemology to engagement? I can sometimes make use of what I was taught, but I was not *taught* to make use of what I was taught. This was not a failing of my excellent mentors, but a necessary failing resulting from the present limitations of the system. If Critical theorizing is to be more than a sideshow to a sideshow, I believe it will be necessary to expand the concept of what it means for a theorist to be engaged. It is not enough to say 'here are interesting ideas I have picked up in my studies; I dump them on your doorstep.' That is to sow our seeds Onanistically on dry sand. If theorizing is to be considered a form of social engagement, the measure of successful theorizing must be the degree to which theorizing facilitates change in the social relationships of power we study. To do so, would involve devoting attention to the development of new institutions and the cooptation, perhaps, of existing ones. The seeds we wish to sow must find fertile ground. In the US, the poverty of linkages between Critical theorizing and the rest of social life was made forcefully to me by a Communist physician explaining how he justified working for merely a single-payer health system rather than fully socialized medicine. His argument was that it is a sad situation when the Communists have to cover all the ideological space to the left of the Republican party. In the UK, an example of this difficulty can be found in the rise and fall of attempts to bring Operational Research out of the corporate boardroom and into the hands of those on the receiving end of public projects (eg Jackson, 1987).

Where are the social service organizations, the think tanks, the political action committees, the labour organizing groups, the student organizing groups who, in the language now fashionable in our B-schools, are the 'customers' of critical theory? Identifying and building these groups is no less important a part of Critical theorizing than is the thinking and writing. On the whole, although we usually act in good faith, we know too much and do too little. Our ideas may be creative in the manner of Gerber's leitmotif comment above, but how often do they lead to innovation when innovation is measured in terms of social change? And let us not forget business leaders. As the once and future 'practitioner,' one thing which impressed me during my academic sojourn was the near-total remapping of issues between those defined by people in business and those defined as academic research problems. This was actually *more* extreme than in the US in my limited experience with the importation of American management knowledge in New Zealand, Thailand, Indonesia and Taiwan. In these countries, I have seen knowledge developed for G7 corporate interests indiscriminately imposed upon culturally and economically alien forms of activity – by the 'natives.'

Based on my historical analysis of the management disciplines, it seems to me that the pockets of greatest vitality in the discipline have come from sites where business people and academics shared a common sense of what problems needed to be solved. Taylor in the steel mills. The Harvard junta at Hawthorne. The US army Alpha group of World War I, which gave American industrial psychology (and advertising!) the clan which guided developments for the next half century. We could mention Bion and the British army, the Aston studies . . . the list goes on. The legacy of wars to personnel research and administrative science in general has been immense. We might look askance at this connection, but we can also use it as a cautionary example that if we wish to stimulate change, then it is all but mandatory that our intellectual efforts be tied to problems that are of concern to a clientele who have the ability to create change in the systems we would wish to influence. Try to find a business leader today well versed in the academic debates current to sociology, economics, or even management. Speaking as somebody who thought of himself as 'the practitioner' even as I came to be defined as a critical organizational theorist, I deeply believe that creating common domains of problem definition with businesspeople is an activity that could be as rewarding as it would certainly be difficult.

A valediction forbidding mourning
[Patience, we're nearly Donne[6]]

On reflection, I realize that my entire *oeuvre* 1988-present has been devoted to attempts to show the pernicious influence of crypto-utopias whose unexamined presence marginalized the views I wished to represent: the attempt to show that, from the perspective of nursing, 'medicine' is not 'healthcare' but *physicians'* construction of healthcare; that 'the employee' is not an eternal *verité* but a construction specific to industrialism and to American values; that 'rationality' is *masculine* rationality; that 'the good of the organization' makes concrete a construction by top management which devalues the legitimacy of diverging beliefs and the needs of all other parties. Because we live in a time where the pillars of our discursive systems are especially out of date (yeah, yeah; Minerva's owl and all that), it is of the utmost importance that we contribute to the production of new knowledge based on present needs and not past constructions.

This leaves us facing two gigantic challenges. One is the need to vigilantly dig out and analyse the crypto-utopian 'objectivity' within which our present constructions, posing as hard realities, drive out, not only all other constructions, but the very idea that we are dealing with constructions rather than Truth. But we must not be deluded that analysis alone will accomplish such a thing. The second challenge is the need to forge alliances with constituencies who can utilize our efforts to forge social change. It is not enough to randomly sow the seeds of new knowledge. We must nurture its growth and measure our efforts, not by what we *know*, but what we have *accomplished* in the world. I will end with a story told at my sister's college graduation.

> A Benedictine, a Dominican and a Jesuit monk were having a glass of wine together when the lights in the refectory went dark. The Benedictine said 'let us meditate on the nature of darkness.' The Dominican petitioned, 'Dear God, please restore to us your light.' The Jesuit got up and changed the fuse.

Be well.

Endnotes

1 From T.S. Eliot's *The Hollow Men*, as you probably know.
2 Best shown in *This is Not a Pipe*, but also elsewhere in his work.
3 Paraphrase from Yeats' poem, 'The Twentieth Century and After.'
4 In a popular mid-1970s American song, a man returning from prison asks his girlfriend to 'tie a yellow ribbon "round the old oak tree"' if she has waited faithfully for his return. I will pass on possible Freudian interpretations of the refrain.
5 In a 1925 speech, American President Calvin Coolidge made the comment that 'the chief business of the American people is business'. It has entered American folk wisdom as 'the business of America is business.'
6 The title is from a John Donne poem. Now, for $400, what beer did Beckett favor?

References

Baudrillard, J. (1988) *America*, London: Verso.
Foucault, M. (1981) *This is Not a Pipe* (J. Harkness, translator), Berkeley: University of California Press.
Jackson, M.C. (1987) Community Operational research: Purposes, theory and practice, *Dragon* 2: 47–56.
Jacques, R. (1996) *Manufacturing the Employee: Management Knowledge From the 19th to 21st Centuries.*
Midgeley, M. (1985) *Evolution as a Religion*, New York: Methuen.

Utopia or ideology: Karl Mannheim and the place of theory

Stephen Ackroyd

There are some fates which befall an intellectual that are almost as damning than not being remembered at all. One is to be recalled for the use of a novel concept or two when the actual contribution is much more significant. It can be argued that Karl Mannheim has been unfairly treated in this sort of way. He is likely to be remembered either when, as here, the notions of utopia or ideology are given another airing; or when some intellectual community rediscovers the founding ideas of the sociology of knowledge. For those with some familiarity with Mannheim's thought, however, there is a puzzle here. Some of the basic propositions that are influential in social science today have obvious affinities with central propositions of Mannheim's thinking. Yet there is almost complete silence amongst contemporary social theorists about him.

What follows is a study of Mannheim's thought which also attempts to tackle the puzzle of his neglect in the contemporary world. It does not claim to be a Mannheimian study of Mannheim but there is, clearly, a substantial influence in the methodology here; as indeed there is, directly or indirectly, Mannheimian influence discernable in the work of many contemporary authors. As with Mannheim, it is assumed here that the social context in which ideas are formed is important in understanding them (see Grey and Garsten, this volume). As he taught, it is assumed here that it is not advisable to take ideas at their face value and to be alert to the possibility of ideological biases in thinking. However, as a study of a particular author, this chapter might be thought out of place in a book devoted to utopia. It is true that the consideration by Mannheim of ideas about utopia is not central to his thinking. Because of this, explicit discussion of Mannheim on utopia is a long time coming in this essay; anyone simply wanting to know more about this is invited to skip to the relevant sections below. But it will be argued that the weaknesses of Mannheim's thinking about utopia is a useful way into the discussion of the value of ideas on this subject in contemporary discource.

Delving into Mannheim's ideas also helps shed light on the question of why he has been so neglected. The verdict of contemporary writers on Mannheim is in stark contrast to the view of him up to a few decades ago, when he was seen as a large if not a towering figure on the intellectual landscape. Mannheim had an extended period of celebrity, following his death in 1947, which lasted until the 1970s. His reputation was high and his influence was strongly felt, not only among sociologists but also among certain professional groups. Mannheim was not a theorist of organizations nor did he have a great interest in particular institutions; but he did, as we shall see, suggest the value of bureaucratic administration. In post-war Britain, many functionaries employed in the post war welfare state – such as planners and educationalists (Stewart, 1956) – were strongly influenced by his thought. After 1970 or so, however, with the exception of those specifically writing about the sociology of knowledge (Barnes, 1974; Longhurst, 1989; Stehr, 1994) – it is as if Mannheim never existed.

In some ways, this is difficult to understand. A great renaissance of British social thought began about the time that Mannheim's direct influence finally evaporated. In the late 1970s, the Robbins reforms were making their effects felt on the British higher education system, and social science was an important area of growth. The newly established plate-glass universities such as Warwick, York, Lancaster, Essex and a few of the older foundations such as Leicester, Leeds, LSE and Durham, became powerhouses in the creation of a new, distinctive, British approach to sociology. This was both critical and theoretical. Yet it is at precisely this point that Mannheim disappears from the plot. The leading figures in sociology today make little use of him.

Anthony Giddens, for example, began his work on social theory at a time when Mannheim's work was still remembered and his reputation was still high (Giddens, 1971; 1973). Even in his early work, which is mainly exegesis of the ideas of the founding fathers, Giddens made much of the capacity of groups to define their reality in particular ways and to act on their definitions of their situation. But the theoretical work that led Giddens to the theory of structuration makes no reference to Mannheim and does not draw on his ideas at all. Another example, that is in many ways even more surprising, is the lack of attention given to Mannheim by Zygmunt Bauman. Bauman is a thinker whose social position and intellectual project are very similar to Mannheim's. Bauman and Mannheim were both émigrés from Eastern Europe, both settled in Britain and made it their intellectual home. Both decided to make us in the English speaking world (seemingly against our better judgment) more self-conscious about the role of ideas in shaping our society and framing our mentality. Yet, signally, Bauman does not draw upon Mannheim or reference his work very much. Remarkably, one of Bauman's first books in English, his *Socialism: The Active Utopia* (1976), selects a similar subject matter to Mannheim's master work, *Ideology and Utopia* (first published in German in 1929), but Bauman makes no reference to any of Mannheim's work. Bauman's slightly later volume, *Hermeneutics and Sociology* (1978) does devote a chapter to Mannheim, but the reader is left in no doubt about the problems with his ideas.

A case for Mannheim's importance can rest on the fact that he was amongst the first to establish the plausibility of social constructionism. There are different conceptions of social construction, of course; but most of them share the basic view that social reality is actively created by participants in social milieux. Constructionism is enormously popular as a basis of thinking and explanation today. Indeed, it is so much a part of the way people think about behaviour, that it is difficult for many to see it as a particular doctrine at all. But one of the things that Mannheim clearly did was to set out propositions that are recognizably constructionist for the first time. It is Mannheim who asserts – as a key proposition of his social thought – that groups of people construct accounts of social reality indistinguishable to them from reality itself. In the essays that were later put together to form his book *Ideology and Utopia* (1936), Mannheim underlined the importance of the perception of social reality by looking in some detail at the connections between specific social locations and the characteristic ways of thinking established by social groups. Thus, several decades before Berger and Luckmann (1967) finally made a developed version of constructionism intellectually compelling, Mannheim had shown very precisely how groups construct particular but systematic views of events and the nature of the world.

Writing originally in 1927 or so, Mannheim proposes the following:

> There arise divergent and conflicting modes of thought which order the same facts of experience into different systems of thought, and cause them to be perceived through different logical categories. (. . .) The multiplicity of possible points of departure . . . and the competition between different points of view colour even the perception of what formerly appeared to be simple and uncomplicated relationships. (. . .) No one denies the possibility of empirical research, but the question of the nature of the facts is a considerable problem. They exist for the mind always in a particular intellectual and social context. (Mannheim, 1936:91. Unless stated otherwise, references to Ideology and Utopia are to the English translation by Wirth and Shils of 1936.)

This passage could have featured, without any noticeable incongruity, in the introduction to Burrell and Morgan's seminal work of organizational sociology, *Sociological Paradigms and Organizational Analysis*, which was published fifty years later in 1979. In view of this, why is Mannheim so little remembered? What can his ideas about utopia tell us to add to our understanding of the idea itself and about the value of his system of thought?

The context of Mannheim's thought

Some details of Mannheim's life and career are fairly well known. He came to Britain – and to writing in English – by a circuitous route. He is a member of what is even today a fairly exclusive band of people – those who have held full professorships in three European countries. Born in Hungary, the son of a Jewish Budapest merchant, in 1894, he was exiled twice: firstly from his native country, which he left for Germany in 1920. His ideas about the social construction of knowledge in general – and his writing about utopia in particular – were produced in the highly creative middle period of his life when he lived and worked in German Weimar Republic. When the Nazis took over, however, he was exiled again, this time to Britain, where he seems to have been content simply to try to apply his ideas and to formulate them in ways that would have more appeal to non-academic audiences. And he accomplished all this in a comparatively short life. He died of a heart attack in 1947 at the age of fifty-three.

As an intellectually precocious student in Hungary, Mannheim adopted liberal and reformist political views early in his life. Although he had had a good deal of familiarity with Marxism and contact with Marxists, his broadly-based education in Hungarian and German universities consolidated his initial convictions. These were that backward semi-feudal countries like Hungary would need to modernize industrially and politically; processes of reform he could see being fostered effectively only by 'progressive' (ie, liberal) political and economic programmes. However, Mannheim came early to the conviction that the path to modernity need not be smooth and the proposition that the middle-classes – although essential for modernization – were often in an exposed position. His experience in later life underlined the difficulties involved in achieving political consensus and the modernization of institutions.

In the ferment of revolution and counter-revolution in Hungary before the First World War, Mannheim aligned himself with a group of intellectuals in Budapest who maintained strict political neutrality. Thinking no doubt that his very public espousal of neutrality would protect him, Mannheim accepted an appointment as a professor of philosophy in the reformed University of Budapest, established following the communist insurrection of 1919. Many other Hungarian university teachers (perhaps more wisely) did not. Mannheim agreed to serve at the invitation of his more eminent colleague in the University, Georg Lukacs (Loader, 1985). Despite his well-publicized neutrality, Mannheim's association with Lukacs and, by extension, the communists, was enough for him to be forced into exile by the deeply conservative Horthy regime when it put down the communist revolt and suppressed its reforms. Mannheim fled to Germany, where he had some academic connections as a result of receiving much of his education there.

Mannheim was hugely successful in Germany. He rapidly secured academic preferment within the elitist (and notoriously clannish) German university system. He rose rapidly from being a doctoral candidate and postgraduate assistant at Freiberg to the position of privatdozent (lecturer) working in Alfred Weber's department at Heidelberg. By the time he wrote about utopia in 1927, Mannheim was actively seeking a more secure position in the German academic establishment and writing copiously. What he produced was a series of long essays. Although these essays were intended for publication, their primary target as readers was the inner circle of the German intelligentsia. The two essays that became the original version of *Ideology and Utopia* were among the highly scholarly productions of Mannheim's most creative years in Germany, 1925–29. Much of Mannheim's writing at this time, and *Ideology and Utopia* is no exception, is a clever blend of traditional scholarship and what was, by the standards of the time, audacious intellectual innovation.

Although presented with all the trappings of high scholarship, these writings were designed to be controversial and to make some bold claims. Mannheim's two essays, one on ideology and the other on utopia, are best understood as two separate and partly contradictory attempts to tackle the problem of the relationship between thought and action. Also we should note that, despite their high level of abstraction and wealth of historical detail, they also represent attempts to conceive of thought in ways that would allow a grip on the relationship between ideas and acts that would be amenable to practical intervention. Considered in this way, the analysis Mannheim offered of ideology proved to be much more influential than his ideas about utopia and, despite the daring and suggestiveness of his analysis of the latter, he did not develop this aspect of his ideas. There seems little doubt that, at the end of the day, Mannheim was extremely distrustful of the capacity of people to act and he was not fully committed to the idea of democracy.

Mannheim's work in Weimar Germany certainly gives a new emphasis to sociological reasoning by focusing attention on the place of thought in new ways. Since Max Weber had put sociology in Germany on the intellectual map in the first two decades of the 20th century, what we might call 'collective thought' had always been part of its subject matter, and there was a great deal of contention about its importance. One thinks of Max Weber's monumental studies in world religion, for example, the religious sociology of Troeltsche or Alfred Weber's speculative sociology of culture (Aron, 1964). Although Weber is theoretically strongly structuralist in much of his writing – as were many other German writers of the time – they usually forbear to propose general theoretical connections between structure and culture, or to establish clearly what are taken to be the fundamental mechanisms connecting social and institutional structures and collective ideas. Mannheim's approach to sociology gives a precise answer to this question by handling collective ideas analytically in a way that only Marxists had treated them hitherto. If you think of political ideas appropriately, for example, Mannheim argues, you can see them as produced by specific groups at or near centres of power. Thus, for him, the central problem is not that of understanding how ideas are produced in society, but to understand in what circumstances ideas may, in their turn, be able to affect society.

The connection between the origination of particular ways of thinking and particular social locations is a theme that Mannheim elaborates in a number of ways from his Weimar early days forwards. His difference from Marxists was to show that it need not be classes that are involved in the formation of political and other ways of thinking, although, for the ideas of specific groups to become widely influential, they would be close to power (rising to or declining from power) if not actually dominant social groups. The specific sets of ideas of such groups nonetheless have the tendency to become widely accepted as true, despite what is, from an analytical point of view, their obvious partiality. The term 'hegemony' was used by Gramsci to identify a more general tendency of a similar kind. Indeed, Mannheim would agree that, so obligatory do these –

essentially social – constructions become, that it is difficult for anyone social-ized into them to think outside of them. However, he adds what Marxists typically would not – that political ideas are *always* partial, reflecting the interests of particular groups – and for this reason they will be, in their origi-nal formulations anyway, defective guides to social action.

What Mannheim does is to use this sociological subject matter (the collective thought of groups) in a way that subtly alters Marxian propositions, so pro-ducing a damaging critique of Marxism and, simultaneously, the recognition that there are several competing forms of thought. Yet his ideas also suggested ways of thinking about contemporary politics which seemed at the time to be both novel and suggestive. Within a historical survey of the character and origins of modes of political thought, Mannheim proposes a radical way of rec-onciling opposed ideologies. In essence his ideas here not only offer a rationale for the reform of politics away from extremes of doctrine (whilst, at the same time retaining some of the distinctive features of different ideas) but also propose that it will be intellectuals who will be able to make the decisive con-tribution to synthesizing ideas. Mannheim's writing was, in fact, politically deft on several levels. To argue for a new role for intellectuals, Mannheim picked up and made expedient use of Alfred Weber's concept of the relatively unattached intellectual. He found new usefulness in this concept – which happened to have been originated by a well-known member of the German intellectual elite. Mannheim argued that the intellectuals – being, uniquely, unattached to any particular group – are capable of seeing beyond sectional interests and this makes them well qualified to propose syntheses of ideas.

Against a background of growing despair amongst German intellectuals, not to mention many ordinary people, concerning their ability to understand (never mind influence) the increasingly chaotic politics of the Weimar Republic, Mannheim's writing could scarcely be more topical or calculated to make an impact. That he caught the attention of the main audience he sought to influ-ence there is no doubt. It is a remarkable fact that, as a result of having some influential academic sponsors, Mannheim (who after all was a Hungarian Jewish émigré) nonetheless obtained a full professorship in Sociology at Frankfurt in 1929. By this time, Mannheim had been in Germany about ten years. To be awarded a chair in this way was recognition indeed. It was an achievement that had evaded many others, including some much more thoroughly assimilated Jewish intellectuals of high ability such as Georg Simmel. That Mannheim's triumph was short-lived merely serves to underline the scale of his achievement and the extent of the liberal reforms that were pushed through in Weimar Germany.

In case it is felt that this account offers only a slighting interpretation of Mannheim's ideas, there is no doubt that he did make a highly creative contri-bution to the political culture of his adopted country. His work clearly placed responsibility for the extent of political turmoil on the educated, and enjoined them to do something about it. On the other hand, it led him to place strong emphasis on ideology and how to overcome it, and to neglect and pass over other ideas. In short, it set Mannheim's own thinking into a distinctive pattern, in which ideas about utopia had little place. The formula that he worked out as his basic theoretical position was as follows: the social determination of the thought of groups, when worked on by intellectuals to produce some kind of reconciliation, potentially allows the effective reconstruction of political and other institutions. This set of propositions did find some kind of application in Britain after the war, in that the development of new educational and other social democratic institutions was understood by the followers of Mannheim in this sort of way. He saw the welfare state as a product of intellectual compromise in the thinking of elites, which, in Britain, in an important sense, it was.

Be that as it may, the complete suppression of the reforms of Weimar by the Nazis (not only its constitution but its emerging culture too) beginning in 1933 is, of course, one of the significant events of 20th century history and, as with so many other people, it had a direct effect on Mannheim's life and career. This was the second time a right-wing regime had made his position untenable. No doubt by this time he was becoming adept at reading the writing on the wall. He rightly foresaw no future for a Jewish intellectual in the Third Reich. Mannheim considered his options and, one step ahead of the Gestapo, he left Germany in 1933 to start his career over again in Britain.

The conception of ideologies and utopias

Despite the fact that his name is indissolubly linked with utopia, anyone interested in mining Mannheim for insights concerning it will find burrowing about in his work unrewarding. What Mannheim has to say about utopia is of interest, and well worth some effort, but the fact is that there is not much to be found outside the pages of *Ideology and Utopia*. The assiduous reader will find scattered references to utopia, in which Mannheim clearly identifies many examples of what he regards as utopian thinking. However, there is almost no sustained analysis of utopian thinking' or why it might be regarded as important' outside the pages of *Ideology and Utopia*. This, together with an encyclopaedia entry on Utopia, comprises his main output on this subject.

The task of identifying what Mannheim said about utopia is made more difficult for English readers by the fact that *Ideology and Utopia* was mangled in the process of translation. The extent of Mannheim's involvement or complicity in this is not clear. When the offer to translate the work came from Louis Wirth in the USA, Mannheim readily agreed and, in due course, he seems to have approved the English version of the full text produced by Wirth and Edward Shils (cf Kettler *et al.*, 1984). However, Wirth also suggested the publication – in the same volume – of a later general essay by Mannheim on the sociology of knowledge as a conclusion. Again Mannheim accepted. However, when it was agreed that the book would also be sold in Britain, Mannheim became more concerned about the content of the text. He was anxious that it should be well received in England where he was now living and working. He therefore insisted on some changes, including changes to the original text. Among these changes was the inclusion of a new introduction, again addressing his general approach to the sociology of knowledge. The addition of a great deal of new material in the shape of a new introduction and a long conclusion made the proposed volume overlong, and, as a result, some fairly deep cuts were made. These included deep cuts in the substantive sections of the original text – especially the chapter on utopia.

The addition of the new introduction and conclusion alone would have very effectively diluted the message in the original work. In the original German edition of the book, the two core essays are mainly exercises in historical interpretation. The consideration of utopia comprised not far short of half of the text. In the first edition of the English version, by contrast, discussion of utopia comprises not more than twenty per cent of the total. Although the translation was improved in a much later edition (1975), the impression given by the English version remains much different from the original German text. The result of all this is that what Mannheim says in English about both ideology and utopia is sometimes obscure, what he says about utopia being especially difficult to follow. The additional text, which appears as the introduction and conclusion, has a quite different emphasis from that of the original work, being much more concerned with interpretation and having been written some years later. Having moved on, Mannheim now conceives of his task in the English edition of *Ideology and Utopia* as that of giving a synoptic account of (his version of) the sociology of knowledge. There is little reason to think that the cuts in the English translation amount to a systematic deliberate re-editing of the text, but there are evidently some new emphases. Loader (1985), who has studied the original German text of *Ideology and Utopia* extensively and in detail, notes not only that the corresponding parts of the English text are shorter but also that the work as a whole has a quite different tone.

There is little doubt that differences between the German and the English versions of *Ideology and Utopia* have led to some different interpretations of the relative importance of the concepts of ideology and utopia in Mannheim's work. Loader (1985) insists that utopia is more important to Mannheim as a theoretical concept than ideology, but this is not the impression anyone reading the English text would obtain. Mannheim's ideas about utopia in the English version of the book are restricted to the last of the three severely cut chapters of the original work. These are themselves now sandwiched between general essays on the sociology of knowledge. More seriously, Mannheim actually fails to make clear a concept of utopia in a way that compels attention and will convince readers of its applicability and importance as a means of interpreting historical processes. The concept makes no further serious appearance in his thinking and writing. Arguably, also, Mannheim distorts events by his use of the concept. The influence of Mannheim's ideas on ideology led him to place much more emphasis on the implications, as he saw them, of his analysis of this latter concept.

The importance of ideology

Mannheim's propositions about ideology are well known and easy to make clear. Ideology is to be understood differently from the way it is by many Marxists. According to Mannheim, ideologies can and do lead to effective action by rising or declining groups to define events in particular ways and to consolidate their situation. Ideologies do not simply serve to justify and defend the interests of a dominant group. Further, ideologies can imply different kinds of claims to generality and inclusiveness. Thus we are led from a detailed discussion of the particular examples of ideology, to the discussion of the notion that there are general ideologies. This is considered to be a particular condition of ideological development, rather than the normal one – as many Marxists would argue – when they deploy the notion of *the* dominant ideology. Mannheim suggests, implicitly against the idea of *the* dominant ideology, a distinction between particular and general conceptions of ideology. He thus argues that there are, usually, several ideological systems of thought extant in an advanced society. Indeed, that there are competing general ideologies, creates the problem of how ideological thought is to be transcended in a special and acute form.

From this, Mannheim's discussion leads to the consideration of consciousness. He argues that, for participants involved in particular milieu who are producing an ideology, their consciousness will be almost completely dominated by the ideology that they espouse. Here Mannheim also discusses the highly contentious notion of 'false consciousness', an idea that he keeps firmly within parentheses. Clearly he believes it is in some senses a highly dubious notion. But he cannot and does not use the obvious problems of the idea of false consciousness as a stick to beat Marxists. This is because he does recognize that false consciousness must exist. He thinks this not because there are systems of thought that are exempt from false consciousness, as some Marxists have suggested, but because the simultaneous existence of several versions of the way the world is implies that they all cannot be right; and very likely none of them are. The key problem of ideology for Mannheim is: once you realize that it is there – and indeed realize that it pervades almost all thought – the question of how people can escape from its clutches immediately arises. He is very interested in the Marxian technique of 'unmasking', and argues that it can be applied to all ideologies. In view of this, Mannheim is, ultimately, some kind of realist in ontology. He does postulate the idea of a reality actually existing. He does not put parentheses around 'reality'. Just as clearly, however, his idea of reality is that it is, in any given instance, highly contested.

Ideology for Mannheim – especially in its general versions – is essentially a partial and somewhat distorted version of what is actual and real. It corresponds, at least in part, to what exists. If it were not so, Mannheim argues, it would not be possible for an ideology to be sustained or for it to be imposed by one group on another. The novelty of this conception is that an ideology does not and cannot completely falsify things. Whatever we may make of this, it does, in turn, allow some initial clarification of the differences between ideology and utopia in Mannheim's thinking. We may glean from what he says that ideologies and utopias are not different from each other in how far they motivate action, but in how far they offer a challenge to any existing social order.

Ideologies close down and stabilize a social order around particular principles of organization and key institutions, whilst utopias open things up by advancing contentious new principles and claims – especially about forms of organization. For Mannheim, utopias offer a much more fundamental challenge to an existing order by questioning its very existence and the founding principles on which it is based. Utopias potentially destabilize society by attempting to advance new patterns of interaction and norms of conduct. A utopia also has the debilitating weakness of not corresponding to reality in any way, shape or form; rather utopia simply counterposes what is claimed as reality with something radically different.

In his discussion of ideology and much of his subsequent work, Mannheim is concerned to attempt to deal with ideology. After his discussion of ideology, Mannheim gives extended consideration to the question of how an account of politics that is not partial and subservient to particular interests is actually to be achieved. He pins his hopes on two ideas: one concerns the developments of the institutions which routinize and order social life; the other refers to the intellectualization of politics. Using a class analysis of Mannheim's methods, we might say that the first of these propositions provides a rationale for the existence of some fractions of the lower middle class, in the shape of state functionaries and professionals employed by them; the second finds and emphasizes a social role for part of the elite of the middle class, in the shape of the intellectuals.

Mannheim has hold of the plausible idea that administration can be substituted for politics and vice versa. Clearly, however, in his view, administration is a much safer alternative. Part of Mannheim's appeal to planners and state functionaries is that he sees a historic role for them in converting problems of politics into matters routinely dealt with by the machinery of government. As they extend themselves, administrative regimes will gradually reduce the areas of uncertainty in which, as it were, raw politics operates. In his attitude towards administration, Mannheim has recognizably social democratic views. By comparison, Max Weber is both more conservative and more pessimistic. For Weber, bureaucracy would lead to the removal of passion and vision from political life, a process that would be very much to its detriment. Mannheim, by contrast, saw the same tendency as a benefit. Indeed, the perception of a broader civil role for bureaucracy is part of the recent polemical defence of bureaucracy by du Gay (2000). Weber himself might have modified his view on this somewhat, had he lived to experience the excesses of Hitler.

Mannheim also thought that developing institutions could not be relied on to close down the arena of politics quickly or far enough to solve the problem posed by the existence of competing ideologies. He undertakes a long review of the history of political thought in the Western world and then argues that the competing ideologies found today are not so much opposing as partly opposing and partly overlapping, and that we are in a better position today to see the overlaps and connections. Also he advances his idea of the potential contribution of the independent intellectual. Although he conspicuously does not give any examples of how it might be achieved, Mannheim does claim that it is possible to believe in the eventual prospect of realizing a new kind of knowledge about politics and imposing it as the obvious way of doing things, based on the work of groups of intellectuals.

Utopia as something different

The thesis we have considered so far shows the imprint of Mannheim's political experience. In both of the countries in which he worked before coming to Britain, the clash of ideologies was severe and the pressing problems of politics could be thought about in terms of suppressing the willingness of people to act on their ideological views. The telling question, for someone with Mannheim's background living in inter-war Germany, is how to respond to a system of politics deeply riven by ideological divisions. His answers, whatever we may think of them, are logical and thoroughly worked through. And yet there is a different thesis expressed in the chapter on utopia in *Ideology and Utopia*. In terms of the thesis Mannheim has put forward so far, it amounts to an incongruous appendage. The fact is that Mannheim's ideas on utopia are outside the main thrust of his ideas and stand in uneasy relation to the main body of his later work and thought.

For Mannheim, utopia is different from ideology in that, instead of tying thought and action down and locking it within a particular and limited view of reality, it involves a direct challenge to an existing social order, potentially liberates thought and dramatically redirects action. It is in fact revolutionary thinking. Mannheim explicitly formulates the nature of utopia in this way, writing very suggestively that: 'Only in utopia and revolution is there true life, the institutional order of society is always only the evil residue which remains from ebbing utopias . . .' (1936:178) He begins his discussion in this chapter by asserting strongly the place and value of utopian thinking in society. This is, that it involves the possibility of breaking out of ideological modes of thought and it offers, therefore, potentially at any rate, another and quite different solution to the problems posed by ideology.

Utopian thinking is significant, Mannheim says, because it disrupts the existing order. He writes: 'Only those orientations transcending reality will be referred to as utopian which, when they pass over into conduct, tend to shatter, either partly or wholly, the order of things prevailing at the time' (1936:173). Thus Mannheim apparently sets aside the habitual, modern view of utopia – that it is, by definition, completely unachievable. He writes in his best Marxisant manner that:

The representatives of a given order will label as utopian all conceptions of existence which *from their point of view* can in principle never be realized. The contemporary connotation of the term 'utopian' is very much according to this usage . . . (1936:176–7, emphasis in the original)

However, Mannheim illustrates his thesis about the 'reality-shattering' character of utopias in surprising ways. He provides four illustrations of utopian thinking in practice. His analysis however, leads him to the conclusion that, in most instances utopianism is a minority activity and short-lived. Despite its uniqueness, it is a historical phenomenon of little importance.

The first example Mannheim cites is the orgiastic chiliasm (millenarianism) of the Anabaptists and other religious sects. The Anabaptists were a schismatic group within post-reformation European Protestantism. Anabaptists believed in the imminent second coming of Christ and the realization of his kingdom on Earth. Over this kingdom Christ would reign for a thousand years. In anticipation of this, Anabaptists thought they should set up new communities modelled on their conception of this kingdom. In the relative fluidity of disintegrating feudalism, argues Mannheim, the Anabaptists, who recruited mainly from very oppressed groups within society, forged revolutionary ideas about the natural order for social life on earth within a basically Christian eschatology. However, so threatening were Anabaptist ideas and practices taken to be that not only the civil powers but also both the Catholic Church and orthodox Protestants sought to repress them (Smart, 1969:577). For Mannheim, however, orgiastic chiliasm stands as a metaphor for a kind of transformative action, action which finds a parallel in more recent social movements. It has affinities with Max Weber's conception of charismatic personality and the idea of value commitment, as well as ideas about the will, discussions of which were still common in German sociology and social philosophy.

Although Mannheim discusses the Anabaptist example at length, clearly the history of Christianity has recurrently produced similar revolutionary movements of various sorts before and since the Anabaptists (Thomas, 1971; Worsley, 1974; Reedy, this volume). The Marxist revisionist, Karl Kautsky (1914), memorably argued that Jesus Christ himself was spokesman for a minority group (of passively resisting individuals) who had broken away from the broader insurrectionary movement against the Romans in Judea. It is interesting to think that the (sometimes overweening) humility which is a persistent emphasis in the personal style of Christians, may have originated as a form of low-level resistance to a colonial power. For Mannheim, however, these religious examples are significant because they identify the tap-root of culturally born dispositions to act. There are some remarkable parallels between this sort of millennialism and that found as the early reactions of some tribal peoples to colonialism (Worsley, 1974).

Next, Mannheim spends a good deal of space arguing that modern liberalism took in and redirected aspects of the chiliastic revolutionary creed. Liberalism, according to Mannheim, takes in chiliastic passion and transforms it into the idea of progress, so that it is no longer an attempted negation of reality but made into some kind of metric by which to assess the progressive transformation of events. Although he writes several pages considering the transmutation of chiliasm into liberal-humanist utopianism, there is in fact precious little in the way of compelling reason to think that liberalism actually has its root in millenarianism. Be that as it may, Mannheim constantly reverts to the discussion of chiliasm. The nearest there is to an actual illustration of the process by which liberal humanist utopianism emerges from chiliasm, is a discussion of some French popular movements before and after the French revolution. Here as elsewhere, the loss of original material fatally impedes full appreciation of Mannheim's thesis.

Arguably, this example and, even more so, the next to be advanced by Mannheim, is less than convincing as an instance of utopianism. This is the example of extremely conservative thought, which can become transmuted into something utopian, argues Mannheim, in a rather different way. This subject matter is also given very truncated treatment. However, with the conservative thought, the idea seems to be that this doctrine, which is in any case not very self reflective, can nonetheless become articulate as a defence of the status quo or some idealized and mythical version of it, when formerly advantaged groups are under severe challenge. Conservatism, potentially, becomes utopian when groups set out to realize in practice what they take to be communities based on perfected conservative ideals. Although Mannheim clearly has the Nazis somehow in mind, this example is not explicitly mentioned. Potentially, of course, German and other modern examples of extreme conservatism are an extreme embarrassment to Mannheim. What the Nazis did was not only to shatter the emerging liberal reality of Weimar but also to sustain an alternative form of society for more than ten years. Franco's Spain survived for more than forty years. In terms of Mannheim's ideas about utopia, however, it is difficult to see these two examples as 'reality shattering'. Liberalism and, even more so, extreme conservatism seem to be basically about preserving reality in a particular form of society against the tides of change that seem to be threatening it. In the terms of Mannheim's other writing, then, these seem to be, almost classically, ideological.

Mannheim's final example of utopianism picks out for discussion certain strands within socialism. Here, on safer ground, Mannheim is prepared to go into some detail and to consider the variety or ideas and patterns of organization within the overall social movement: he argues in fact that the general tendency of this movement is to produce organized parties and to develop ideologies. Such developments may be seen as the failure of the utopian spirit. As Mannheim describes socialism, then, it is only utopian to some degree. Utopianism is generated and preserved only in the interstices of such movements. As with Christianity, so in socialism, he argues that only distinct and historically restrictive examples are authentically utopian. Within socialism, it is anarchist groups in particular that are likely to produce versions of socialism that seek the just society on earth, in the here and now, and which are authentically utopian. Anarchism, of course, is suspicious of formal organization and for this reason it is difficult if not impossible to institutionalize. No doubt this explains its tendency to fail to survive (though see Reedy's chapter in this volume).

Three of Mannheim's examples of utopianism – certain sects within Christianity, revolutionary anarchists sects and extreme conservative movements – do display some interesting similarities, which are worth discussing. It is important to note, however, that in this view, utopian currents only occur within broader movements and then only express themselves in action in special circumstances. Hence, although he begins by robustly defending the significance of utopian thinking, holding that its key characteristic is its potential for the transformation of society, the only examples that are actually cited are essentially failed experiments, put into action by extreme groups within much broader movements having a generally different character. The fact is that his two modes of analysing historical events – as ideologies or utopias – are not in fact compatible. Once having ruled out the possibility of there being higher forms of truth, he is disbarred from preferring one body of ideas over another. On this ground he cannot prefer utopias to ideologies. Once having given the concept of ideology precedence in analysis, the place left for the transformative action of utopian thinking is small indeed.

The (in)significance of Mannheim's use of utopia

That there can be ideas that produce dramatic but real change in social organization is the idea that Mannheim is toying with in his discussion of utopia. In his prior discussion of ideology, however, Mannheim has effectively ruled out the possibility of this, and mapped out a path of social development which does not need or have a place for radical challenge from below. There is thus no very good reason for including this material in his account. Mannheim's discussion provides another – but radically different – proposition about the way change might be secured than he has proposed in other parts of his book. In support of this proposition, there have been several good summaries of the argument of *Ideology and Utopia* which make little reference to the material on utopia at all. (See, for example, Lichtheim, 1965; Bauman, 1978.) It is a tribute to his qualities as scholar, as opposed to propagandist, that Mannheim retained these elements in later editions of *Ideology and Utopia*.

However, it does seem clear that, as Mannheim handles it, the idea of insurrectionary utopia is considered only in order to be subtly disparaged and set aside. The robust assertion with which he introduces the idea of utopia, according to which 'The representatives of a given order will label as utopian all conceptions of existence which *from their point of view* can in principle never be realized' is followed by a discussion of examples of utopianism that are often obscure and so seldom realized in fact that they hardly qualify for serious attention. It turns out that, from Mannheim's point of view, especially as he developed his ideas in later life, utopias are empirically and also theoretically unimportant.

Mannheim's account of utopia is full of damaging equivocations and qualifications. Unlike ideologies – which are forged by groups in power or close to power – utopias, as Mannheim considers them, are forged and put into effect by tiny (and, usually, manifestly ineffectual) minorities. Although some of these groups did actually bring their utopias into existence they did so for only very short periods and they all failed in the longer term. In addition, to argue that there are reactionary utopias, such as conservatism, is itself to dilute drastically the idea that they are 'reality shattering'. Taken together, the attributes of utopias as Mannheim describes them are highly prejudicial to the proposition that utopian thinking can be truly transformative. Mannheim's account of utopia is damaging to the idea that utopias – as ideal forms and patterns of relationships – can not only be imagined but also put into practical effect, so permanently changing the world. It is clear that, for Mannheim, real progress is simply not produced in this sort of way. Utopias cannot do this because, unlike ideologies, they do not correspond to what is real.

One of the ways of describing utopias that Mannheim introduces is to designate only some as 'active utopias' – with the implication that some utopias are passive (1936:187). If, however, utopias are by definition 'reality shattering' the notion of an inactive utopia is something of a problem. In this context, it might be useful to compare Mannheim's use of the concept utopia with that by Bauman. Can it be mere coincidence and accident that Bauman does not discuss Mannheim's use of the concept but nonetheless uses exactly the same term as Mannheim – active utopia – in his book about socialism? There is little of Mannheim's damaging equivocation in Bauman. The use of the term active utopia is as far as the similarity extends. Whereas Mannheim argues that the majority of socialistic thought is ideological – and only a small proportion of it utopian (and therefore potentially 'reality shattering') – for Bauman (1976) the whole socialist project is an active utopia. Following Bottomore, Bauman describes socialism as 'the counter-culture of capitalist society' (Bauman, 1976:36). He writes: 'Socialism has been, and to some extent still is, *the* utopia of the modern era . . . It should be clear that . . . to classify socialism as a utopia does not belittle its immense historical significance. On the contrary, . . . whatever inspiring power socialism can justly boast is drawn from its utopian status' (Bauman, 1976:36).

The use of utopia today

Although Bauman's identification of socialism as a utopia is an insightful idea – and an improvement in so many ways on Mannheim's excessively focussed account of utopias – it is not a reliable guide to the relevance and value of utopia as a concept for use in general social theory today. For reasons not adequately understood, any idea of the radical transformation of societies is not a negotiable idea at this time. For this reason, even seriously identifying with or being interested in utopian ideas – let alone espousing them – is to invite ridicule. But this discussion is not unique in demonstrating that, more often than not, ideas used in political and social debate are not intrinsically progressive or conservative but must be judged one or the other according to context. In case it is thought that the above statement represents relativist backsliding on the part of an alleged realist, on the contrary, it is only by having a firm grip on the real character of social change that it is possible to decide which concepts might be useful to find a way through the quagmire.

Although sociology has often (and sometimes with some justification) been unmasked as a species of socialism it would be tactically unsound to make any such parallel explicit. Today it is better to argue along the lines set out by Robert Nisbet (1962). Nisbet suggests that, in a certain limited sense, utopianism is an element of all useful and effective social theory. If we think of utopias as idealizations and utopian thinking as designating imaginative proposals about what social arrangements *could be like*, this suggests that utopian thinking is a necessary ingredient or aspect of social theorizing. Such idealistic conjectures unite ideas otherwise as different as Durkheim's notion of organic solidarity and Marx's idea of socialism. This is the sense in which it is appropriate for social theory to be utopian, and all useful social theory is so.

However, such an observation is far from being a general endorsement of the relevance of utopian ideas to theory. Used in other ways, utopia is unlikely as a model. Because it does not exist anywhere in reality, any explicit model of utopia is capable of containing multiple ambiguities. This alone renders utopian thinking *per se* questionable as a template for social theory. For this reason indeed, any known utopia is highly susceptible to rationalistic critique; and this has been so since the idea of utopia, as popular expression of an ideal society, was invented.

For example, in his dissection of Thomas More's *Utopia*, Peter Ackroyd (1998) shows that the deeply conservative More was out to lampoon and discredit the very idea of utopian thinking – especially to the extent that it might be useful guide to the emancipatory imagination of ordinary people. His main weapon was ironic and satirical internal critique. At the time it was written (1515), More's *Utopia* was exclusively addressed to the highly cultured European administrative elite and was not intended for a wider readership. More's readers were a group whose status as a highly educated people with some influence was deeply compromised by their servitude to temporal and/or spiritual authorities with absolute power. This position predisposed them to be sceptical of and to want to parody general expressions of human idealism. More's *Utopia* seems to be this: a lampooning of the very impulse for people to think they might design a better society. More, of course, was in one way highly aware of his servitude, finding the strength to resist the temporal power only through acceptance of the prior and higher authority of the Catholic Church.

John Ruskin described More's *Utopia* as: 'perhaps the most really mischievous book ever written' (Kinney, 1979). Accordingly, Ackroyd writes:

> *Utopia* is an ambivalent and ambiguous work in which various absurdities are paraded in the most apparently innocent and unsatirical manner. But it also harbours various contradictions which render the account . . . . . very suspect indeed. The counter argument, the case against Utopia in effect, is contained within the narrative itself. (Ackroyd, 1998:171.)

More and his chums no doubt had some good fun at the expense of common man at the time he wrote. In the longer term, of course the joke was on More, who, in his elitist sophistication, greatly overestimated the discriminatory powers of his readers in subsequent generations. This subverted his mockery in the longer term. Instead of subverting the appeal of utopia, he greatly added to the vitality of the thinking he wished to discredit.

Radicals are faced with a paradox. They know there is a need for idealism, but they also know that explicit avowal of idealism, in many periods of Western history, exposes them to ridicule. It is argued here that they need to be covertly utopian. Despite his initial interest in Utopia, Mannheim does not draw this conclusion. The whole thrust of Mannheim's work, in the forms that it developed after Weimar, was to deny the need for idealism.

Conclusions on Mannheim

Mannheim was not a thorough-going democrat in the sense that he believed democracy always to be the best way of organizing social affairs. He recognized its importance only as a long-term goal. He was by disposition an intellectual, and an elitist intellectual at that. He gravitated towards the intellectual elites of every country in which he lived, and was preoccupied with the outlook and composition of the leading groups in the societies with which he was familiar. The active cultivation of the German intellectual elite by Mannheim, and their sponsorship of him, has been touched on already. When he came to England his tendency was exactly the same. He joined and, indeed, was influential in constituting, a group of intellectuals in this country, which used to meet before and during the Second World War in London and elsewhere. That the groups he joined had members with widely differing views, did not seem to bother Mannheim at all. Just as he brought together the work of Lukacs and Weber when in Germany and tried to synthesize them, so he cheerfully tried to co-operate with arch conservatives such as T.S. Eliot. It is not recorded how far (if at all) Eliot's belligerent rejection of Mannheim's belief in social democracy as a political goal affected him.

The bias in Mannheim's views in favour of the middle classes, which leads him to be predisposed to favour them and their activities, has been noted many times. He has been identified by both Marxists and liberals as a spokesman for the middle class (see Loader, pp. 116–120). Such a bias has also been given some support in this account. Arguably, it is this bias that fixes Mannheim's ambivalence, which is, at times, indistinguishable from antipathy towards utopianism and which leads him, ultimately, to put more faith in (and to prefer) the activities of bureaucrats over those of idealists. But this is not – as will now be argued – also the key to understanding the limitations of Mannheim's views about social construction. Mannheim recognized the capacity of groups to form their own identities but he also recognized the necessary limits to such processes. At the end of the day, Mannheim's work leads to the conclusion that people have much more capacity to fear change and consolidate existing realities (through the elaboration of ideologies) than he sees in the possibilities for freedom resulting from their capacity to invent and to live out utopias. In this he was undoubtedly correct. But was he so for the right reasons?

It has been argued here that Mannheim was a species of realist; his thinking is, to that extent, inimical to the relativism that is often tacked on to the idea that social groups construct their own realities today. Often today, the capacity of groups to construct themselves is used to defend the moral if not the actual right of self-created groups to exist. Social constructionism, the observation that groups do as a matter of fact construct themselves, is taken to support a basic democracy of group rights to do so; tendencies that might be labelled as relativist or fundamentalist constructionism.

According to this, the capacity of groups to produce their own reality somehow establishes the legitimacy of their sense of reality and the ethicality of their being able to insist on what they see, in fact, to be reality. It is difficult to rebut this insidious doctrine by discussing the relative merits of the cultural systems from which a sense of reality springs. On the other hand, history suggests that any situation in which distinct subcultures or ideologies are both recognized and tolerated is rare. In the history of the world, it is much more usual for materially strong cultures to drive out and extirpate the organization and cultures of the weak. It is not sufficient, therefore, to rest content with the principle that one culture is as good as another.

Mannheim clearly has a realistic understanding of this sort of thing; and his whole project is to understand how best to avoid the overt exercise of power. He clearly grasped that reality – if defined simply as the capacity to be construct a sense of itself – is extremely vulnerable. The independent life of dissenting groups and organizations, as Mannheim knows very well, is routinely crushed out of them by the ideological and material power of dominant groups. Also, as he rightly thought, to establish something new, the existing institutional matrix and its ideological carapace has to be reconfigured. Obviously, this cannot be achieved by ideas alone. But he wilfully ignored this conclusion in much of his mature work, taking the social democratic line that societies can be reformed from the inside.

Bibliography

Ackroyd, Peter (1984) *T.S. Eliot*, London: Hamish Hamilton.
Ackroyd, Peter (1998) *The Life of Thomas More*. London: Chatto and Windus.
Aron, Raymond (1964) *German Sociology*. Glencoe Illinois: Free Press.

Barnes, Barry (1974) *Scientific Knowledge and Sociological Theory*. London: Routledge.

Bauman, Zygmunt (1976) *Socialism: The Active* Utopia. London: George Allen and Unwin.

Bauman, Zygmunt (1978) *Hermeneutics and Social Science: Approaches to Understanding*. London: Hutchinson.

Bauman, Zygmunt (1989) *Modernity and the Holocaust*. Cambridge: Polity Press.

Berger, Peter and Luckmann, Thomas (1967) *The Social Construction of Reality*. Harmondsworth: Allen Lane.

Burrell, Gibson and Morgan, Gareth (1979) *Sociological Paradigms and Organizational Analysis*. London: Hienemann.

du Gay, Paul (2000) *In Praise of Bureaucracy*. London: Sage.

Floud, Jean (1959) 'K. Mannheim', in A.V. Judges (ed.). *The Function of Teaching*. London: Faber and Faber.

Giddens, Anthony (1971) *Capitalism and Modern Social Theory*. Cambridge: Cambridge University Press.

Giddens, Anthony (1973) *The Class Structure of the Advanced Societies*. London: Hutchinson.

Kinney, A.F. (1979) *Rhetoric and Poetic in Thomas More's Utopia*. New York: Malibu.

Kettler, David, Volker, Meja and Stehr, Nico (eds) (1984) *Karl Mannheim: Structures in Thinking*. London: Routledge.

Lichtheim, George (1965) 'The Concept of Ideology' in G.H. Nadel (ed.) *Studies in the Philosophy of History*. New York: Harper and Row.

Longhurst, Brian (1989) *Karl Mannheim and the Contemporary Sociology of Knowledge*. London: Macmillan.

Loader, Colin (1985) *The Intellectual Development of Karl Mannheim*. Cambridge: Cambridge University Press.

Mannheim, Karl (1936) *Ideology and Utopia* trans by Louis Wirth and Edward Shils.

Nisbet, Robert (1962) *Community and Power*. London: Oxford University Press.

Panitch, Leo and Leys, Colin (eds) (2000) *Necessary and Unecessary Utopias: The Socialist Register, 2000*. Woodbridge, Suffolk: Merlin Press.

Smart, Ninian (1969) *The Religious Experience of Mankind*. New York: Scribeners.

Stewart, W.A.C. (1956) *Karl Mannheim on Education and Social Thought*. London: George Harrap.

Stehr, Nico (1994) *Knowledge Societies*. London: Sage.

Thomas, Keith (1971) *Religion and the Decline of Magic*. London: Weidenfeld and Nicholson.

Worsley, Peter (1964) *The Trumpet Shall Sound*. London: Granada.

Autonomy as utopia or dystopia

David Knights and Hugh Willmott

Introduction

This chapter explores a contemporary conventional wisdom of western culture: the understanding that autonomy is an unalloyed virtue, a version of utopia to be pursued without qualification precisely because it is viewed as unequivocally desirable and virtuous. The modern association with individual or collegial freedom, self-determination and self-expression give autonomy its laudatory and seductive appeal.

Autonomy is not a utopia in the sense of a vision of a good place – such as the Utopia imagined by Thomas More or the utopian vision that inspired the architects of Huxley's *Brave New World*[1]. In the modern world, Utopias continue to be imagined: utopias are being actively devised, developed and studied[2]. That said, we are inclined to view this interest, including the present volume, as a minority pursuit that is unlikely, in the contemporary context of widespread cynicism and disillusionment with grand(iose) experiments and their associated 'grand narratives', to have a mass appeal. We avoid seeking to contribute to a debate about specific utopias or dystopias since they are often difficult to distinguish, as one person's vision of virtue is another's view of vice. Instead we believe that it is relevant to give attention to practical, mundane utopian efforts – efforts that are often so taken for granted as to be almost unrecognizable as utopian in inspiration (see also Law and Mol, this volume). Amongst these we count 'autonomy', a desired condition that, as we have just noted, is widely assumed to be an unalloyed virtue, a version of utopia to be pursued without qualification or challenge.

Yet, when subjected to critical scrutiny, the call to become autonomous can, we contend, be seen to have a dark side when the self-discipline of subjects is directed toward undeniably evil rather than virtuous objectives. The twin tower terrorism of September 11th could clearly be seen to have been perpetrated in the name of the autonomy of those who choose to sacrifice their lives for a strong and, it might be said, utopian religious cause. Such appeals are not unequivocally distinct from other versions of utopia that are often criticized for their programmed rather than self-determining characteristics. There are numerous examples of these programmed utopias in John Carey's (1999) anthology but what they share in common is the elimination of real people (ibid. xii) and this is why the ideal of autonomy can coexist with what in this world would seem its opposite – a programmed world. Whether it is the New Lanark Mills of Robert Owen or more recent science fiction narratives (see Lightfoot and Lilley, this volume), they seem readily to combine the notion of autonomy or freedom with oppressive control. Mindful of how the other utopian visions – from Plato to More or from Hitler to Skinner – entertain practices that are, arguably, oppressive, we should be attentive to the potential of autonomy to be dystopic in the name of self-determination.

Ambivalence about the notion of autonomy resonates with the ambiguous status of utopia. Semantic confusion[3] has led to utopia being associated with a good place rather than its correct meaning as no place or nowhere (Carey 1999:xi), in the sense that utopias are and must remain fanciful places. They can fire the imagination and inspire practical endeavours but they can never be realized and, in this sense, they exist nowhere. Be that as it may, utopia is commonsensically understood as a good place that, in principle at least, is realizable. Conversely, the term dystopia emerged to convey its opposite: a bad place. Here we follow Carey (1999:xi) who suggests that:

> To count as utopia, an imaginary place must be an expression of desire. To count as dystopia, it must be an expression of fear.

Here we are interested in exploring the seductive, disciplining and potentially misleading effects of autonomy. This exploration is, we suggest, consistent with understanding the embrace of utopias by those seeking the 'good life', or a good place, while recognizing that utopias are, and must remain, figments of our imagination, existing no place or nowhere.

Utopias are imaginary places but they are places imagined within particular historical and cultural contexts that are productive of the desires they articulate. For example, it is difficult to contemplate the utopia hilariously described in the final chapter of Julian Barnes' *A History of the World in 10 1/2 Chapters* as situated anywhere but in a world of unrestrained consumerism. Likewise, the desirability of autonomy, as a possible utopia, is coloured, in the contemporary context, by historically specific notions of freedom, self-determination, independence, individualism and so forth, to which an unequivocally positive value is routinely assigned in modernity. It is implausible to believe that 'autonomy' has a universal, uncontested or invariable meaning any more than to believe that meanings of utopia remain unchanged over time.

'Autonomy' does not *describe* or even point towards some condition or state of mind that exists in the world. Rather, it is a way of imbuing the world with a particular meaning (or meanings) that provide a way of orienting ourselves to the social world – by, for example, ascribing degrees of autonomy to a nation state, a work group or the job allocated to a particular employee. Whatever meanings are attributed to 'autonomy', they are forged and negotiated in particular historical and cultural contexts that are framed within relations of power and knowledge[4]. Broadly speaking, the contemporary meaning of autonomy is associated with the desirability of, and capability ascribed to, institutions, groups and individuals making their own decisions about how to understand and manage their lives. Increased autonomy is regarded as desirable; conversely, reducing or restricting autonomy is construed as a negative, unappealing prospect.

The argument of this chapter comprises three, related elements. First, we begin by locating our position in relation to the influential arguments of Isiah Berlin. We elaborate this view that the contemporary positive value ascribed to 'autonomy' is largely a legacy of modern, humanistic thinking reinforced by the Enlightenment and popularized in the modern era through a liberal political consensus. Second, we examine what the ascription of equal rights of all to self-determination means for those disciplined by such principles. Specifically, we attend to ideas of 'responsible autonomy' and 'empowerment' that have become increasingly influential in thinking about management and organization during the past couple of decades. Third, and finally, we interrogate conceptions of autonomy advanced in two of the most important philosophers of the 20th century – Habermas and Foucault. What they share, but in very different ways, is a disillusionment with a liberal tradition of thinking exemplified by Berlin. For Habermas, autonomy is a distinctive and unequivocally positive human quality whose full realization is impeded and distorted by social institutions. He points to the possibility of quasi-autonomous reason detecting and dispelling forms of distortion and oppression so that the form of life anticipated in his concept of the 'ideal speech situation' can be realized. By contrast, Foucault's scepticism about the possibility of power being removed from institutions and forms of communication leads him to be equally sceptical about autonomy. He identifies the danger of the regulative idea of becoming autonomous operating to turn us back on ourselves, thereby tending to (further) isolate us from those who could be a source of collective strength in resisting what we have been made to become (Foucault, 1982). Instead of treating autonomy and reason solely as a means to, or end of, a utopian social life, Foucault invites an interrogation of their power effects. This ambivalence accommodates the understanding that the regulative idea of autonomy may problematize prevailing conventions and disciplines, with the consequence of enabling self-determination and expression; but it may also legitimize forms of tyranny in the name of reason. Autonomy and reason are, therefore, not essentially utopian or dystopian in their effects.

Thinking about autonomy

The idea of autonomy as a utopia to which contemporary, modern human beings routinely aspire is lucidly articulated by Berlin (1958:131):

> I wish my life and decisions to depend on myself, not on external forces of whatever kind. I wish to be the instrument of my own, not of other men's acts of will. I wish to be a subject, not an object; to be moved by reasons, by conscious purposes, which are my own, not by causes which affect me, as it were, from the outside . . . I wish,

above all, to be conscious of myself as a thinking, willing, active being, bearing responsibility for my choices and able to explain them by reference to my own ideas and purposes.

We suggest that Berlin's formulation of autonomy rests upon a conception of the individual as a sovereign agent who, asserting ownership of 'reasons', 'purposes' 'choices' and 'ideas', is clearly differentiated from 'external forces', 'the outside'. This conception of agency is grounded in the Cartesian dualism between mind and matter, or subject and object. Human beings are invoked as cognitive agents who act on the world, including their own bodies, in accordance with a reasoned set of self-interests or purposes. Agency in this conceptualization is self-determining, rather than a complex outcome of self-other relationships, interactions and interpretations. Absent is any acknowledgement of how the self, to which Berlin ascribes sovereignty, is a manifestation of historically and culturally bounded interactions, rather than a 'subject' or 'inside' that stands above and beyond the 'objects' comprising its 'outside'.

It is difficult to imagine how the construction of Berlin's sovereign self is possible without engaging the 'forces' that he would regard as 'external'. Thinking and willing, whether in respect of 'autonomy' or anything else, is learned and developed through processes of interaction within traditions of thought and through practices of will formation in which 'subjects' are participants, not observers or consumers. The very process of self-identification as a subject who is differentiated from its 'object' (s) is a social process. The practices – of thinking, willing, choosing, bearing responsibility, etc. – to which Berlin attributes 'autonomy' are socially embedded or situated; they are not, in our view, plausibly conceptualized as the manifestations or possessions of a sovereign, cognitive being.

Does it follow from this that autonomy is an illusion? It does *if* we follow Berlin in conceiving of 'autonomy' as the *sovereign* possession and exercise of will, reason or purpose. What is illusory, arguably, is the ascription of *ownership* of autonomy-generating practices to the self. It is mistaken to conceptualize the self as *a sovereign entity* that is governed by its 'own acts of will', 'choices' and 'purposes'. Autonomy is more persuasively conceived as a *regulative idea* that calls for, promotes and engages particular kinds of persona and actions. Habermas, for example, believes that the aspiration and quest to become autonomous can encourage critical self-reflection upon the credibility and value of established ideas and practices, with the prospect that they become actively chosen rather than passively received and followed. The processes of reflection and action that are ascribed to the motivating effects of autonomy as a regulative idea are not illusory. What is termed 'self-determination' or 'self-mastery' in discussions of autonomy is real or substantive in its effects; and these effects are plausibly attributed to autonomy as a regulative idea insofar as the ideal of autonomy promotes and legitimises particular kinds of action and agency that are described as 'autonomous'. What then is at issue is the social context in which autonomy as a regulative idea is embraced. This context may foster a critical and self-reflective evaluation of autonomy as a regulative idea but, equally, it may assume the desirability of autonomy in ways that feed upon, and contribute to, anxiety, fear and insecurity. Perversely, fear which Carey (1999) identifies as expressive of dystopias can be a product of the dominant discourse of autonomy when, for example, it acts to push people back on their own devices and makes them feel socially isolated (Foucault, 1982). With within the context of Western capitalism insofar as the self is disciplined by the discourse of autonomy, the outcome may be an anxious preoccupation with survival and success.

Embraced as a regulative idea, autonomy has what Foucault terms 'truth effects' to the extent that subjects identify with its value and participate in processes of self formation that are deemed to confirm it. Acts of will and decision are routinely but mistakenly ascribed to the self. More plausible, we contend, is a conception of the self as a fluid medium of discursive practices through which 'selfhood' is represented in historically and culturally variable ways (eg as sovereign or as predestined by God) and through which human existence is regulated or disciplined. Becoming autonomous, then, is a paradoxical project. The very construction of 'a life and decisions' that 'depend on myself' is reliant upon participation in social practices that make possible the formation and identification of what Berlin (1958:131) sees as '*my own* ideas and purposes'. That it is paradoxical, however, does not mean that it is incoherent or meaningless. Instead of dismissing autonomy as 'illusory', it is possible to appreciate and value it as an historically and culturally available idea. An idea that, nonetheless, merits the same measure of critical scrutiny that its embrace, as a regulative idea, commends to the interrogation of other appealing, yet potentially dystopian, visions and claims.

Modernism, humanism and autonomy

In a sacred world, the position and decisions of human beings are ascribed to the designs of 'other worldly' forces, such as the grace of God. Whether events or actions are abhorrent or admirable, they are interpreted as God's will – a will that is ineffable, beyond human understanding. In modern humanism, by contrast, the will of 'man' (sic), rather than magical forces or the word of God, becomes the centre and measure of all things.[5] Becoming autonomous is tantamount to becoming fully and perfectly human.

Human actions, however vicious or vile, are represented as willed by (wo)men. History is understood to be open-ended rather than preordained, and it therefore presents the possibility of rendering the world responsive to human control through the development and imposition of will-power – a power that is attributed to the individual, putatively autonomous human being. In principle, the social world is susceptible to rational interrogation and transformation as any transient sense of closure is produced by the worldly will of modern individuals[6].

Modern humanism and liberal political philosophy

In contrast to classical beliefs in God or the divine right of Kings to determine the fate of their subjects, modern humanism is founded upon the understanding that there is a natural equality between all humans to determine the course of their own lives. Each human being is conceived to have the (natural) right autonomously to exercise his or her powers of self-determination. These powers are considered to be axiomatic to the potential of human existence As Carroll (1993:3) has expressed this idea,

> The axiom on which the humanist rock was to be forged was put as well by Pico della Mirandola in 1486 as by anyone: 'We can become what we will' . . . So the humanist fathers put their founding axiom: man is all-powerful, if his will is strong enough. He can create himself. He can choose to be courageous, honourable, just, rich, influential, or not . . . Out of his own individual will he can move the earth.

The humanist belief in autonomy is an integral part of the Cartesian legacy of subject-object separation and the project of the Enlightenment. Here Reason is enjoined to challenge dogmatism, superstition and other diverse forms of compulsion that present themselves as beyond questioning and doubt. Conceived as 'all-powerful' and 'creative', everyone is considered to be equipped with the will to 'move the earth'. Humanism re-makes the human condition: the modern, autonomous individual is released from a pre-rational subordination to tradition and unquestionable authorities that assigned individuals to an object(ive) station in life with its accompanying roles and scripts. Only the autonomous individual is robustly sceptical about everything outside of the human mind, including his or her social destiny.

Since the Enlightenment at least, the quest for autonomy or self-determination has become a normal preoccupation. Indeed, it is possible to say that the very sense of personhood, identity and purpose of modern people is forged, 'disciplined' or 'empowered' within the discursive formation of humanism where notions of autonomy and sovereignty of the self occupy a central place. Adulthood and maturity are routinely equated with emotional and intellectual independence. Modern legal systems assume rational autonomy: the attribution of guilt can only be justified where the subject is assumed to have been capable of making rational and autonomous decisions. Except in certain extreme circumstances, minors and the mentally ill are excluded from the normal process of justice precisely because they are not yet fully 'masters' of, or are deemed to have lost, this rational autonomy. To lack or deny a desire for actions that attract the sobriquet of autonomy risks being seen to inhabit a degraded or spoiled identity deficient in will-power and/or maturity. To ignore, disregard, or fail to fully respond to the call of autonomy places in question one's standing and stature as a human being. Autonomy then becomes inseparable from what it is to be human.

The humanist idea of the autonomous individual is celebrated and defended in liberal political philosophy, exemplified in Mill's (1859) *On Liberty*. Founded on the principle that the liberty of each individual must be respected and protected, the 'right' to self-autonomy or sovereignty is restricted only insofar as the actions of the individual intrude upon the liberty of others. Except in this circumstance, there can be no rational justification for restricting a person's liberty by compelling him or her to act or refrain from acting, or threatening a punishment if s/he refuses. Forms of reasoning, persuasion or entreaty alone should be used without resort to force. Making a clear division between the narrow sphere of activity that limits or polices the actions of others, and an extensive sphere that is exclusively the individual's, Mill (ibid: 103, cited in Lindley, 1986:6) contends that

> The only part of the conduct of anyone which is amenable to society, is that which concerns others. In the part which merely concerns himself, his independence is, of right, absolute. Over himself, over his own body and mind, the individual is sovereign.

Mill's philosophy is hostile towards ideas, policies and practices that countenance paternalistic interference in the lives of others. Such benevolence is seen to have the effect of compromising rather than facilitating self-determination. More questionable is the claim that 'the individual' has sovereignty of his/her mind when, arguably, its contents and operations are historically embedded and culturally organized, though not determined, by its formation through processes of social interaction and reflection. Although heuristically helpful, it is questionable whether autonomous and heteronomous forms of action can be clearly distinguished. Certainly it is possible to identify (heteronomous) forms of action that are pursued out of habit, ritual or 'blind' obedience. Yet, even actions that are ostensibly the product of 'autonomous' deliberations involving the identification and assessment of alternative courses of action depend upon processes of will formation and decision-making that are learned through social interaction. A condition of assessing alternative forms of action is the individual becoming an object to him/herself, and it is only through interaction with others that it is possible to identify oneself as an object of decision.

As Mead (1934:138) puts it, the person 'becomes an object to himself only by taking the attitudes of other individuals towards himself within a social environment or context of experience and behaviour in which both he and they are involved'. In other words, any claim to be or become 'self-determining' is to be treated sceptically since it implies a separation of the sphere of 'the individual' from 'society'. Arguably, it is only through the medium of (modern) 'society' that the very idea of the (potentially) autonomous individual – as an 'attitude' derived from the other – is developed, positively valued and pursued. This understanding presents a direct challenge to the liberal assumption that the sphere of the private individual can be separate and distinct from public or political life. The so-called autonomous choices of individuals are already infused with political judgments and evaluations of what is just and legitimate. The very liberal notion of respecting and sustaining the autonomy of individuals in a way that is compatible with preservation of others' opportunity to act autonomously is itself an outcome of political deliberation. In particular, it reflects a consideration of the potential disorder that would follow the 'nasty, brutish and short' behaviour of individuals pursuing their self interests regardless of the effect on others (Hobbes, 1651, see also Grey and Garsten, this volume).

Autonomy at work

From diverse perspectives, work has been examined and represented in terms of the presence or absence of 'control'/'autonomy'. As Halaby and Weakliem (1989:549), in a comprehensive (though US-centric) review of this literature, have observed, 'the choice and discretion workers exercise over the substantive and procedural aspects of their jobs – labelled "control" by some and "autonomy" by others – has been a prominent theme of numerous treatments of the workplace'[7].

Recently the call of autonomy at work is evident in the value placed, by employers and employee representatives alike, upon 'empowering' workers by giving them more control, choice or discretion in their working lives. The mutual benefits to employer and employee of moving away from close supervision over highly specialized tasks towards greater 'involvement', 'participation' and 'self-actualization' in decisions and processes were first prompted during the 1950s and 1960s (eg Argyris, 1957; Likert, 1961; McGregor, 1960)[8]. This 'humanistic' thinking has been regularly revisited and amplified in the intervening years. Most management fads and fashions – such as TQM, BPR and Knowledge Management – rehearse the value of greater autonomy for individuals and/or groups at the workplace. Summarizing this thinking, Potterfield (1999:xi) notes that:

> the overall arguments are that (a) the fast-paced, ever changing, chaotic business environment demands creative, flexible, loyal, and highly motivated employees; (b) to attract and motivate these sort of employees, organizations would have to develop more democratic organizational structures that offer employees greater autonomy, freedom, and participation in decisions that affect their working lives; and (c) the increasingly well-educated citizenry would balk at working within the constraints of traditional 'command and control' organizations and would demand that the same democratic ideals and practices that are valued in the larger society be evidenced in the workplace.

Here Potterfield is attempting to summarize, rather than endorse, the kinds of arguments that are deployed by advocates of increased employee 'autonomy'. On Potterfield's account, increased interest in 'autonomy' has been inspired primarily by an instrumental interest in attracting and shaping the kind of employee who is capable of working effectively in a 'fast-paced, ever changing, chaotic business environment'. A commercial imperative demands (self-managing) employees at all levels who will respond creatively and flexibly, but also loyally, to changing situations without incurring the cost and delay of waiting for their superiors to instruct them on how to proceed. Any moral concern to introduce more 'humane' practices that provide 'greater autonomy, freedom, and participation in decisions that affect their working lives' is subordinated to this commercial imperative. In allegedly changed circumstances, employees' 'rich and varied, if incoherently organized and under used, insights and experiences' (Eccles, 1993:13 cited in Potterfield, 1999:12) are assigned a positive, rather than disruptive, value.

This formulation is ideologically unstable, however, as it harbours a contradiction between, on the one hand, the representation of increased employee autonomy as a commercial imperative and the commonsense idea that autonomy involves increased self-determination including the possibility of pursuing lines of action that might subvert or refuse such imperatives. This contradiction invites a reframing of the issue that privileges the expectations ascribed to a 'well-educated citizenry'. A coincidence is identified between, firstly, the 'democratic ideals and principles' that allegedly infuse the larger society and thereby shape employee expectations, and, secondly, the preferences of employees who are demotivated by 'traditional "command and control" organizations'.

Most accounts of autonomy and empowerment, such as those developed by prominent management theorists, represent changes in work in terms of opportunities to exercise greater freedom, choice, discretion, etc. These changes are frequently framed in terms of commercial imperatives but their demands are morally neutral, or even progressive, since they are seen to require 'democratic ideals and principles' to be introduced into the workplace, and thus enable people to become as employees what they already are as citizens. Even accounts of increased autonomy that place its introduction in the context of the development of strategies of management control assume that organizing work in ways that grant greater autonomy to employees is mutually beneficial – in the sense that it confers greater status, meaning, authority, etc. upon the employee and enables them to be more adaptable and productive whilst also reducing supervisory overheads.

Revisiting 'responsible autonomy'

This case has been eloquently made by Andrew Friedman (1977) whose work is most closely identified with the critical examination of Responsible Autonomy as an alternative human resource strategy to Direct Control[9]. Both strategies address the question of how to secure the *capacity* of labour to be productive, and thus 'to create more value in the labour process than it costs to produce that labour power' (ibid: 77). The principle difference between the strategies, Friedman argues, is that the latter (DC) 'treats workers as though they were machines', whereas a Responsible Autonomy (RA) strategy 'attempts to harness the adaptability of labour power by giving workers leeway and encouraging them to adapt to changing situations in a manner beneficial to the firm' (ibid: 106). This 'encouragement' to exercise autonomy in a way that is responsible (ie, 'beneficial' to the employer) is understood to be attractive to employees because it enables workers to feel 'as though they were not alienated from their labour power' (ibid: 106).

To understand the logic of this argument, it is necessary to appreciate the foundation of Friedman's thinking in Marx's discussion of the alienation of labour within the capitalist mode of production. From a Marxian perspective, the alienation of labour occurs when labour is sold, as a commodity, to an employer. Following its sale, the employer is legally authorized to instruct the worker to do what s/he (the employer/manager) requires (ibid: 77). Ultimately, the employer/manager can mobilize the force of law to secure the productive application of employees' labour power, or to terminate their employment. All variants of the DC strategy are viewed as coercive, the assumption being that coercion is necessary because employees are fundamentally lazy and, in the absence of direct control in the form of close supervision and instruction, will contrive to withhold effort.

Variants of the RA strategy, in contrast, are understood to reduce, or even remove, employees' sense of alienation from the ideal of exercising autonomous control of their labour. RA strategies, in contrast to those based upon DC, are distinguished by how they encourage sellers of labour to experience their work in ways that make it seem non-alienated. This is done by employers and managers 'accentuat(ing) the positive, peculiar aspect of labour capacity, its malleability' or adaptability (Friedman, 1986:98). The work of those subjected to a RA strategy is not directly controlled through mechanisms of close super-vision, machine pacing or set procedure, leaving some discretion and choice over how tasks are performed. Instead of seeking to eliminate the adaptability/ unpredictability of human labour power, which is the aim of DC strategies, RA strategies strive to harness this peculiar capability and thereby foster active consent, rather than resigned compliance or resistance, to productive activity.

It is the exercise of discretion that justifies the attribution of 'autonomy' to employees' actions, albeit that it is an autonomy viewed by non-managerial com-mentators as a more subtle or 'indirect' alternative to a DC strategy for secur-ing the subordination of labour to capital. In what does the subtlety of this strategy reside? The answer favoured by humanist Marxists like Friedman is that employees have an innate tendency or desire to exercise autonomous control of their labour; and that this impulse is frustrated when labour is sold, as a com-modity, to an employer who is legally able to determine how it will be deployed. A limitation of this thesis is that it cannot account for the willing subordina-tion of employees to strategies of DC and/or RA, except by appealing to some notion of 'false consciousness'. It is simply assumed and asserted that labour is not alienated prior to its sale; and that only 'false consciousness' prevents labour from restoring its non-alienated condition.

The assumption of humanistic Marxism, embraced by Friedman and many other labour process analysts, is that labour arrives at its point of sale in an unalienated status. It is as if the potential of 'labour power' exists in an historical vacuum whereas, we argue, it is indelibly coloured by its process of formation in which habits and skills, however rudimentary or common, are acquired. No question, the sale of labour routinely involves a loss of control over its use and application for employees, as others – managers, supervisors – determine how it is to be deployed. But it still may be possible to appreciate how, prior to its sale, labour is not an independent sovereign subject since it is already decentred. That is to say, labour, like other forms of subjectivity, is already embedded in complex power-knowledge relations before entering any particular labour market. For this reason, it is a mistake to assume that labour necessarily strives, consciously or unconsciously, to become non-alienated or even to respond positively to strategies of management control that appear to enable a move in that direction. That such striving does occur is attributable to powerful discourses that value and commend it rather than to any condition of human nature that compels it. Of course, in modern society we are all subjected precisely to such powerful discourses, prevalent among them a humanism and enlightenment reason that 'naturalizes' our desire for autonomy.

Accepting this standpoint makes us sceptical that employees will either react positively to changes that are represented as allowing them to exercise greater discretion or that they will be more or less seduced and duped by the opportunity to act more 'autonomously'. Consequently we are led to question both the former 'progressive' managerialist and the latter humanist Marxist assumptions about labour. The response of employees to opportunities or demands for more autonomy or empowerment may be expected to vary in accordance with context and political orientation (Knights and McCabe, 2000)[10]. For this reason, to the extent that they expand, rather than restrict, individual worker responsibility, RA strategies may be experienced by some employees as overly demanding and anxiety-provoking and by others as confirming a positive sense of self-identity (ibid.). While in the latter case, autonomy may stimulate productive power and employee commitment to the organization, as has often been recorded as the effect of teamworking (Barker, 1999), the impact on more sceptical employees is to unsettle them and even to render them unproductive. Regardless of support or opposition, most employees feel obliged to comply with, or even embrace, opportunities or demands for responsible autonomy. At the very least then, the outcome may be stress and burnout as employees are required to assume a degree of responsibility that exceeds the powers of autonomy that are ascribed to them. This occurs as enthusiasm for employee responsibility blinds managers to the limits of capitalist employment relations and their own reluctance to relinquish their managerial prerogative. Employee resistance to RA is often stimulated because of the extra-curricula demands (eg social activities outside work) of programmes designed to generate company identification (Knights and McCabe, 1999). In these and certain other circumstances, Direct Control strategies may be preferred by employees to RA on the basis that then the workplace obligations will be more than highly circumscribed.

From this standpoint, resistance to RA strategies is not an irrational act undertaken by individuals who, in Friedman's (1977:106) words, are 'essentially free and independent, but have alienated their labour power'. Instead, resistance to managerial pressures to work more independently or to exercise greater discretion can be a perfectly understandable response. It is a way of preferring the security of routine provided by DC and/or refusal to become entangled in a regime of subordination that aspires to colonize more, rather than less, of their labour power. However, the difficulty of this resistance and refusal should not be underestimated, given the utopian attributes assigned to autonomy both inside and outside the workplace in the age of enlightenment.

A basic problem with formulations of 'responsible autonomy' and associated ideas of empowerment and self-actualization, whether *managerial* or *Marxist* in inspiration, is that they uncritically embrace a discourse that perceives increased autonomy as a utopian goal. As we have noted, the valorizing of autonomy in this way is unequivocal in managerial versions of such thinking, the justification of which was examined at the beginning of this section. Working life as well as corporate performance will be improved, it is contended, by ensuring that employees have the opportunity to exercise 'self-direction and self-control' (McGregor, 1960:56). Or, for managerialists who doubt that a spontaneous consensus of individual needs and corporate objectives can be assumed, 'culture strengthening' is commended. This involves an active management of consensus through establishing a framework of values 'in which practical autonomy takes place routinely' (Peters and Waterman, 1982:323). Marxian-inspired discussions of managerial strategies characterized by 'responsible autonomy' also favour a utopian conception of autonomy that is understood to be compromised by disingenuous managerial efforts to align workers' interests with those of employers or 'top managers' (Friedman, 1986:99). For the apologists of managerialism, autonomy at work would be perfectly realized when (a) the business environment permits it; (b) managers attract and motivate employees by developing more 'democratic organizational structures' (Potterfield, 1999:xi); and (c) society has evolved to the point at which employees are capable of working effectively in organizations that have moved beyond a reliance upon 'command and control'. In Marxian analysis, in contrast, autonomy is fully realized when labour is no longer sold as a commodity and, as a consequence, regains its non-alienated, 'free and independent' (Friedman, 1986:99) quality. Again, there is no recognition of the potentially dystopian consequences of seeking to pursue the recovery of a non-alienated utopian existence presumed to exist prior to the commodification of labour. In failing to see the pursuit of autonomy, whether post or pre the commodification of labour, as less a reflection of human nature than a function of enlightenment rationality and its associated discourses, Marxists are just as capable as managerialists of reinforcing the separation of subjects from one another.

Having illustrated our position by reference to ideas of autonomy developed within management and Marxist accounts of work, we now further explore the ambivalence and ambiguity surrounding the idea of autonomy by reviewing how Habermas and Foucault assess its significance.

Theorising autonomy: Habermas and Foucault

In this section, we explore the relevance of ideas developed by two key contemporary thinkers, Habermas and Foucault, for interrogating and clarifying the meaning and significance of autonomy in modern society and especially its appeal within the workplace.

For Habermas and Foucault alike, 'autonomy' is a critically important idea for interpreting and changing contemporary social practice. Their respective deliberations on autonomy are positioned in relation to Kant's response to his rhetorical question 'What is Enlightenment?. For Kant, the significance of the Enlightenment is that it offered a 'release from [the] self-incurred tutelage' where social forces inhibit the capacity to apply reason 'without direction of another'. Kant contends that we are in a state of 'immaturity' when we uncritically accept or simply 'bank' the expertise of someone else – such as blindly accepting a doctor's instructions on a recommended diet (see Knights and Willmott, 1999, Ch1). In his discussion of Kant's ideas, Foucault contends that the Enlightenment did not provide human beings with reason that they previously lacked. Rather, it presented *the socially organized* opportunity to use reason autonomously: '*Sapere aude!* "Have courage to use your own reason!" – that is the motto of enlightenment' (Kant, 1963:3).

As Kant's injunction to be courageous also indicates, he was very much aware of the presence of forces that impeded the autonomous application of reason. For exponents of Critical Theory, Habermas included, the challenge is to develop a *critical science* that is dedicated to exposing and thereby challenging the presence and irrationality of such forces. The mission of this science is to generate forms of knowledge that, by overcoming the ossifying habits and seductions of 'self-incurred tutelage', 'determine when theoretical statements grasp invariant regularities of social action as such and when they express ideologically frozen relations of dependence that can in principle be transformed' (Habermas, 1972:310). This is exemplified in the kind of ideology critique favoured by Friedman (1977, 1986) where he identifies managers conferring 'status, autonomy and responsibility' (Friedman, 1977:6) upon workers as they try to 'win their loyalty to the firms ideals ideologically' (ibid). For Friedman, this involves a form of ideological manipulation, or distorted communication in Habermasian terminology. Its intent, he argues, is 'to have workers behave *as though* they were participating in a process which reflected their own needs' (ibid: 101, emphasis added) or 'as though they were not alienated from their labour capacity' (Friedman, 1986:99).

For Foucault, in contrast, the challenge posed by Kant's 'motto of enlightenment' resides not in the significance of the irrational forces that must be exposed and transformed through the production of critical science. Rather it is in the injunction to *practise* reason or *embody* the emancipatory possibilities of modernity, whilst remaining aware that the demand for a self-referential and self-disciplinary subjectivity of humanistic endorsements of autonomy, can be the greatest confinement of all. In our discussion of autonomy we have endeavoured to show how the understanding of autonomy favoured by both Marxists like Friedman and the mainstream managerial literature, merits sustained critical scrutiny. Otherwise there is no guarantee that the pursuit of autonomy will not contribute to the very forms of oppression that it claims to challenge and overcome (Knights and Willmott, 2001).

Habermas

For Habermas, the idea of autonomy resides at the centre of his metanarratives about emancipation from dogmatism and the compulsive demands of critically unexamined habitual conduct. Autonomy, Habermas argues, is a necessary condition of critical self-reflection that facilitates emancipation from dogma. But the process is not atomistically individual or asocial. Thus, in contrast to Berlin who conceives of the subject exclusively in terms of individual purposive-rational action (see earlier), Habermas believes this to be embedded in and ultimately dependent on the meanings that flow from, and are reproduced by, symbolic interaction and communicative relations. Consequently, critical reflection is conceived as a social process that is at once enabled and constrained by the particularities of its historical self-formation. It is not so much the consciousness of individuals as their communicative inter-actions that can become (unnecessarily) dogmatic, restricted or distorted in ways which provoke productive challenges to repressive power. Communicative discourses are therefore both the vehicle for, as well as the target of, emancipatory challenges and social/political transformations.

A key question, for Critical Theorists and for Habermas in particular, is how the outcome of critical reflection is justified as more truthful or less distorted, and therefore more enlightened or less irrational, than what preceded it. On what basis are such claims about emancipation to be defended? Habermas's response has been, firstly, to argue that the very act of communicating is founded upon the anticipation of unconstrained and transparent dialogue characterized by him as 'universal pragmatics' (Habermas, 1976); and, secondly, to suggest that the notion of an 'ideal speech situation'[11], deduced from this insight into the conditions of communication, logically provides the (counterfactual) basis for judging the truth of any claim.

In practice, the assessment of truth claims is recognized to be compromised by historical residues (eg institutionalized social inequalities of class, gender, race and disability or political exclusions) of communicative distortion that it cannot transcend. Truth claims even about the ideal speech situation must await the realization of the latter before they can be consensually validated. Nonetheless, for all its imperfections, the modern condition is understood to harbour the possibility of closely approximating the ideal speech situation in which a collectively forged rational will is consensually produced by the unconstrained force of the 'better' argument. The autonomy of acting subjects', Habermas (1973:89) argues, is guaranteed insofar as a communicative ethics exposes the forces that are shown to impede its full realization.

All those engaged in communicative acts are seen to be persuading others of the validity of their truth claims. In the ideal speech situation, they do so without resorting to anything other than the 'force' of their arguments. Habermas's theory of communication does not, however, assume the existence of an autonomous subject of reason who champions the development of a more rational discourse. Unlike Kant, for whom it is the autonomous individual who is the guarantor of the rational will, Habermas stresses the importance of the structure of language and communication (ie universal pragmatics). As he puts it, 'What raises us out of nature is the only thing whose nature we know: language. Through its structure, autonomy and responsibility are posited for us' (Habermas, 1972:314). It is the structure of language and communication, not an autonomy attributed to human beings, that underwrites and anticipates the possibility of forging the rational will of autonomous subjects out of an unforced consensus.

Anthropologically a degree of 'autonomy' is a condition of emancipatory action inasmuch that the cultural process of 'raising us out of nature' is attributed to or, better, exemplified by, actions that are autonomous with respect to the imperatives of nature. The natural energy of the individual 'libido, [that] has detached itself from the behavioural system of self-preservation and urges towards utopian fulfilment' (ibid: 312), is what drives the autonomous impulse to mobilize natural capacities to extend the possibilities of human life beyond the confines of the repertoire of nature. In short, because human energy is no longer locked into a continuous battle for biological survival, it can be diverted to projects of social improvement. But it is the communicative ordering of the social world through language that facilitates or impedes the impulse of participants to struggle with, and overcome, restrictions and distortions that are at once discovered by and detected in 'the cultural break with nature'. From this it is clear that Habermas's thinking about autonomy poses a radical challenge to the Kantian concept of autonomy. Kantian autonomy rests upon a pure, ahistorical concept of the 'rational will' that can identify timeless, universal maxims. Habermasian autonomy, in contrast, rests upon the situational production of 'rational will' through unconstrained communicative consensus.

Foucault

Habermas's optimism about the possibility of an ideal speech situation, even as a regulative idea, sharply contrasts with Foucault's understanding of the possibilities of freedom. Foucault is much more ambivalent about the autonomous subject and enlightenment reason. They are not rejected out of hand but, alongside many other discourses, enlightenment reason and autonomy are regarded as potentially dangerous. Unlike Habermas, Foucault believes that power is synonymous with social relations and therefore is deeply sceptical of any analysis that perceives or even anticipates a human discourse free of power. Accordingly, he eschews the humanist faith in autonomy as the basis for emancipation and the 'good society'. Why? Because the imposition of autonomy is for Foucault the very source of an economy of power that displaces the more barbaric strategies of a pre-modern era. Physical torture of subjects was necessary within classical regimes where transgressions were perceived as a violation of the body of the sovereign and their peoples. Within a modern regime, hierarchy, normalization and the examination of case files can be seen to remove the necessity of torture in a range of institutions from prisons to factories. Human autonomy is normalized as a condition and consequence of subjective self-discipline (Foucault, 1980; 1982). Enlightenment reason and the demand for self referential autonomy can be linked to the particular gaze (Foucault, 1979) where subjects are conscious of a disciplinary standard even when there are no physical signs of its presence.

As a discourse of modernity, the danger of autonomy is that it exerts a seductive power – a power that can make it a most oppressive discourse, as it imprisons us in its plausible moral reasoning and its rational promise of self-determination. That said, Foucault (1984) does not reject enlightenment reason and the autonomy that it seeks to sustain. He simply remains ambivalent, recognizing how, despite its potential to operate effectively as the greatest confinement (Foucault, 1982), the appeal to reason and autonomy is our only resource in seeking to resist any power that is deemed to be oppressive – including the very demand that we be autonomous, self-referential subjects. Foucault regards the pressure to be either 'for or against the Enlightenment' (Foucault, 1984:43) as a kind of blackmail from which no amount of dialectical nuance of seeing rationality as both good and bad can help us escape. What is needed is for us to interrogate how we as subjects 'are historically determined, to a certain extent, by the Enlightenment' (ibid.) in order to discover 'what is not or is no longer indispensable for the constitution of ourselves as autonomous subjects' (ibid.). This means being for reason *and* against unreason, including what may be regarded as the unreason(able) and potentially dangerous claims about the possibility of discourse free from power made by Habermas.

Foucault's distinctive form of pluralism warns against the excesses of absolute knowledge while, contrary to some of the claims of his critics (cf. Knights and Vurdubakis, 1984), not sliding into a position of complete relativism. It also involves him refusing to conflate or confuse discourses of humanism with those of the Enlightenment. While highly complex, the Enlightenment was a 'set of events' and 'historical processes', of which a key feature, argues Foucault, was an intellectual and philosophical concern with 'the mode of reflective relation to the present' (ibid. 44). Humanism, by contrast, is a set of themes concerned with a diversity of value judgements, dependent on the different historical contexts in which it occurs. In its different forms, humanism has been both linked with, and opposed to, Christianity, religion in general, science, socialism, existentialism, and even fascism (ibid.). Foucault sought to illustrate the tensions and differences between the Enlightenment and human-ism partly to avoid their confusion, specifically arguing that they have tended to be more opposed than conflated, particularly in the 19th century (ibid. 45).

While humanism is capable of endorsing any philosophy or practice that gives pre-eminence to human values, the Enlightenment restricted its support to reflective and autonomous reasoning. The point of overlap between the Enlight-enment and humanism appears to occur only in the 20th century, when the idea of human autonomy becomes the central preoccupation. For humanism, the preoccupation with autonomy reflects a universal view, whether secular or sacred, of the significance and elevation of the human individual. In the 20th century, enlightenment beliefs have been less preoccupied with what Foucault identified as their principal 18th century theme – our 'reflective relation to the present'. Instead, they have focused on the centrality of individual reason and rationality, which requires a belief in the autonomous subject as its condition of possibility. Being not so much for reason as against unreason enables Foucault to reject the individualising effects of humanistic thinking while retaining some conception of autonomy (ie our reflective relation to the present) handed down to us by the Enlightenment.

Being able to stand apart from what others seek to impose upon us demands a degree of autonomous self-reflection, even though what often we might seek to oppose are precisely those individualizing consequences engendered by a philosophy of autonomy. This use of autonomy to oppose individualization can easily be seen as contradictory but it is part of the subtlety of Foucault's analysis that underlies his refusal to be for or against the Enlightenment. His stress on 'our reflective relation to the present' rather than reason and rational-ity enables him to use the Enlightenment against itself. This reflexivity makes it possible to challenge the current preoccupation with autonomy and its rela-tionship to the processes of individualization that turn 'individuals back in on themselves' (Foucault, 1982).

For Foucault, autonomy cannot be the utopian ideal of a communicatively competent discourse unconstrained by power. The embeddedness of discourses of autonomy in power – knowledge relations renders them decidedly danger-ous. The Truth can only be realized through social consensus but this occurs as an effect of power. For it can transform individuals into subjects that secure their sense of meaning, purpose and identity through participation in discursive practices that are a reflection of particular power-knowledge relations (Knights, 1992). Deterministic, or should we say, pessimistic interpretations of Foucault are inclined to describe these outcomes as a dystopia – the 'sweat shops' of work intensification and non-stop technological surveillance (Fernie and Metcalfe, 1998, Sewell and Wilkinson, 1992). What such interpretations neglect are the ever – present discontinuities of control and discipline as well as the resistance and recalcitrance of subjects (Knights and McCabe, 2000) that may refuse to identify with the subjectivities imposed by power.

Discussion

For Habermas, the basic problem with Foucault's ambivalent orientation to autonomy is that his claims lack normative grounding (Fraser, 1996) in anything equivalent to the ideal speech situation. Habermas demands a transcendental framework that can act as a benchmark for assessing truth claims. Otherwise, claims to truth are viewed as arbitrary and uncompelling. Habermas revises the Kantian autonomous subject of reason, arguing that subjects are inescapably interpellated within forms of communication. Accordingly, the autonomous subject is conditional upon the critique and transformation of communicative practices that currently deny or distort its realization.

The merit of the ideal speech situation, for Habermas, is that it acts as a basis for the consensual validation of competing claims. In the absence of such an evaluative framework, truth claims are considered to remain idiosyncratic, involving subjective judgements of taste rather than a systematic process of inter-subjective assessment. Autonomy is, for Habermas, a condition and consequence of the exercise of critical reason. It makes possible the detection of, and appeal to, the ideal speech situation as a regulative ideal for debunking claims that impede the pursuit of autonomy by imprisoning and distorting it within asymmetrical relations of power. Only in the ideal speech situation is autonomy fully and freely expressed as the remaining impediments to its unqualified realization are convincingly challenged.

Habermas complains that Foucault is unable to provide normative foundations for his claims. But Habermas' vision of autonomy is founded upon a particular understanding of the Enlightenment to which Foucault does not subscribe. Foucault is not persuaded by criticisms levelled against what Habermas (1987:276) characterizes as a 'presentistic' and 'relativistic' position. For Foucault, Habermas's search for such foundations is at best elusive and at worst fanciful. Foucauldians are therefore untroubled by the Habermasian assault, except perhaps insofar as they regret Habermas's failure to recognize or respect their principled refusal to yield to a totalizing conception of Enlightenment. As we noted earlier, Foucault is neither 'for' nor 'against' Enlightenment, and is critical of those who enlist its discourse to support their role as cognitive, and also moral, police who possess a monopoly of truth about the Enlightenment. This occurs as Habermasians proceed to use their conception of Enlightenment – distilled in the formula for the ideal speech situation, for example – to assess the virtue of other, competing efforts to exercise critical reason. Rejecting both the pursuit of the Holy Grail of normative foundations for truth claims and a conception of critique that is 'oriented retrospectively toward the 'essential core of rationality' that can (allegedly) be found in the Enlightenment, Foucault commends an approach – a critical ontology – that is:

> oriented to the 'contemporary limits of the necessary', that is, towards what is not or is no longer indispensable for the constitution of ourselves as autonomous subjects (Foucault, 1984: 43).

Foucault takes autonomy as a given of western social life but, in contrast to Habermas, refuses to understand it as an irrefutable utopian good. Unlike Habermas, he sees the danger in autonomy as well as its benefits. He invites us to contemplate what baggage the autonomous self, however reflective, carries with it since it would appear to be a condition and consequence of an enlightenment rationality that reflects and reinforces particular modes of truth. In short, while autonomy facilitates our refusal to be what we have become, it is important to recognize how autonomy also conceals from us the very self-formation of subjectivity as a relation of power and knowledge. This concealment is especially efficacious with respect to those aspects of the self (eg sexuality) that we treasure as autonomous. It could then be precisely Foucault's questioning of the humanistic, autonomous self and especially its philosophical form of a separation between subject (mind) and object (matter) that leaves him *less* deluded about autonomy. He is willing to use autonomy against itself rather than, along with humanists, pursuing it as a utopian means of protecting us against the oppressions of political tyranny or economic exploitation. In this sense, Foucault sees neither utopia nor dystopia arising out of a faith in autonomy and reason.

Foucault is more concerned with how we can refuse the subjectivity of autonomy where it has the effect of individualizing subjects or isolating them from one another. But his approach to its realization is very different. Habermas is preoccupied with the normative foundations of claims that he wishes to make about dogmas or other impediments to autonomy. In contrast, Foucault commends direct intervention into specific spheres and relations, such as those between the sexes, the representation of illness or madness, and so on. His version of critique, or critical ontology, is dedicated to the immediate process of becoming other than we are. It is to showing what is superfluous, redundant or obstructive to the practice of 'constituting ourselves as autonomous subjects' (Foucault, 1984:43). For Foucault, autonomy is a practice kept alive through practice, and not something that must await its validation within the ideal speech situation. Of course, for Habermas, this is unsatisfactory and indeed dangerous as it appears to license any claim, provided it 'passes' as action, that disrupts the 'limits of the necessary', to promote autonomy instead of subjecting claims to rigorous evaluation by reference to a favoured regulative idea.

Conclusion

Our concern in this chapter has been to interrogate the identification of autonomy as a commonsense utopia: an unquestioned aspiration that may never be wholly realized but is nonetheless regarded as a desirable, virtuous goal. Without either confirming or denying the claim that human beings are innately and/or potentially autonomous, we have explored how the notion of autonomy is constructed as an ideal that exerts 'truth' effects in its routine disciplining of subjectivity. We have elaborated this understanding by reference to the world of work, where ideas of empowerment have been highly influential during the past decade or so, and to the thinking of Foucault and Habermas.

When we considered the sphere of work, we considered discourses on autonomy developed from opposite ends of the political spectrum – managerialist reformers and Marxist critics. Both subscribe to the idea of autonomy as a virtue. Despite their political differences, they share a view of humanistic progress arising incrementally (managerialists) or through violent social change (Marxists). Neither contemplates the possibility that the labour process may involve considerable ambivalence both for employers and employees. They each support a vision of autonomy on behalf of employees without reflection on the potential danger of imposing and promoting a narcissistic and individualistic demand for personal achievement and self-realization.

In addressing the appeal of autonomy as a form of mundane utopianism, we have followed a line of thinking that is closer to Foucault than to Habermas. This is not to say that we wholly reject Habermas's utopian faith in an autonomy that is free of unnecessary controls or constraints perpetrated by relations of asymmetry. But we are sceptical about the idea that rational argument can be the ultimate or sole arbiter of social intercourse. Relatedly, we are concerned about Habermas's obliviousness to the dystopian possibility that autonomy might be the most confining and disciplining of discursive demands. That said, we recognize how at times Foucault (1982) gives the impression that the panoptic society is upon us, having the effect of simultaneously individualizing and totalizing the subject. However, at other times, he stresses resistance such that a fully individualized and totalized subject would seem an impossibility. Most of the time, Foucault (1977; 1980) avoids such universal grand narratives and focuses on the concrete sites (eg prisons, hospitals, and schools) where power-knowledge relations and struggles of resistance are played out. It is within such relations and struggles that the autonomous self is both a resource and an outcome. Power is routinely exercised to develop, appeal to, secure or reinforce an autonomous sense of self or identity, as our discussion of the 'empowering' management strategy of 'responsible autonomy' (Friedman, 1977) sought to demonstrate. But resistance to such power draws precisely upon the same sense of autonomy, often couched in, for example, issues concerning human dignity or equal rights and opportunities.

In conclusion, it is perhaps appropriate to return to the limited comments we made at the beginning of this chapter regarding the concept of utopia. If the original meaning of utopia is retained, then autonomy can be seen as utopian in the sense of it representing no more than a vision that inspires the imagination rather than a blueprint of a future concrete state of affairs. The autonomy anticipated by Habermas's ideal speech situation conforms to this conception of utopia but Habermas does not contemplate its potentially dystopian effects. Should we accept the more commonsense definition of utopia as representing the 'good' society, then along with Foucault we should remain sceptical and ambivalent about the attribution of utopian values to autonomy, recognizing that the pursuit of autonomy can be as dangerous as its denial. For us, the value of utopias and utopianism resides less in their visions of good or better societies that, in any event, effectively demand 'the elimination of real people' (Carey, 1999:xii) than in the invitation they unwittingly extend to reflect critically upon the utopian promises and residues present within everyday anticipations of the good life.

Notes

1 For a very extensive listing of Utopian literature from the 16th century to the present day, visit the New York Public Library website at http://www.nypl.org/utopia/primarysources.html

2 Visit, for example, the Utopia Pathway Association at *http://www.angelfire.com/co/harmony/utopiapa.html*, the Utopian Studies Society at http://www.utopianstudies.org/ and the Society for Utopian Studies website at http://www.utoronto.ca/utopia/. A comprehensive gateway to information on utopia is at *http://users.erols.com/jonwill/utopialist.htm*).

3 The confusion relates to the first syllable of the word utopia being associated with the Greek word for good – eu. See Parker, this volume.

4 Of course, 'autonomy' is by no means unique in this respect as all concepts secure their meaning and value through particular power–knowledge relations.

5 It is worth stressing that we are concerned here with a modernist conception of humanism that is not that form of humanism said to be founded by the pre-Christian philosopher Cicero who, 100 years before Christ, translated the ancient Greek philosophers for Roman consumption. While there are a number of contrasts, for our purposes it is simply that the autonomous subject was not a part of the ancient philosophies whereas it is an essential element in modern versions of humanism. This is not to suggest that modernity be characterized by a singular universal humanist discourse. There is a diversity of such discourses – Christian, existentialist, Marxist, Freudian – but they share one common belief in treating the human being at the centre of the universe. Indeed Foucault (1984) has argued that 'humanism is too diverse and inconsistent to serve as an axis for reflection' (Quoted in Townley, 1999:301).

6 For Kant, autonomy is conceived in terms of the exercise of a *rational* will to identify *universal*, self-ruling maxims. In later humanist thought, influenced by existentialist thinking, autonomy is conceived as a leap of faith, rather than rational calculation, to a fundamentally arbitrary (rather than rationally defensible) value-position. For Weber, for example, this leap may be rationally framed and informed but it is not rationally calculated (see Willmott, 1993; Alvesson and Willmott, 1996).

7 Amongst such studies they include the classic studies by Walker and Guest (1952), Gouldner (1954), Blauner (1964) as well as Marxist studies (eg Braverman, 1974; Burawoy, 1979; Clawson, 1980; Friedman, 1977).

8 As with all aspects of innovation, it is possible to find even earlier versions of these strategies of involving employees more in the work activity. Jacques (1996:156) sees parallels to the job enrichment/enlargement literature in the industrial psychology of Scott and Clothier (1923).

9 While there is not space here to discuss it in detail, this analytical distinction is in danger of being reified as if management had no choice but to adopt one or other of these polarized approaches. We distance ourselves from such a view, for as Knights and McCabe (2000a) argue: 'these distinctions are not in practice alternative approaches to management let alone polar opposites. For power and control is only necessary because those over whom it is exercised are free and autonomous to behave in ways contrary to that desired by those exercising the power. Consequently, power is always about persuading others to use their autonomy in a 'responsible' manner' . . . 'power is exercised on the actions (power) of others; if this were not so, subordinates would be subject to domination and their behaviour simply determined'.

10 In this study, although by no means exhaustive of possibilities, we found 3 common responses to teamworking and its demand for responsible autonomy that we labelled the 'bewitched' who

welcomed it and the 'bothered' and 'bewildered' who were more sceptical or highly critical (Knights and McCabe, 2000).

11 The ideal speech situation includes, for example, equal chances of all participants to engage in the dialogue. For Habermas, the ideal speech situation operates in the process of communication and is anticipated by it. In this sense it is a regulative idea but it is an idea presupposed by all communication rather than one that is identified, as one possibility, by it.

References

Argyris, C. (1957) *Personality and Organization*, New York: HarperCollins.

Barker, J. (1999) *The Discipline of Teamwork*, London: Sage.

Berlin, I. (1958) 'Two Concepts of Liberty' in I. Berlin, ed., *Four Essays on Liberty*, Oxford: Oxford University Press.

Blauner (1964) *Alienation and Freedom*, Chicago: Chicago University Press.

Braverman, H. (1974) *Labor and Monopoly Capital*, New York: Monthly Review Press.

Burawoy, M. (1979) *Manufacturing Consent: Changes in the Labor Process Under Monopoly Capitalism*, Chicago: University of Chicago Press.

Carey, J., ed. (1999) *The Faber Book of Utopias*, London: Faber and Faber.

Carroll, J. (1993) *Humanism: The Wreck of Western Culture*, London: Fontana.

Clawson, D. (1980) *Bureaucracy and the Labor Process*, New York: Monthly Review Press.

Du Gay, P. and Salaman, G. (1992) 'The Cult(ure) of the Customer', *Journal of Management Studies*, 29, 5: 633.

Eccles, (1993) '*The Deceptive Allure of Empowerment*', Long Range Planning, 26, 6: 13–21.

Ezzamel, M. and Willmott, H.C. (1998) 'Accounting for Teamwork: A Critical Study of Group-Based Systems of Organizational Control', *Administrative Science Quarterly*, 43, 2: 358–396.

Fernie, S. and Metcalf, D. (1998) '(Not)Hanging on the Telephone: Payment Systems in the New Sweatshops' Paper No.390, Centre for Economic Performance.

Foucault, M. (1977) *The History of Sexuality Part One*, London: Tavistock.

Foucault, M. (1979) *Discipline and Punish*, Harmondsworth: Penguin.

Foucault, M. (1980) *Power/Knowledge*, (ed.) Gordon, C. London: Harvester Wheatsheaf.

Foucault, M. (1982) 'The Subject and Power' in H. Dreyfus and P. Rabinow, *Michel Foucault: Beyond Structure and Hermeneutics*, Brighton: Harvester Press, pp. 208–226.

Foucault (1984) 'What is enlightenment?' in P. Robinow (ed.), *The Foucault Reader*, London, Penguin.

Fraser, N. (1996) 'Michel Foucault: A "Young Conservative"?' in S.J. Hekman (ed.) *Feminist Interpretations of Michel Foucault*, Pensylvania: Pensylvania State University Press, pp. 15–38.

Friedman, A. (1977) *Industry and Labour: Class Struggle at Work and Monopoly Capitalism*, London: Macmillan.

Friedman, A. (1986) 'Developing the Managerial Strategies Approach to the Labour Process', *Capital and Class*.

Gouldner, A. (1954) *Patterns of Industrial Bureaucracy*, New York: Free Press.

Habermas, J. (1972) *Knowledge and Human Interests*, London: Heinemann.

Habermas, J. (1973) *Legitimation Crisis*, Boston: Beacon.

Habermas, J. (1976) 'What is Universal Pragmatics?' in J. Habermas, *Communication and the Evolution of Society*, London: Heinemann.

Habermas, J. (1987) *The Philosophical Discourse of Modernity*, Oxford: Polity.

Halaby, C.N. and Weakliem, D.L. (1989) 'Worker Control and Attachment to the Firm', *American Journal of Sociology*, 95, 3: 549–591.

Hobbes, T. (1651) *The Leviathan*, London.

Jacques, R. (1996) *Manufacturing the Employee: Management Knowledge from the 19th to 21st Centuries*, London: Sage.

Kant, I. (1963) *Kant on History*, ed. L.W. Beck, New York.

Knights, D. (1992) 'Changing Spaces: The Disruptive Power of Epistemological Location for the Management and Organisational Sciences', *Academy of Management Review*, Vol. 17 No. 3, July, pp. 514–36 also in M.B. Calas, and L. Smircich (eds) *Postmodern Management Theory*, Vermont, USA: Ashgate Publishing Company, 1997, pp. 171–194.

Knights D. and McCabe D. (1999) 'Team drives and private lives: team and gender tensions in a call and processing centre', Delivered at the 3rd International Workshop on Teamworking at Royal Holloway, University of London, 14–15th Sept.

Knights, D. and McCabe, D. (2000) 'Bewitched, Bothered and Bewildered: The Meaning and Experience of Teamworking for Employees in an Automobile Company', *Human Relations*, Vol. 53 No. 11, pp. 1481–1517.

Knights D. and Vurdubakis T. 'Foucault, Power, Resistance and All That', in J. Jermier *et al*, editors, *Resistance and Power in Organizations*, London: Routledge, 1994, pp.167–198.

Knights, D. and Willmott, H. (1999) *Management Lives: Power and Identity in Work Organisations*, London: Sage.

Knights, D. and Willmott, H. (2001) 'Autonomy as a narrative of oppression and of the oppressed' presented at the Narratives of Oppressors and Narratives of Oppressed stream at the CMS Conference, July 11–13th, UMIST, Manchester.

Likert R. (1961) *New Patterns of Management*, New York: McGraw-Hill.

Lindley, R. (1986) *Autonomy*, London: Macmillan.

McGregor D. (1960) The Human Side of Enterprise, New York: McGraw-Hill.

Mead, G.H. (1934) *Mind, Self and Society*, Chicago: University of Chicago Press.

Peters, T. and Waterman, R.H. (1982) In Search of Excellence, New York: Harper and Row.

Potterfield, T.A. (1999) *The Business of Employee Empowerment: Democracy and Ideology in the Workplace*, Westport, Conneticut: Quorum.

Scott W.D. and Clothier R.C. (1923) *Personnel Management: Principles, Practices and Points of View*, Chicago: A. W. Shaw and Co.

Sewell, G. and Wilkinson, B. (1992) 'Someone to Watch Over Me: Surveillance, Discipline, and the Just-in-time Labour Process' *Sociology*, 26, 2, 271–191.

Townley, B. (1999) 'Nietzche, Competencies and Ubermensch', *Organization*, Vol 6 no 2 pp. 285–305.

Walker, C.R. and Guest, R.H. (1952) *The Man on the Assembly Line*, Cambridge: Harvard University Press.

Willmott, H.C. (1993) 'Strength is Ignorance; Slavery is Freedom: Managing Culture in Modern Organizations, *Journal of Management Studies*, 30, 4: 515–552.

Local entanglements or utopian moves: an inquiry into train accidents[1]

John Law and Annemarie Mol

British Railways: a National Crisis in Confidence

In 1996, after nearly fifty years in public ownership, the British rail network was privatized. As a part of this, what had been single organization, British Rail, was broken into a set of different units which were individually sold off. Prominent among these were Railtrack plc (owner of the track, stations, signalling and other infrastructure), more than twenty train operating companies (TOCs) which received franchises to run trains (usually with government subsidies), and three companies which owned and leased rolling stock[2].

This privatization and the consequent fragmentation was (and remains) controversial. There were successes – traffic and rail use substantially increased after privatization, at least until the events we describe below, in part because of increased services and improved passenger facilities. At the same time, however, the railway was subjected to intense public scrutiny and criticism. Fare levels, unreliability, delays, poor rolling-stock, overcrowding, lack of co-ordination between the different train operating companies, all of these were the subject of widespread complaint. But our particular interest here is in safety – and a series of more or less serious accidents.

Accidents and incidents between 1996 and early 2001 are listed in Table 1. Some are much more serious than others, but three were particularly significant, both in their scale, and their role in generating a sense of crisis and shaping debate about railway safety in the UK. These are: the Southall collision in September, 1997; the Ladbroke Grove collision in October 1999; and the Hatfield derailment in October 2000.[4] A few words on each.

The Southall collision, in which a high speed passenger train which passed through a danger signal and collided with a freight train, became the subject of a major public inquiry[5]. However, before this Inquiry reported it was overtaken by the second collision between two passenger trains at Ladbroke Grove. This was particularly horrific, with greater loss of life and injury, in part because of the speed of impact and in part because of a devastating fire. The national sense of emergency that followed was also, however, because this accident took place on the same stretch of track (the approach to London's Paddington station) and was the result of a similar error (a train passing a signal at danger). Was there

Table 1: Recent Railway Accidents in the UK[3]

Date	Location	Deaths	Injuries	Cause
8 Aug, 1996	Watford South	1	6	Signal Passed at Danger, Collision
19 Sep, 1997	Southall	7	150	Signal Passed at Danger, Collision
8 Jan, 1999	Spa Road	0	4	Signal Passed at Danger, Collision
23 Jan, 1999	Winsford	0	27	Signal Passed at Danger, Collision
18 Jun, 1999	Cookham	0	0	Near miss on automatic level crossing
5 Oct, 1999	Ladbroke Grove	31	414	Signal Passed at Danger, Collision
18 Oct, 1999	Lewes	0	0	Signal Passed at Danger, Collision
17 Oct, 2000	Hatfield	4	70	Derailment caused by broken rail
19 Oct, 2000	Stafford			Derailment caused by broken rail
26 Oct, 2000	Virginia Water			Derailment caused by slippery rails
1 Nov, 2000	Bristol			Collision caused by brake failure
28 Feb, 2001	Selby	10	70	Collision caused by road vehicle

something systematically wrong with the organization and the management of the British rail system? This was the question. The accident led to a further public inquiry, which became a forum which explored not only the proximate causes of the crash, but also possible background factors including management style and competence, the role of privatization, the relation between profit and safety, and the commercial and organizational fragmentation of the railway system[6].

Public confidence in the railway system, already seriously undermined as a result of these two accidents, suffered a *coup de grace* with the derailment which took place about a year later at Hatfield in October 2000. The circumstances of this accident were quite different. A train travelling on an open stretch of track in the countryside north of London was derailed at about 185 kilometres per hour. The first three vehicles stayed on the track, the middle coaches stayed upright, but the buffet car towards the end of the train fell on its side and part of its roof was ripped off. It rapidly became clear that the accident was caused by neither driver nor signal error but rather by rail failure. A length of rail about 35 metres long had simply disintegrated into approximately 200 pieces as the train passed over it[7].

The immediate result was a decision by Railtrack to impose draconian speed restrictions on large parts of the British rail network while it inspected the track and re-railed where necessary. The consequence was chaos. For many weeks there were no published train timetables for any part of the UK. Journeys took twice or three times as long as before the restrictions – and were often altogether impossible.[8] As thousands of kilometres of track were inspected, and hundreds of kilometres replaced, system timetables were still slow and disrupted more than six months after the derailment. More generally, the industry was widely seen as having suffered a major setback in terms of financial and passenger growth, and public confidence. Tensions between the train operating companies and Railtrack, usually well-concealed, were surfacing regularly in the media, and Railtrack started to suffer considerable financial stress – stress which, about a year later, was to lead to it being put into receivership.

Interlude: the Good

What to make of this sorry tale? We do not comment directly on rail safety in this chapter (though our argument has some implications for this[9]). Instead we are interested in what philosophers call 'the good'. Train accidents signal a lack of good: they offer participants and observers an occasion to mourn, to regret, and to find fault. But how? Philosophy has a rich tradition of painstakingly seeking to establish standards for 'the good': good technology; good knowledge; good management; good policy; good action. Here, we work differently. Instead of seeking to frame 'the good' ourselves, we explore how others go about this task.[10] For this is an everyday activity. Attempts to differentiate between errors and achievements, failures and successes, falsehoods and truths, problems and solutions, or catastrophes and triumphs (the terms vary), are not the prerogative of a specialist academic discipline. Most everyday practices make use of, or try to create, scales to measure or contrast 'goods' and 'bads'. This opens a space for an *empirical philosophy*. An ethnographic interest in practice can be combined with a philosophical concern with 'the good' to explore which 'good/bad' scale is being enacted, and how this is being done[11]. It is the latter question we engage with here: the *mode* of handling 'goods' and 'bads' in the context of the various British railway accidents.

Thus, the Selby crash aside, the accidents were not treated as an act of fate. They were set up, instead, as a consequence of human failure. For instance, this is Finn Brennan, East Finchley branch secretary of the train driver's union, ASLEF, after Ladbroke Grove:

> What makes me most sick and angry is when they talk about the 'accident at Paddington.' That was no accident. It was no accident that ATP [Automatic Train Protection] was not put in. It was a political and financial decision. Railtrack managers have blood on their hands.[12]

This is an accusation. Particular actors are being accused and called upon to justify themselves and account for their actions. And we will argue that this is a *utopian* mode of engaging with 'the good'. This is because, with the loss of the irony implied in the origins of the term 'utopia', utopian modes for dealing with the good came to suggest that perfection is possible: that the absence of good is not necessary. Thus they evoke the possibility of a tension-free zone: a place or a situation where there are no clashes between what one might call, in the plural, different goo*ds*. And with this comes another characteristic feature: utopian modes of dealing with the good are necessarily discursive.

We are saying, then, that in utopian modes 'the good' is disentangled both from other goods and from the practicalities of non-discursive life. Material and practical entanglements make it impossible to serve a single, purified 'good'[13]. Such entanglements do not sustain utopias. There are, however, other modes of dealing with 'the good' as well. In complex, mundane, material practice 'the good' tends to figure as something to tinker towards – silently. So this is our position: that while utopian modes of relating to the good pose as *really* good, as better than best, we are suspicious of their disentangled discursivity. In a world where verbal justification and numerical accounting have become increasingly important, stressing the specificities of non-discursive practice and speaking up for silence are becoming matters of urgency. Instead of seeking to purify systems with more and more 'rationalization' it would be better to attend more to the complexity of sites and situations where there are many goods which are sometimes incompatible and may even be inarticulable.

'ATP is the only way of getting the drivers to stop'

The Selby derailment in February, 2001 was caused by a vehicle running down a motorway embankment onto a main-line railway track. It rapidly became clear that this vehicle had left the road at a point before the crash barrier precisely intended to stop such an incident – which meant that it had travelled a long way, perhaps 50 metres, before coming to rest. The result was an accident widely regarded as 'freakish'[14]:

> . . . at this stage the accident appears to have been just that, a dreadful concatenation of random events. Subtract any one of them – the vehicle leaving the road a moment later, the freight train a moment earlier – the result might have been altogether different.[15]

Even so, the accident quickly produced its crop of bright ideas and questions. For instance *The Guardian* printed seven letters about the Selby accident two days later on March 2nd. Amongst these, two suggested that road traffic in general was a bad, one doubted the efficacy of motorway safety barriers, one suggested that Railtrack and the Highways Agency had not undertaken a 'proper risk assessment' of barriers on roads close to railways, one imagined the need to fit seat belts in trains, and one asked why a freight train was in any case carrying imported coal through the middle of the huge South Yorkshire coalfield.[16]

What is interesting about these letters is that in a few column inches we discover at least six different versions of the good and six implicit demands for justification[17]. The implication was that someone should have known, someone should have done better, someone had failed. And the overall public coverage of Selby also generated numerous versions of the good. In the guise of news reports, possible reasons for the scale of the accident were rehearsed. There was plenty of talk of the need for crash barriers:

> Questions will have to be asked about the condition of the road surface and the roadside barriers on the bridge at the time of the accident, and about the strength of

barriers on roads that take large volumes of traffic above other highways or railway lines[18].

Then there were comments about the means of escape from trains after accidents:

> However, there were calls for a review of barriers to protect roads and track, especially high-speed lines, and of methods to escape from crashed carriages.[19]

Doubts were expressed about the absence of a heavy locomotive at the front of the train:

> Crash investigators were examining whether the 30-tonne driving car on the GNER express had sufficient weight to be leading the train and whether the train would have remained on the rails if the 80-tonne locomotive had been leading, instead of being at the back.[20]

And questions were raised about procedures for alerting drivers if vehicles fall onto the track, including train-mounted radar equipment and other methods:

> In France they have a system of trip wires, so that if a vehicle falls off a bridge trains are automatically brought to a halt. Could we not implement such a system here?[21]

These, then, were some of the suggestions or questions raised in and through the media in the two or three days immediately after the Selby collision. They differ, but they share a tone of indignation. They all suggest that there was a single weak point in the system that should not have been there. The accident was 'unnecessary' because it might have been prevented. Easily.

The Hatfield accident was not caused by an obstacle on the line, but by a broken rail. In the media coverage afterwards, questions were asked about why the track was not replaced after cracks were detected in the rails. Some of the responses were interesting. Responsibility (it was said) lay in part with the way privatization had shifted repair work from a single organization to an army of contractors and subcontractors, working to tight deadlines and costings, in an antagonistic contractual culture:

> The first consequence was the breakdown of the old comradeship, which used to mean that problems were easily spotted, repairs made, and people could talk to each other. Track workers operated in gangs and knew their stretch of rails like their own back gardens. Instead, workers became nomadic, moving to the next job with little or no local knowledge and instructions not to talk to rival workers except via a supervisor miles away.[22]

Another good, then, is being evoked here. This does not have to do with better road surfaces, roadside barriers, leading locomotives, or trip wires. It has to do with comradeship and group solidarity. Written down in this way it seems so obvious. But why? Perhaps this is because it has been disentangled from the complexities that led to changes in work practice in the first place; or perhaps it is because it is simply detached from other goods, full stop. As are the claims, in the context of reporting on the Ladbroke Grove and Southall collisions, about another equally self-evident solution, that of ATP (Automatic Train Protection System):

> Experts believe ATP could have prevented both disasters. Tony Cima, 46, from Stroud, Gloucestershire, who attended [. . . a] rally [in London], survived the Paddington crash last month. He said he still had awful memories of the accident. 'The worst thing was being unable to help people, I could have done more for them,' he said. 'ATP is the only way of getting the drivers to stop. We don't want a cheapskate alternative.' Campaigners want better rail warning systems.
>
> Addressing the gathering, London mayoral hopeful Ken Livingstone said: 'The more you look at Railtrack's involvement in the railways, the more it looks like a gravy train for its investors and less like a modern integrated train service for the public.'[23]

This kind of argument spilled over the pages of the papers. ATP was not installed but it should have been. If it had been, then the accident would certainly have been prevented. But then, if we go back a little bit to December 1998, we find the papers overflowing with a quite different public preoccupation:

> On Wednesday the Commons Transport Committee said the Mark I carriages – some of which date back to the 1960s – posed a danger to passengers. There are still about 2,000 of these doors in service.[24]

In public discourse not very long ago, then, it was slam doors that were a bad, bad for safety[25].

The dis/entanglements of panaceas: mobile utopianism

Over no more than three years the location of failure, and of the solution needed to put it right, has moved many times. The 'good' evoked in media coverage of train accidents, has shifted between crash barriers, ATP, carriage and especially door-design, and procedures for detecting and correcting metal fatigue in rails. We could extend the list. But what is important here is that at the moment they are voiced, these 'goods' are all pressed with singular urgency. And to stress the urgency the papers do not just let the experts speak on, say, ATP, but seek the spokespeople whose concerns we are most likely to respect. For instance, accident survivors. But, however much we may want to support (and believe) someone whose right to talk grows out of his or her physical suffering, there is a problem here. This has to do with the relation between the different goods. Where does one good leave the others? Where does ATP leave the issue of rail metal fatigue? Or slam doors? Or any of the other elements that are crucial to railways? Juxtaposing quotes about virtues, however virtuous each of them may individually be, has a very specific overall effect in the context of public debate.

Taken by itself each 'good' seems to call for total commitment. Any deviation from such total commitment is inappropriate. With the benefit of hindsight, it is cast as something that might or should have been foreseen. Any specific deviation is treated as an accountable failure in responsibility. But in combination the various accusations produce a different effect. Taken together they evoke a 'good' that is *multiple* as well as *mobile*. The juxtaposition of complaints generates multiple versions of the good – and more or less effortless moves between them.

Since each 'good' is presented in a further newspaper article, and since such articles are read one by one, separately, no requirement of discursive consistency is imposed. Each version of the good is thus disentangled from all others, a discursive island unto itself. And the various 'goods' are not just disentangled from each other, but also from any executive responsibility. In the media it is possible to propagate versions of the good without any commitment to seeing them through into action or policy. Thus we are confronted with something which we might think of as *mobile utopianism*. This is a mode relating to 'the good' that disentangles itself from discursive coherence and material embeddedness, while imposing a rapid but constantly shifting insistence on accountability.

'A cold, distasteful evaluation'

The Ladbroke Grove Rail Inquiry was set up in the aftermath of the Ladbroke Grove collision. This, as we have noted, was particularly horrific. Many were killed, and many of the survivors were grievously injured, some in the fierce fire which followed. No-one involved with this accident was anything other than shocked. In order to prevent an accident like in the future it was important to learn what went wrong and make sure that it never happens again. Such was the purpose of the Inquiry. It was established to explore both the proximate and the background causes of the accident, and make specific recommendations for subsequent executive action.

Under an experienced Scottish judge, Lord Cullen, the Inquiry was quasi-judicial in form. Barristers representing both the Inquiry itself and various interested parties including victims and relatives of the bereaved, the companies involved, and relevant trades unions, presented evidence. The Inquiry took statements and called witnesses who gave verbal testimony and were cross-examined. The proceedings were open and widely reported, with public access, a press gallery, and a web-site.[26] The web-site offers outsiders access to the high density zone of the Inquiry, where in a well delineated place and a comparatively short space of time a variety of modes of relating to 'the good' were brought together.

One mode for handling the 'good' is introduced into the Inquiry by the Ladbroke Grove Solicitors' Group which represents the victims and families of the bereaved. Here is the group's barrister, addressing the Inquiry:

> Our clients want to hear in this Inquiry how the Thames Trains' directors justify their decisions. They want to hear too why it was that, without seemingly a whimper, Railtrack and Her Majesty's Railway Inspectorate as the safety authorities allowed Thames Trains to decide not to fit ATP.

We came across ATP (Automatic Train Protection System) above. In this a computer on board a train, processing data about signals and track conditions (such as fixed speed limits), overrules the driver if s/he is going too fast, and stops the train or slows it to a safe speed. The High Speed train in the Ladbroke Grove collision was fitted with ATP though this was not switched on. The Thames Train (which passed the red light) was not. But – here is the nub of the argument – it appears that had the Thames Train been fitted with working ATP, the accident would have been avoided (the same is not the case for the High Speed Train where its operation would have made much less difference.)[27] So why was it not fitted? This was a crucial question for the Ladbroke Grove Solicitors' Group. To quote their barrister again:

> Now, with the tear-stained benefit of hindsight . . . even on the basis of a cold, distasteful evaluation of £2.5 million per life lost, the benefits of fitting ATP must far outweigh the costs. They wait to hear Thames Trains' commitment that costs will no longer be an obstacle.[28]

Cost, we are learning, should not be an obstacle to safety. Safety should be prioritized. It is a greater good than any other. And if ATP is a means to this end, it is called for immediately. In other locations survivors of the crash also speak up as advocates of ATP. Three examples:

> ATP MUST be fitted on all lines, and the trains using them, where train speeds frequently exceed 75 mph or where there are heavy freight trains. This means on all lines except rural branch lines. TPWS must be fitted to the remainder. ATP must be fitted *immediately* to all trains that frequently run over lines already fitted with ATP.[29]
>
> As one of the Paddington crash survivors, 82-year old Eric Skentelbery, stated: 'Money takes second place to lives. What does a billion pounds mean anyway? If you lose a battle it is the general's fault not the soldiers'.'
>
> Another survivor, Amanda Williams from Wokingham, said: 'It is totally ludicrous. Train companies are making a huge profit so why are they not investing it back into the system? We should have bought the fail-safe safety network ATP. It may have cost £750 million but what price do you put on a human life?'[30]

The trades unions made also similar arguments.

> Shunting responsibility on to a dead driver brought an angry response from union leaders with Bob Crow, an assistant general secretary in the main RMT union, accusing the companies of trying to 'wash their hands' of the tragedy. 'Blaming the staff is not good enough. We will always get human error but you have to look at why this happened,' said Mr Crow. 'If Automatic Train Protection [ATP] had been fitted this would never have happened. Railtrack has refused to install it because it costs money.' The human cost of failing to protect passengers and workers is now enormous. The travelling public knows where the real blame lies.[31]

The dis/entanglements of absolutism

Two things are going on here. First, there is an argument which says that Thames Trains (and other railway companies) could well afford to invest in ATP: it was only greed which stood in the way. And second, there is an argument which suggests that it is simply inappropriate to value human life in terms of money at all: cost-benefit calculations are outright inappropriate. We will deal with the first approach later. Here we are concerned with latter, the idea that human life does not have a money value and that to calculate it in this way is 'cold' and 'distasteful'. This suggests that human life is beyond evalution, an absolute, and an absolute good – which means, in this context, that an investment in ATP (or some other appropriate safety system) is also an absolute good.

The idea that human life has absolute value co-exists very uneasily with the cost-benefit world of the management of Thames Trains. Indeed, it co-exists very uneasily with the idea of cost-benefit analysis. The consequence is that it is discursively dangerous to raise doubts about safety measures in a context where such a commitment to absolutism is able to shape debate. Indeed, the then head of Railtrack, Mr Gerald Corbett, came unstuck on just this issue when he talked about the pursuit of perfection, and by implication rail safety in the following terms:

> . . . in commercial life and in big organizations things are not perfect. It is a journey and you never, ever arrive at the destination.'

This unfortunate choice of words, which provoked tears and outrage, greatly contributed to his resignation a week later on November 17th 2000.[32]

A mode of relating to the good that has trouble co-existing with others deserves to be called *absolutism*. Reminiscent of Max Weber's value rationality (*wertrationalität*), it implies a logic of black and white[33]. Of clear right and clear wrong. A single version of the good and the attempt to strive after it, after perfection. To be able to adhere to this a set of clear moral, organizational and technical certainties is required. This means that certain and specific kinds of objects, processes and realities are relevant because they help us to think about, articulate, and implement this absolute version of the good. Here (but this is just one version of absolutism) human life and then by implication, the ATP system. Such are the links, the relevant links, the relevant entanglements, in constructing this particular version of the good.[34] And then it follows that everything else – any other link or possible entanglement – is inappropriate. Not simply arguments about cost, but anything that tends to undermine human life (for instance real or supposed technical or managerial incompetence) has to be disentangled, separated. Absolutism is about disentangling one value, here human life, from anything which tends to dilute its incommensurable value.

This, then, is *utopian absolutism*. It is an absolutism utopian in character because it will never be achieved. It may lead to the resignation of managers, but however great the executive implications of the Inquiry, its recommendations will not be based on an absolutist commitment to the value of human life. So what is going on here? Traditionally absolutism was a prerogative of the high and mighty, the governmental style adopted by a particular kind of monarch. But this is no longer the case in the context of an Inquiry where it is introduced into debate by victims, survivors, family members and their barristers. It is introduced because this may be the only way for such relatively powerless participants to get themselves heard. If they don't treat their own lives (and the lives of those they have lost) as having absolute value, then who will treat them as having any value at all[35]? For safety easily gets lost or devalued when other goods come crowding in – or so those who use absolutist arguments tend to fear. Here is *The Guardian*:

> At the inquiry into the Clapham rail disaster of 1988, before railway privatisation, British Rail publicly expressed its commitment to 'absolute safety' saying that this 'must be a gospel . . . paramount in the minds of management'. Yet immediately on privatization this commitment was abandoned. Instead of talking about absolute safety, the newly created railway companies such as Railtrack and Great Western trains began to talk about cost benefit analysis and the value of saving a life.[36]

'A system that needs balancing'

After the Hatfield derailment in October 2000, the national inquiry into the state of the railways in the UK continued with added urgency. As a part of this, the House of Commons Select Committee on the Environment, Transport and Regional Affairs Committee met shortly after that derailment to question Mr. Corbett and two of his colleagues about Hatfield and Railtrack's response[37]. They were asked about the Railtrack stewardship of the rail network – of how it had tackled its management task. The point was to find out if they had done so well – or not. But what is to manage well, what 'good' is important in this context, and how is it handled?

> the railway is a system, and of course we want cost reduction, everyone wants it to be more efficient, everyone wants better train performance, everyone wants better safety, everyone wants more trains, but it is a system that needs balancing. . . .[38]

What is striking here is that it is not just a single 'good' that is being mentioned, but a series of them. Cost reduction, efficiency, train performance, safety, more trains. This variety of 'goods' is not distributed between different articles, sites or situations. They are being brought together in just a few lines as part of a 'system that needs balancing'. The metaphor of balance recurs:

> What we have actually done [by imposing speed restrictions and checking the quality of the track] is reduce the likelihood of a broken rail, but, at the same time, of course, we have also reduced the train performance. And, if you think about it, there is a complex balance between speed, punctuality, number of trains on the network and safety, and that is, I believe, harder to manage now than it was; but that is the challenge, that is what we have to do.[39]

A 'complex balance'. And there are other metaphors that do similar work. Mr Steve Marshall, Mr Corbett's successor, talks of 'juggling':

> *FT*: . . . customers, dealing with the regulator, politicians, all the rest of it. How are you going to prioritize or balance that? How do you approach that wide range of things you have to do?

> *Marshall*: It's always going to be a huge juggling act. That is what Railtrack is, and therefore it's how you best manage that juggling act. But I hope we signalled two of the key priorities in the board changes that I announced within two days of taking the job. One is the focus on the customer . . . The other . . . is really emphasizing beefing up our engineering skills[40]

Management is a matter of complex balance, a 'huge juggling act'. But this begs the question of how the various 'goods' that need to be balanced relate together. Are they consistent, or can they be rendered so? This is an open question. Here's the House of Commons Select Committee:

> It has been suggested that there may be conflict between passenger and freight growth, demands for better train performance and requirements for a greater emphasis on safety. Mr Corbett told us that fragmentation of the rail industry at privatization has made it more difficult to resolve that conflict. Conversely, the Rail Regulator has argued that 'a safer railway is where trains are well-maintained and run on time on a reliable infrastructure; good management of performance and safety are entirely consistent and inseparable'.[41]

In an absolutist mode, the pursuit of profit and the pursuit of safety are simply incompatible. The Rail Regulator, however, takes what he calls 'performance' and 'safety' to be not only consistent, but, more strongly, inseparable. Mr Corbett is somewhere in between. The relation between the different 'goods' of profit and safety is indeed in tension, he says, and it has become more difficult to resolve that tension than it was in the past – but this what managers are paid to do: to balance and to juggle. There is tension between the goals (the different goods at hand pull in different directions) but compromise should be sought (it is possible to put together an arrangement which will somehow hold them together)[42]. Here is Mr Corbett underlining this once again:

> *Q.* So would you agree with the Regulator when he said, in the *Financial Times*, 'good management of performance and safety are entirely consistent and inseparable'; would you agree with that assessment?
> *Mr Corbett* I think that if you overemphasize one particular part of the equation you affect the other part, and I think that good management is about balancing it.[43]

But how is balance achieved? This may be done by exercising *judgement*. Here is Mr Corbett responding to a hostile question from a member of the Select Committee:

> *Q.* How many times do people at Railtrack have to fail before they are asked to resign?
> *Mr Corbett* That is an impossible question to answer. I have changed quite a lot of people at Railtrack, and this is one of the fundamental problems you have; how fast do you go. On the one hand do you go slowly because you want to preserve the railway skills; on the other hand do you want to go fast because you want to try to make it better and respond to the challenges?[44]

On the one hand. On the other. Judgement juxtaposes different aims in terms of specific and local considerations. There are no general rules. Even if, alongside judgement, balance may also be achieved by mobilizing 'equations' (as Mr Corbett revealingly suggests above). For instance, there was the algorithm used by Thames Trains to determine that it was economically unjustified to put ATP into its trains[45]. Managing is full of algorithms. Here is Mr Corbett gesturing at another in the course of the Ladbroke Grove Inquiry:

> The regulatory economics of Railtrack's affairs and how we charge for train paths and the true marginal cost of those train paths is extremely complex and it is inconceivable that anyone at that [junior] level of the organization had the remotest idea, quite frankly.[46]

Train paths, income from train paths, the marginal costs of train paths, consequent investment decisions – he is telling us that all of these can be calculated by someone who, by training, has become sufficiently sophisticated. If one knows how they can all be taken into *account*.

If managing is a matter of balance, brought about by judgement and calculation, then something that goes wrong depends on an 'unbalanced' decision. For instance, was Railtrack right to close the main line between Glasgow and England at a few hours notice for three days in the immediate aftermath of the Hatfield derailment? Many, including Mr Corbett, thought not. They thought that the 'broader issues' (read goods other than that of safety) were not taken into account:

> *Q.* So do you think in this instance that we have got a situation where local managers panicked, and subsequent evidence suggests that that was the case, because there was nothing found that was wrong in that section, was there?
> *Mr Corbett*: Whenever you ultrasonically test, you do find defects, and then you deal with the defects. I do not think they panicked, I think they interpreted an instruction in a particular way without thinking about the broader issues, and I think it was unfortunate that there was not more communication.[47]

This suggest that, if the 'local managers' erred, their error was to move too far in the direction of absolutism, a perfectionist commitment to safety. They should have taken more than just a single 'good' into account – or their superiors, with their broad overview, should have told them to do so.

The dis/entanglements of managerialism

Managerialism is a method for responding to the idea that we live in an imperfect world. Indeed it is a way of responding to the idea that we live in a doubly imperfect world. First, it is imperfect because we may make the wrong judgements or the wrong calculations, as in the case of the closure of the Glasgow west coast line. This is always likely to happen because circumstances may change, indeed can be expected to do so, chronically. And second, the world is imperfect because, more generally, we cannot in any case have overall perfection. Such is the nature of a trade-off. Too much of one good undermines some other good. Too much safety, not enough trains. So there is no black and white. Instead the world is irreducibly complex, impure, multiple.

Max Weber again catches the logic at work here:

> Action is instrumentally rational (*zweckrational*) when the end, the means, and the secondary results are all rationally taken into account and weighed. This involves rational consideration of alternative means to the end, of the relations of the end to the secondary consequences, and finally of the relative importance of different possible ends.[48]

The crucial phrase here being: 'the relative importance of different possible ends'. So the issue is one of *judgement*, of finding ways of drawing together different and heterogeneous materials and goods. And then possibly (though not necessarily) as a somewhat separate issue, of articulating and *justifying* their temporary, relative importance, their momentary balance[49]. For managerialism justifies to others (shareholders, regulators, government ministers, committees of inquiry).[50] But (as various commentators on the topic of reflexive modernity have noted) managerialism also chronically takes the measure of the different and irreducible goods and accounts for the way it balances between these, not only to others, but also *to itself*.[51]

In managerialism as in mobile utopias, there are no absolute substantive goods. Instead their multiplicity is acknowledged. There is, however, a commitment to action, to seeing things through. This commitment is absent in mobile utopianism but is shared with absolutism. However, unlike absolutism, managerialism knows no fixed links. Every substantive link, connection and commitment is assessed for its current salience and may either be retained or abandoned. 'All that is solid melts into air.' But since managerialism is always reassessing, this implies dedication and skill in discursive justification: the mobilization of materials of all kinds. Technical objects, financial calculations, organizational practices, employee relations, politicians – managerialism entangles itself with all of these. They all have to be held together in an iterative and reflexive process of heterogeneous engineering and reflexive justification. There is only one fixed point: the ability to articulate and evaluate one's actions. Which suggest that in managerialism one good is, in the end, more equal than the others. It is a good that tends to be set aside as non-substantial, 'merely' procedural, a question of method. It is the all but unquestionable good of being accountable for one's judgements.[52]

Unlike absolutism, managerialism is not a way in which those with little power can hope to get themselves heard at an Inquiry. Instead it is reflected in the very *format* of inquiries. For whatever specific form these take, they are always arenas where a variety of actors are pressed into articulating what they judge to be relevant. And once they are articulated, all these issues can then be taken into account by a judge, a chair or a committee in the form of a 'report' that offers a well balanced judgement about how to prevent similar disasters from happening again.

**'On that day I could not recollect the time at all.
It was just over so quickly.'[53]**

About twenty-five kilometres from the site of the accident in Ladbroke Grove
is the Slough Electronic Control Centre. Here signal men, poring over terminals
and keyboards connected with tracks and signals, control the trains into and
out of Paddington station – and for many kilometres beyond. Like Mr Corbett
and his colleagues, these men ended up giving evidence to the Ladbroke Grove
Inquiry. The major question here was what happened in the few seconds between
the moment it became clear that the Thames Train had passed a signal at danger
and the instant of the collision itself. The issue was whether the signallers could
have done anything to avert or reduce the scope of the disaster. And, as a pre-
liminary to this: what did they actually do?

One account of those critical instants – between twenty-one and twenty-five
seconds – would run so:

1. Mr David Allen, the signaller at the relevant workstation wasn't actually
   looking at the screen when the Thames Train went through the red signal.
   Instead, since the signalling was automatic, he was reading some important update documents.
2. When the train went past the signal, the audible alarm went off – a tweet-
   ing sound that immediately attracted the attention of all three signallers
   in the control-centre.
3. Hearing the alarm, Mr Allen looked at a special display, the 'alarm
   screen' to see what kind of alarm was involved (the audible alarm warns
   of seven different kinds of danger, only one of which is a train passing
   a signal at danger). The alarm screen told him that it was, indeed, a signal
   passed at danger (SPAD) – and he shouted 'We have a SPAD' to his colleague in the control centre, Mr James Hillman.
4. Then he looked back at the main 'schematic' screen to identify the particular signal that had been passed at danger and find out which train
   had done so (there were numerous other trains on the move that
   morning).
5. Next, expecting to hear on the cab secure radio telephone from the driver
   of the train that he realized his error and had stopped, Mr Allen looked
   again at the schematic screen and saw the display change once more. This
   time it showed that the Thames Train had moved into the next block of
   track beyond the signal. This again triggered the audible alarm.
6. With this information he realized that he was dealing not, as he had
   expected, with a train that had not quite stopped in time at the signal but
   had nevertheless come to a halt safely some distance further on. Instead
   he was dealing with a 'runaway train'.
7. He looked back at the 'schematic screen' and saw the visualization of the
   other train, the High Speed Train. At this point he realized that there
   was imminent risk of a collision between the two trains.

8. He set the appropriate signal to danger for the High Speed Train. This was a manoeuvre that involved shifting to an alternative and more detailed display, in which he used a trackball (It turned out that the train had already passed the signal in question, and it was too late).

9. His colleague in the box, Mr Hillman, had by now left his own work-station to join Mr Allen, and was sending out an emergency stop call to the Thames train – an operation which involved half a dozen keystrokes on the keyboard.

10. Mr Allen then set further signals to red to stop other trains entering the Ladbroke Grove area – again using the trackball – and put in place a series of safety interlocks to hold those signals at red.

11. And then they watched with horror – and finally shock – as they realized it was all too late. Barring an act of God, the two trains were going to collide.[54]

Did Mr Allen and his colleagues act as they should have?

> If a train passes a signal at danger without authority the signaller must immediately arrange for the movement to be stopped by the most appropriate means and take any other emergency action.[55]

This is one of the relevant rules. But did they follow it? Did they act 'immediately'? And did they act using 'the most appropriate means'? Some thought not. This is from the closing statement of the Thames Trains barrister:

> The evidence of the signallers is most troubling and gives rise to serious concern. Central to it, in order to send an emergency stop message to Driver Hodder [who had passed the signal at danger], what was required was to make just five key strokes on the keyboard. The evidence is that that can be performed in no more than two seconds. . . . assuming that Driver Hodder responded promptly, an emergency 'stop' message sent up to 17.55 seconds after he passed signal 109 would have had the effect of preventing the collision.[56]

The suggestion is that Mr Allen didn't do this. Instead he delayed.[57] More than a few times in the course of the Inquiry he indeed appears defensive about this. Here he is being asked whether there were (as data tapes seemed to suggest) indeed between twenty-one and twenty-five seconds between the alarm going off and the collision itself.

> *Q.* Does that timing match your recollection of events?
> *A.* Yes. I would say, yes, but I cannot recollect the time factor. It is all very well saying that you have got, you can actually map minutes or seconds. At the time, during the time that was happening I couldn't recollect the time at all.[58]

And here is another example of his vagueness, again about time:

> *Q.* Are you able to help us as to how long it took you to attempt to alter those points?
> *A.* I can't say for sure, sir.
> *Q.* Well, are you able to give us any estimate?
> *A.* All I can say, sir, is it is seconds. There was too much going on at the time to actually record any time.[59]

The indeterminacy about time sometimes comes with indeterminacy about the order of events. Here is another of the signallers, Mr Thomas Siddell:

Q. Mr Siddell, did you actually go to workstation 1 after Mr Hillman had been there?
A. Yes.
Q. How soon after?
A. To be honest, I cannot really remember if it was before I silenced the alarms on my workstation or after.
Q. But by the time you –
A. I think it was after, because I went across to relieve Dave [Allen], to chase him off the way because he was shocked.[60]

The dis/entanglements of tinkering

The suspicion that speaks from the questions is that Mr Allen and his colleagues, in a state of shock after the accident, realized that they should have tried to contact the Thames Train driver more quickly. If so, then their vagueness about time and the order of events signals defensiveness mixed with distress (Mr Allen was reduced to tears at the Inquiry). The Cullen Report itself suggests that there was undue delay.

> If management had applied the lessons of past SPADs, and if signallers had been adequately instructed and trained in how to react to a SPAD, it may well be the case that the signaller would have been able to send the emergency message in time to enable to Turbo to be brought to a halt before it fouled the path of the HST.[61]

Whether or not this is right (and it is contested by the official account by the Health and Safety Executive[62]), something else is going on, too. This is that the Inquiry requires of the signallers that they translate their daily work into a set of clear and distinct answers to definite questions. That they translate a fairly seamless flow of action, a set of practices embedded in a specific material location, from that location into a setting that is quite different in character. That they disentangle themselves from screens, tracks, noises, coffee breaks, working hours, false alarms, and shock, and entangle themselves with words that are supposedly 'about' these.

If, as is the case, discursive justification is the predominant style of an Inquiry then this implies that those who speak there have to meet various requirements. They have to *speak*. Their speech has to show overall discursive *coherence*. And it cannot just flow on, but has instead to separate out events and order them. Speakers have to commit themselves to discursive *distinction and discrimination*. Here is Mr Allen responding to the question of a barrister:

> You have been describing a process that involves identifying the problem, analysing a situation, taking a decision and acting on it. Now, in one of your statements you have talked about monitoring and determining the overview. Did you mean anything different from what you have been telling the Inquiry by that?
> *Mr Allen* No, sir[63]

So on the one hand we have Mr Allen talking of 'monitoring and determining the overview'. On the other hand we have a barrister who talks about 'identifying a problem', 'analysing a situation', ' taking a decision' and 'acting on it'. The difference between the two glosses is subtle, but it is also real. The barrister's talk performs a greater degree of discursive decomposition. It creates more discrete units. Further it strings these out more clearly through time. And as a part of this it identifies a moment of decision, a moment that follows appropriately once a problem has been first identified and then analysed. The model of judgement being offered is linear. And at a particular point (the point of decision) everything comes together. All of which is in contrast to Mr Allen's own characterization of the events in question. Less discursively decomposed, it produces fewer units, its timeline is not so clear, and in particular there is no discrete moment of decision.

When asked about this in as many words, Mr Allen agrees that his account and that of the barrister mean the same thing. He accepts the barrister's translation of his words and does not insist on the difference between them. Despite this, *we* would like to insist that they are different. This is because it leads us to a further mode of 'doing good', and one that is not utopian, if only because it is non-verbal in character. For it is a striking characteristic of the practice Mr Allen tries to present to the Inquiry that its specificities are not primarily linguistic. Words form a part of it, but they are as likely to be shouted ('We have a SPAD') as they are to be spoken calmly. Words may be written, too, on paper (in training records, on worksheets) or appear on computer displays. But what is crucial is that these words form a *part* of what is going on. They do not stand outside the process itself. In this they are different from most of the words at Inquiries where people tend to talk about 'decision making' (or other events) that have taken place *elsewhere*. In the control room words are one kind of element among many. There are other signals to respond to (for instance audible alarms warning of seven different kinds of danger), and to send out (by shifting between screens, using trackballs and keyboards). What is more, in the control room words are inseparably tied up with actions. The different alarm keys each work in a different way. Some send out warning signals to people who may or may not perceive and pay attention to them. And others may cut the power on large parts of the railway system.

If all goes well and the trains arrive on time at their destinations, then the work of the signalmen leads to 'good'. If the trains come to a standstill, or, worse, if there an accident, it does not. But if it is not 'good', then how might one decompose the flow of events into separate entities to pinpoint a 'wrong act' or a 'bad decision'? This is what the barrister is after at the Inquiry (where everyone is outside the process itself). He is discursively decomposing and recomposing the chain of events of the fatal day. It is what the Inquiry does when asking the signalmen to account for their actions second by second. But it goes against the logic ingrained in the practice itself. This is one in which different relevancies come together. Where they flow on, disrupt one another, go into turbulence, or suddenly form a vortex. Our point is not only that in the daily practice of the control centre no single 'good' takes precedence over all the others. It is also that there are not multiple 'goods' waiting to be balanced in that practice. However much the 'good' of the control room is composed and put together (through assembling working hours, instructions, habits, key-boards, displays, signals, and so on) it cannot be satisfactorily divided into different components. Neither the work nor the 'good' it seeks to achieve are discursively distinguished. There are no discrete elements to be balanced or added up into coherence. It is all rather a matter of *tinkering*.

Viewed in this way, Mr Allen's statement 'I cannot recollect the time factor' takes on a different significance. It no longer looks like a possible attempt to avoid responsibility. Instead it indexes the way in which practice unfolds in uncertain and relatively unaccountable ways. It resists entanglement in a world of decomposition and recomposition, and stays faithful to the process of tin-kering towards the good implied in the practice of the control centre. It is a refusal, or an inability, to submit to the idea that 'the good' of the control centre is accountable elsewhere, whether as a matter of managerialist trade-offs or as an absolutist utopian commitment to some articulable end. And it is as far away as one can get from mobile utopias that know it all, but do so little. Tinkering towards the good, we want to suggest, is set of local and embodied entangle-ments. Of *doing*, without knowledge-in-words that is separable from it.

Unsurprisingly, then, it is difficult to articulate the practices of tinkering at the Inquiry.[64] The latter spent several days trying to unravel the mysteries of the control centre, to put them into words. And despite all this effort it proves almost impossible to talk about the practical tinkering of the signalmen in a way that doesn't immediately make them seem shoddy, sloppy, slow off the mark, or dis-tracted. This should not surprise us very much. After all, a variety of traditions in social science have suggested that the flow of practice converts only partially into words. There is *always* something incomplete about such a translation – our own account above included. Translation is always also a betrayal.[65] But what turns this banal fact into a problem, is that when an embodied and localized version of the good is betrayed in a translation, it very easily takes the features of a bad:

> On any view, [the delay] cannot be justified, although it can perhaps be explained by the prevailing practice at Slough IECC.[66]

The accusation that the work of the signalmen was 'bad' is moderated. There is a 'prevailing practice' that (perhaps!) forms an 'explanation' for it. But an explanation falls short of the good more highly appreciated at an Inquiry, that of 'justification'. So this is what is lost when one accepts that the barrister's talk and Mr Allen's story at the Inquiry are the same. What becomes invisible is that the work of Mr Allen and his colleagues simply cannot be represented in words, let alone in the particular way of talking appropriate to an inquiry. For their day-to-day practice of tinkering doesn't allow discursive decomposi-tion and overall justification. While in an Inquiry silence is impossible. Silent work gets turned into a refusal to talk. Having little to say comes out in the form of the repeated and embarrassed acknowledgement that: 'I do not remember'.[67]

Different utopias

Utopianism, as Louis Marin observed, is about a happy place that is not a place.[68] It disentangles itself from the mundanities and complexities of situated practices and locates itself in a discursive space instead. This is not just a matter of striving after the good (or maybe a combination of goods) but a very particular mode of doing so.

The first mode of striving after the good we have considered is obviously utopian. We have called it *mobile utopia*. This expresses itself in a relatively free floating discourse, far removed from an urgent commitment to act. It tends to come in the form of accusations. The accused have failed to meet some high standard, or another. This is the trick of mobile utopianism: that it does not stick to anything for long. Unlike absolutism it does not press a single good. And unlike managerialism, it does not painstakingly try to balance various goods against each other. Mobile utopia is not situated in some specific place but neither does it attempt an overview. Instead there are repeated moments of heated indignation. And each time a good-that-wasn't-realized is projected as the counterfactual of an actual situation. But when they are juxtaposed these moments leave a sense of lack, of failure. And of empty hands.

Then we considered *absolutism*. Here again there is accusation. *The* good, not any good, but *the* good is neglected, the good that should have taken precedence over all the others. The rhetorical shape of absolutism stems from a time and place where a single authority could seek to impose a single good. Absolutism was an *imposed utopia* (and one that was bound to get nasty if only because it *was* imposed). But the absolutism we have witnessed here is quite different. If people with little power want to get themselves heard in crowded and noisy discursive arenas, they need to speak with extra force. And one of the techniques for doing so is to try to borrow power from the former absolutists. A value may be made more valuable by calling it absolute. This is a *utopianism of despair*.

At first sight *managerialism* does not seem utopian. This is because it is an answer to the imperfections of the world. It recognizes that different 'goods' are in tension with one another, and understands that balancing between them is a crucial but precarious task. But we have argued that there is a third mode of utopianism at work here. For in managerialist discourse we discover a shift to *procedure*. Handling the tensions between different goods in a proper way, balancing between them wisely, and being prepared to articulate one's actions and account for them – these are turned into meta-goods. Risk assessments, audits, Inquiries and other ways of staging accountability become powerful. No longer treated as managerial techniques among others, for which there may be a (delineated) place, they become the very space we are made to inhabit. A space in which endless reflexive questions are being asked, but one that is put beyond question itself. Managerialism thus incorporates a *hidden utopia*. Reflexive and justificatory discourse is the good that it celebrates.

We have also considered one radically non-utopian mode of relating to the good: that of *tinkering*. This is quite different because it is located. It takes place somewhere, and rather than being an afterthought it is immersed in the present. It has less to do with thought, but is more a matter of matter, of the body, of practice. A practice in which there are material objects, flickering screens, bleeping sounds, rails, weather. A practice, moreover, where one may have worked for four hours, or twelve, or be out for a tea break; and where one may (or may not) be worried about one's colleagues. The good, in this place, is neither single nor divided. But if tinkering is both complex and non-discursive, this has unfortunate consequences elsewhere. It means that its specific modes of dealing with the good tend to look like failures when they are called to account in other contexts. Discursive justifications always betray the specificities of tinkering.

What does this imply? Obviously we do not suggest tinkering should always be accepted at face value. It does not necessarily bring goods. But if justifications of tinkering do not get to its heart, then this suggests that we need instead to shift questions, and to explore how goods are actually enacted in the practices of tinkering. What is avoided as bad practice? What is sought after? How do people get committed to their work, come to care for what is at stake there? These are the kinds of questions that need to be explored. For if we are committed to and care for the quality of practice/s then further high modern self-reflection and additional requirements for accountability are unlikely to help. Instead tinkering deserves to be investigated in its own terms. However difficult it may be to find the words. However much *terms* are not what tinkering is about.

Notes

1 We are grateful to Kevin Hetherington and Vicky Singleton for discussions about many of the arguments developed here; and to Jeannette Pols for her friendly but justly ferocious comments on a previous version of this text.

2 There were many additional actors – which included the Rail Regulator, the relevant part of the government safety authority, the Health and Safety Executive, a newly created Strategic Rail Authority and (important for the present story) a plethora of subcontractors, and sub-subcontractors, some large and some not, which worked for Railtrack and maintained the railway infrastructure. In late 2001 (as we complete the final draft of this paper) the future structure of the industry is uncertain. In large part because of the events discussed in this paper, Railtrack is in receivership.

3 The details are drawn in part from the links shown on the official Health and Safety Executive Railway Inspectorate's web site. See http://www.hse.gov.uk/railway/rihome.htm#Accident.

4 Selby, though a serious accident, is somewhat different. As we suggest below, it appears in general that the responsibility for it is taken not to lie with the railway system.

5 See http://www.southall-rail-inquiry.gov.uk

6 Details are to be found at the Inquiry's website, at http://www.lgri.org.uk/ and in the Cullen report. See (Cullen 2001).

7 For further details see http://www.hse.gov.uk/railway/hatfield/interim2.htm

8 See the Financial Times website for details of the cost (estimated at £600 million on January 15th, 2001). http://news.ft.com/ft/gx.cgi/ftc?pagename=View&c=Article&cid=FT3NCP0VZHC&live=true&tagid=ZZZYF7I2B0C&subheading=transport. Note that a large part of this bill represented compensation for the Train Operating Companies.

9 These are explored more fully in Law (2000).

10 In the field of science studies, the shift from articulating norms to studying the way they are practised was made in relation to epistemology. For exemplary studies see Barnes (1977), Latour and Woolgar (1979) Shapin and Schaffer (1985). In political theory there has been an analogous shift from justifying good action to analysis of how people justify their actions in the work of Boltanski and Thévenot and their colleagues. See, for instance, Boltanski and Thévenot (1987), Boltanski (1990), Thévenot (2002), and Dodier (1993). The shift is also currently being made in ethics. See, for instance, Harbers, Mol and Stollmeijer (2002).

11 One might explore how the 'goodness' of particular activities grounded: in scientific studies (for instance through trials); in reasoning and argument (as in ethics); and no doubt there are other possibilities. Or one might analyse how people relate to what they themselves take to be good: proudly, reluctantly, ambivalently? And then again: one might analyse what failure is turned into: an occasion for guilt, for shame, for punishment, for learning, for retreating? The list of possible questions is long, and the present paper is simply the first step in a much larger project of studying *doing good*.

12 Quoted in http://www.univ-nancy2.fr/CEAA/CRESAB/text-railways-nuss.htm

13 These terms entanglement and disentanglement have been developed by Michel Callon and Vololona Rabeharisoa. See Callon (1998a; 1998b) and Callon and Rabeharisoa (1999).

14 GNER, the company which owned the passenger train was described in the *Financial Times* in March 2nd 2000 as talking of a 'freak sequence of events'.
http://globalarchive.ft.com/globalarchive/articles.html?id=010301001437&query=Selby

15 The quotation is from the *Guardian* leader of March 1st, 2000 available at
http://www.guardian. co.uk/selby/story/0,7369,444635,00.html.

16 *The Guardian* March 2nd, page 25.

17 And the public arena propensity to seek justifications when something goes wrong was reflected in a BBC encounter with the weary government minister, Mr John Prescott, when he visited the Selby site a few hours after the accident. In this the BBC tried to cross-examine him about the inadequacy of the motorway safety barrier. This exchange appeared on the 1.00 pm News on BBC1 on 28th February, 2001.

18 http://www.guardian.co.uk/selby/story/0,7369,444348,00.html 37:4 (153:156), 2nd March, 2001.

19 http://globalarchive.ft.com/globalarchive/articles.html?id=010301001437&query=Selby;   39:2 (57:59), 1st March, 2001.

20 http://www.guardian.co.uk/selby/story/0,7369,445299,00.html;   36:1   (131:134),   2nd March, 2001.

21 http://news.bbc.co.uk/hi/english/uk/newsid_1196000/1196790.stm   43:1   (76:78),   2nd March 2001.

22 http://news.ft.com/ft/gx.cgi/ftc?pagename=View&c=Article&cid=FT36IGKIHJC&live=true (20:11 (101:107)) (FT, 22nd Feb, 2001, page 4)

23 http://news.bbc.co.uk/hi/english/uk/newsid_507000/507691.stm 50:1 (57:70), 6th November, 1999.

24 http://news.bbc.co.uk/hi/english/uk/newsid_232000/232283.stm 45:1 (67:69), 1st December, 1998.

25 Slam doors, present in every compartment and operated by passengers, were the standard on post-war local routes. These have since been replaced by many fewer doors that are operated by the driver or guard.

26 The website, which includes transcripts of all evidence, is at www.lgri.org.uk/.

27 See the Third Interim Report of the Health and Safety Executive, Section 2. The Report is published at http://www.hse.gov.uk/railway/paddrail/interim3.htm.

28 www.lgri.org.uk/transcript/11mayam.htm (4:11 pages 9–13 (290:392)).

29 From Alan Macro's personal home page at
http://www.amacro.freeserve.co.uk/rail-safety.htm#ATP.

30 Both these citations are from Privatization Disaster: Time to RENATIONALIZE the railways! Rob Sewell Socialist Appeal Railways special, Socialist Appeal, Issue 73, at www.socialist.net/ 73/railways.html.

31 'How a mistake led to mayhem', Kevin Maguire, Matt Wells and Keith Harper *The Guardian*, Thursday October 7, 1999, at http://www.gu.com/traincrash/Story/0,2763,201534,00.html

32 See http://www.lgri.org.uk/transcript2/10novam.htm, page 31, and additional BBC reporting at http://news.bbc.co.uk/hi/english/uk/newsid_1016000/1016708.stm.

33 See Max Weber (1978), pages 24–26.

34 In the context of ATP this raises serious difficulties. ATP is expensive, yes, but its reliability has also been questioned. Furthermore, there are ever-present questions about the way in which safety systems can increase as well as decrease hazards. See Charles Perrow (1984) and John Law (2000).

35 We are grateful to Jeannette Pols for suggesting this argument to us.

36 Louise Christian, *The Guardian*, Wednesday October 6, 1999, 'They kill to save money: Why haven't proper rail safety measures been introduced?' http://www.guardianunlimited.co.uk/traincrash/Story/0,2763,201546,00.html

37 See the House of Commons Environment, Transport and Regional Affairs Committee, First Report, 'Recent Events on the Railway', published at http://www.publications.parliament.uk/ pa/cm200001/cmselect/cmenvtra/17/1703.htm#a1

38 http://www.publications.parliament.uk/pa/cm200001/cmselect/cmenvtra/17/0110105.htm 26:1 (27:34) paragraph 62. (House of Commons – Environment, Transport and Regional Affairs – Minutes of Evidence, Select Committee on Environment, Transport and Regional Affairs Minutes of Evidence).

39 http://www.publications.parliament.uk/pa/cm200001/cmselect/cmenvtra/17/0110104.htm, 25:9 (55:63) paragraph 41. (House of Commons – Environment, Transport and Regional Affairs – Minutes of Evidence, Select Committee on Environment, Transport and Regional Affairs Minutes of Evidence).

40 Interview with Steve Marshall by Juliette Jowit, Financial Times, 7th December, 2000; at http://news.ft.com/ft/gx.cgi/ftc?pagename=View&c=Article&cid=FT33MKCQGGC&live=true (4:17 (77:92))

41 http://www.publications.parliament.uk/pa/cm200001 /cmselect/cmenvtra/17/1703.htm#a1 32:17 (524:541) paragraph 21 (House of Commons – Environment, Transport And Regional Affairs – First Report Select Committee on Environment, Transport and Regional Affairs).

42 The compromise may, in part, be between long and short term goods. See Interview with Steve Marshall by Juliette Jowit, Financial Times, 7th December, 2000; at http://news.ft.com/ft/gx.cgi/ ftc?pagename=View&c=Article&cid=FT33MKCQGGC&live=true (4:17 (77:92)).

43 http://www.publications.parliament.uk/pa/cm200001/cmselect/cmenvtra/17/0110104.htm, 25:9 (413:420) paragraph 58. (House of Commons – Environment, Transport and Regional Affairs – Minutes of Evidence, Select Committee on Environment, Transport and Regional Affairs Minutes of Evidence).

44 http://www.publications.parliament.uk/pa/cm200001/cmselect/cmenvtra/17/01101010.htm, 31:3 (181:190) paragraph 179. (House of Commons – Environment, Transport and Regional Affairs – Minutes of Evidence, Select Committee on Environment, Transport and Regional Affairs Minutes of Evidence).

45 'Our clients . . . observe that though Thames Turbo trains . . . were not fitted with ATP on cost benefit grounds. Thames Trains' cost benefit analysis concluded that over 20 years it would cost them £8.2 million. . . . This, it was calculated, would prevent only an estimated one fatality at a saving, valued at the standard 1998 Railtrack figure, of £2.49 million, together with a saving of £0.47 million in respect of disruption. The net cost of ATP was, thus, a mere £5.26 million over 20 years. . . . It seems incomprehensible to my clients that the directors of Thames Trains, reflecting in 1998 on the 7 dead and 151 casualties of the Southall crash, refused to spend these modest sums . . . In the same year, 1998, in which the Thames Trains directors rejected ATP fitment . . . they paid out the dividend to shareholders of £4.23 million. In 1999 they paid a further dividend of £3.25 million. Our clients observe that by restricting their profits, Thames Trains could

comfortably have paid in two years the whole 20-year cost to equip their trains with ATP . . . and still given away well over £2 million in dividends.' www.lgri.org.uk/transcript/11mayam.htm (4:11 pages 9–13 (290:392)).

46 Ladbroke Grove Rail Inquiry, Transcript of Proceedings, morning of 18th July, 2000, page 75, lines 9–13; at http://www.lgri.org.uk/18julam.htm 89:40 (1987:1991).

47 http://www.publications.parliament.uk/pa/cm200001/cmselect/cmenvtra/17/0110107.htm, 28:2 (96:118) paragraph 108. (House of Commons – Environment, Transport and Regional Affairs – Minutes of Evidence, Select Committee on Environment, Transport and Regional Affairs Minutes of Evidence).

48 See Max Weber (1978), page 26.

49 The term 'drawing things together' is the title of an important paper on centres of control by Bruno Latour. See Latour (1990).

50 It may or may not, of course, experience the need to make its tradeoffs publicly accountable (and there are, as is obvious, also different publics – in the present context, the general press with its concern for safety, and the financial press which is more concerned with profit, investment and growth). The circumstances of the railway industry in the UK have certainly been unusual in the level of general accountability.

51 The most obvious point of entry into this large literature is Anthony Giddens' (1990).

52 It is difficult to find any countervailing argument in the face of what appears to be a very general commitment by right and left alike to accountability in Euro-American public life. But for an important opening, see Luc Boltanski (1990).

53 The quotation comes from www.lgri.org.uk/transcript/30mayam.htm – 92:24 (1618:1619), page 58, lines 6–7.

54 This account is derived from www.lgri.org.uk/transcript/30mayam.htm (1064ff), page 36ff, and www.lgri.org.uk/transcript/30maypm.htm.

55 www.lgri.org.uk/transcript/30mayam.htm – 92:7 (1009:1014), page 24, lines 33–35.

56 www.lgri.org.uk/transcript/27julpm.htm – 84:31 (1589:1602), page 50, lines 16–25.

57 The testimony also explores something else that he didn't do. This was to press the 'signals on' button. This is a way of rebooting the entire signal system, but also sets every signal in the area to red. If the signals on button had been pressed it might, perhaps, have averted the accident. It would also, and this is part of the argument, have caused large disruption to the rail system and a series of dangerous emergency stops by other trains. See www.lgri.org.uk/transcript/ 30mayam.htm – 92:19 (1834:1843), page 66.

58 www.lgri.org.uk/transcript/30mayam.htm (1119), pages 39–40, lines 25–3.

59 www.lgri.org.uk/transcript/30maypm.htm 93:17 (493:499), page 175, lines 5–13.

60 www.lgri.org.uk/transcript/30maypm.htm 93:16 (1872:1881), pages 121–122, lines 22–1.

61 Cullen (2001), page 3.

62 'The amount of time taken by Signaller Allen to react to the occurrence of the SPAD does not seem unreasonable, given the decision-making process required based upon the technology, in particular the quality of the displays available to him.' At www.lgri.org.uk/transcript/30maypm.htm – 93:3 (359:371) page 116, lines 21–25. The quotation comes from the report of the official Health and Safety Laboratory.

63 www.lgri.org.uk/transcript/30maypm.htm – 93:18 (44:50) page 105, lines 16–22.

64 There is a large literature on tacit knowledge and the relation between formulations and practices. See, for instance, Harry Collins (1975), and Lucy Suchman (1987).

65 See Michel Callon (1986).

66 www.lgri.org.uk/transcript/28julam.htm – 85:22 (1217:1221), page 43, lines 9–13.

67 In an interview with sociologists a person is similarly pushed into talking. Faced with an informant who didn't do so, Callon and Rabeharisoa began to appreciate this refusal as a political act – or rather an attempt to remain private, outside the political arena where one needs to justify one's actions. See Callon and Rabeharisoa (1999).

68 On utopia, see Louis Marin (1993) and Kevin Hetherington (1997). On purity and impurity see Bruno Latour (1993). On the disentanglement of discursive locations to produce happy and simple places, considered in another mode, see Donna Haraway (1997).

References

Barnes, Barry (1977) *Interests and the Growth of Knowledge*, London: Routledge and Kegan Paul.

Boltanski, Luc (1990) *L'Amour et la Justice comme Compétences:Trois Essais de Sociologie de l'Action*, Paris: Metailié.

Boltanski, Luc and Laurent Thévenot (1987) *Les Économies de la Grandeur*, Vol. 32 Cahiers du Centre d'Études de l'Emploi, Paris: Presses Universitaires de France.

Callon, Michel (1986) 'Some Elements of a Sociology of Translation: Domestication of the Scallops and the Fishermen of Saint Brieuc Bay', pages 196–233 in John Law (ed.), *Power, Action and Belief: a new Sociology of Knowledge?* *Sociological Review Monograph*, 32, London: Routledge and Kegan Paul.

Callon, Michel (1998a) 'An Essay on Framing and Overflowing: Economic Externalities Revisited by Sociology', pages 244–269 in Michel Callon (ed.), *The Laws of the Markets*, Oxford and Keele: Blackwell and the Sociological Review.

Callon, Michel (1998b) 'Introduction: the Embeddedness of Economic Markets in Economics', pages 1–57 in Michel Callon (ed.), *The Laws of the Markets*, Oxford and Keele: Blackwell and the Sociological Review.

Callon, Michel and Vololona Rabehariso (1999) 'Gino's Lesson on Humanity', Paris: Ecole des Mines de Paris.

Collins, H.M. (1975) 'The Seven Sexes: a Study in the Sociology of a Phenomenon, or the Replication of Experiments in Physics', *Sociology*, 9: 205–224.

Cullen, Rt. Hon Lord (2001) *The Ladbroke Grove Rail Inquiry, Part 1*, Norwich: HSE Books, Her Majesty's Stationery Office.

Dodier, Nicolas (1993) *L'Expertise Médicale: Essai de Sociologie sur l'Exercise du Jugement*, Paris: Métailié.

Foucault, Michel (1979) *Discipline and Punish: the Birth of the Prison*, Harmondsworth: Penguin.

Giddens, Anthony (1990) *The Consequences of Modernity*, Cambridge: Polity Press.

Haraway, Donna J. (1997) *Modest_Witness@Second_Millenium.Female_Man©_Meets_Oncomouse^TM: Feminism and Technoscience*, New York and London: Routledge.

Harbers, Hans, Annemarie Mol and Alice Stollmeyer (2002) 'Food Matters: Arguments for an ethnography of daily care', *Theory, Culture and Society*, forthcoming.

Hetherington, Kevin (1997) *The Badlands of Modernity: Heterotopia and Social Ordering*, London: Routledge.

Latour, Bruno (1990) 'Drawing Things Together', pages 19–68 in Michael Lynch and Steve Woolgar (eds), *Representation in Scientific Practice*, Cambridge, Mass: MIT Press.

Latour, Bruno (1993) *We Have Never Been Modern*, Brighton: Harvester Wheatsheaf.

Latour, Bruno and Steve Woolgar (1979) *Laboratory Life: the Social Construction of Scientific Facts*, Beverly Hills and London: Sage.

Law, John (2000) 'Ladbroke Grove, or How to Think about Failing Systems', http://www.comp.lancs.ac.uk/sociology/soc055jl.html.

Marin, Louis (1993) 'The Frontiers of Utopia', pages 7–16 in Krishan Kumar and Stephen Bann (eds), *Utopias and the Millennium*, London: Reaktion Books.

Perrow, Charles (1984) *Normal Accidents: Living with High Risk Technologies*, New York: Basic Books.

Shapin, Steven and Simon Schaffer (1985) *Leviathan and the Air Pump: Hobbes, Boyle and the Experimental Life*, Princeton: Princeton University Press.

Suchman, Lucy (1987) *Plans and Situated Actions: the Problem of Human-Machine Communication*, Cambridge: Cambridge University Press.

Thévenot, Laurent (2002) 'Which Road to Follow? The Moral Complexity of an 'Equipped' Humanity', forthcoming in John Law and Annemarie Mol (eds), *Complexities: Social Studies of Knowledge Practices*, Durham, N.Ca.: Duke.

Weber, Max (1978) *Economy and Society: an Outline of Interpretive Sociology*, ed. Guenther Roth and Claus Wittich, Berkeley: University of California Press.

Utopiary: utopias, gardens and organization

Gibson Burrell and Karen Dale

Utopian thinking, in a broad sense (Kumar, 1989:19–20), is more than More. It encompasses our capacity as humans for the free-floating imagination of how things could be different and better. As such, its history surely must be as old as humanity. Organization Studies inhabits little else other than capitalist spaces of production and consumption and may seem woefully devoid of such valuable traditions. But in the parallel world of the Other, it has its own particular utopian legacy. This strand of utopian thinking, that envisages better alternatives to the organization of production, has been a powerful force both in literature (eg Saint Simon, Morris, Chernyshevsky) and in attempts to instigate communities of practice (eg Owen, Fourier, Cabet). However, in this chapter we do not intend to subject conceptions of the organization of production to further scrutiny, but to turn this on its head and consider its Other – the *production of organization* (Cooper and Burrell, 1988). We believe that utopian thinking illustrates some common principles around the production of organization (which we discuss below) and these, we would argue, may well reflect back upon the ability of utopias actually to render a change to the organization of production.

The second element in our exploration of utopian thought is another aspect that is conventionally overlooked in organization studies: *spatial organization*. Space and place are fundamental to utopias. In the Christian tradition, for example, the story begins in a paradisiacal garden and ends in the Holy City, both obvious utopian images of placement. Thomas More's very play on 'no *place*' and a 'better *place*' in coining the word is clearly central to this and, as we will show, utopian visions have a powerful link to geographical, physical, and spatial notions of social organization. Within the range of spatial images, we have chosen to take *the garden* as our reference point (see also Munro, this volume). Again this may appear on the surface to be almost the opposite of the subject of the organization of production. Certainly these days, although this is a relatively recent phenomenon, gardens are associated with leisure and consumption. They are linked with nature and the rural, whereas our geographical imagination of production (though not necessarily its actuality) is thoroughly urban. Therefore, Gardens and Utopias often go hand in hand – but in complex and contradictory ways. For where and when the world has solved the problems of organizing production, what remains to be imaginatively ameliorated is the equally significant task of the production of organization. And it is to the garden that many utopians have turned as helpful in their plot. Gardens appear to be sites for the production of other defensible forms of organization that are somehow 'closer to Nature'. But it has been shown in many places, including Euripides's description of how the Bacchae treated those of an Apollonian bent (Euripides, 1973:215–218) and The Old Testament's narrative in Genesis of the events leading up to the Expulsion, that the garden is a place of mystery and power and pain, as well as harmonious enlightenment, equality and pleasure. What does become apparent is that gardens, as with other social spaces, are places of multiple interpretations and these include the readings of the present authors as well as those of utopian writers.

Therefore, before starting down this path, perhaps we should say something about our approach in this chapter. We will borrow a little from Deleuze and Guattari. In their metaphor of vegetation, the place of the structured tree of knowledge with its brown narrow trunk a-topped by a mature lushly green growth and an open canopy of surface approaches gives way, as Deleuze and Guattari talk, to an exploratory rhizome. What we are trying to do in this chapter takes the form of the exploratory rhizome rather than the logical straight lines of the arboreal. In the manner of the subterranean rhizome the matter we consider is de-territorialized: it is not the usual home ground of organization studies. The rhizome wanders in a multiplicity of forms that are hard to see and hard to predict in their location. Unlike the aborescent tree that is visible, hierarchical and predictably straight, the rhizome assumes very diverse forms as it ceaselessly establishes subterranean and grounded connections. Likewise, the multiple forms of social organization imagined in utopian works are not limited to notions of organization rooted only in rationalism and effectiveness. Thus neither utopian writers nor those that seek to give meaning to them need to be governed by the disciplinary conventions of adding to the tree of knowledge and kneeling in homage to the conventionally workaday. We seek then not to be proper 'garden historians' but to make rhizomatic connections between different historical periods, across different discourses and different interpretations of relatively well-known social phenomena.

Through three elements of the *production of organization*, particularly of *space* and especially in the place of the *garden*, ('marginal' as they are currently to Organization Studies), we seek to use this approach to explore what utopian thought might have to contribute to our understanding of organizations and organizing. We do not shy away from drawing unconventional conclusions.

Obscuring and securing the spatial production of organization

Within the context of this chapter we wish to focus on utopias as essentially riven with paradoxes and contradictions. We seek to look at one particular facet of utopianism that seems crucially important. Namely, that the reproduction of social relations which both *obscure* and *secure* organization (Burawoy, 1985:82) are parallel processes within utopian thought. On one hand, utopias present the security of reasoned and managed alternatives but at the same time occlude and obscure both old and new forms of control and deception. Utopian space is always ambiguous.

With regard to the *obscuring* of organization there are a few hints in Cooper and Burrell (1988:103, 106–7) about what the term 'the production of organization' could mean. First, there is the Foucauldian notion of 'genealogy', which, through its sketches of a history of the present, implies that some sense of how organization gets produced today and yesterday is crucial. Second, organization is produced within situations marked by uncertainty, disorder and imbalance, as something remedial. Organization is also an automatic reaction to impending threat. Hence, organization is defensive as well as reactive. But organizational principles are constantly being subjected to self-recursion and doubt. The necessity of self-reference in any organizational principle dictates that each principle contains its own opposite and for each programme there is an unprogramme. Every strategy contains deviations and errors. Finally, Lyotard's (1977) suggestion that there is a complex play of active operations that bring organization alive, which he calls the '*mise-en-scene*', is important. Drawing upon the concept in producing live theatre, he implies that very many items can affect the way in which a performative impact is made upon those involved. Organization exists within such performative, existential gaps that lie beyond strategy, knowledge and coherent discourse. What we perceive amidst successive entrances and exits is confused complexity. The core of organization, given all this, is a vortex.

With regard to the *securing* of organization, we would suggest that there are similar organizational features within very many utopias. At first, these themes look like a coherent formal strategy for the attainment of utopian existence. They are the obvious principles of:

1. *Protection.* The utopia offers the spiritual, political, physical and moral protection of the community around its membership
2. *Boundaries.* Utopias are consistently presented as being separated off from the non-utopian or even dystopian world by clear lines of demarcation.
3. *The 'beastliness' of the outside and the 'bestliness' of the inside.* We mean by this that the boundary is meant to contain within it all that is perceived to be best and worthy of nurture whilst at the same time holding outside what is beastly in the world of nature.
4. *Control.* Utopian thought does not usually speak of 'control' but rather of 'harmony'. Many utopias have sought harmony as their objective, but harmonious living often means that 'individuals' (if such are deemed to exist) are prevented from behaving in ways that they might think appropriate, in the interests of maintaining the peace.
5. *Patterns.* Utopian existence is often meant to follow pre-determined patterns of behaviour that have been laid down before the community is even

settled. As we shall see in the Garden Cities of early 20th century Britain, Sir Ebenezer Howard laid down that none in the community had the right to change his highly prescriptive 'master' plan.

6. *Formality*. Utopian thought often follows the notion that jurisprudence is important to the community and lays down rules that are meant to be formal, objective and understood by all. Formality here is to do with the in-built stasis and the resistance to change that such structured thinking implies.

These six principles, outlined above, appear to us to be predicated upon the securing of organization in the face of 'disorganizing' tendencies. The securing of the production of organization along formal bounded 'lines' is to be found in very many utopian imaginings. But so too is the parallel production of the obscuring of the irrepressible, uncontrollable wilderness within which formality is valued. Every utopia is also a dystopia, for the first is predicated upon the second. Every utopia attempts to secure the 'best' and obscure the 'beastly'. Every utopia attempts this boundary-work spatially. And so too does every garden.

One side of the garden brings out strongly the structural-spatial elements (cf. Massey, 1984:99) of the production of organization which we describe here as 'utopiary'. Thomas Jefferson's image of 'Virginia' was of the suppression of the wilderness and the expression of the 'Garden of the World', green, well-ordered and of continental size in which agricultural endeavour was the highest rung of achievement. It fits in with this utopiarian strand very well (Kumar, 1987:74). But there is also another side of the garden – the aspects of which do not fit easily with our conception of organization, which elude our categories and boundaries and which we might describe as the 'other side' of the production of organization. So on one side, we see the principles of boundary, formality, planning and design, matter in its place, control: in other words – management. On the other side, however, we see the connections with spirituality, fecundity, sexuality, pleasure, playfulness, surprise and the unpredictability of nature, even where it is gardened. These paradoxes and contradictions in the garden are ones that resonate with the two authors. One of us loves pruning and taming, and holds up the walled garden as their ideal; the other loves abundance, the romanticism of the wild, and the blurred boundaries of the cottage garden. The production of organization is the articulate securing of moral principles and axioms whilst obscuring the imperfect grasp held by humanity of what to do for the best. In the chapter we hope to play with this tension.

Utopiary: The spatial organization of utopias

A key historical dimension of the production of organization is: which conceptualizations of space become conceivable, and which are rendered inconceivable? Thomas More's *Utopia* is a model of a tightly organized spatial form and represents a perfected golden age of small town living. Harvey (2000:160) tells us that for More 'Utopia is an artificially created island, which functions as an isolated, coherently organised, and largely closed space economy'. *Utopia*, first published in 1516, envisages its capital, Amaurote, as being set in the centre of the island. The primary form of organization is not to be the guild but the family and the neighbourhood. The organization of the household is to be regularized (Davis, 1993:24). The streets are to be 20 feet wide and every house has to have both a street door and a garden door, for the Utopians have a zeal of gardening which 'is increased not merely by the pleasure afforded them, but by the keen competition between streets, which shall have the best kept garden' (in Mumford, 1961:325). Gardens are at the heart of Utopia. Country life and sports were to be encouraged and agriculture was to be the one common pursuit of both men and women. Utopia, amongst many things' is an important spatially organized image that allows us to explore the formal principles of organization by which human beings in the west have sought to understand the ways in which their lives might be made better. Harvey (2000:161) goes on to suggest that utopias 'become with More's initiative, a fertile means to explore and express a vast range of competing ideas about social relationships, moral orderings, political-economic systems, and the like.' Marin (1984) however, in keeping with the (partial) origin of the term to mean 'No-place', suggests that utopia is a pure signifier without any meaningful referent in the material world. So, given this immateriality, is there any point in seeking to understand utopian thought as if it refers to spatial organization in particular? Foucault (1974) recognizes the spatiality of utopia in positive ways: 'Utopias afford consolation: although they have no real locality, there is nevertheless a fantastic untroubled region in which they are able to unfold: they open up cities with vast avenues, superbly planted gardens, countries where life is easy, even though the road to them is chimerical' (in Harvey, 2000:183).

In this particular spatial order of things, we find the suggestion of a movement through the social spaces of utopia: starting in the city, moving 'out' into the suburbs where one finds the garden, thence into the countryside proper with its fields, and then Foucault talks of a road that is chimerical. Perhaps the last hints at the wilderness, the place of non-human beasts and monsters that might prove the antithesis of the fundamentally humanist utopia. These four zonal notions will run throughout the chapter and whilst we appreciate that they force space into two dimensions rather than allowing it three, we, like many before us (cf Kumar, 1987:5–7), find this annularism useful. Utopian thought can be seen, we will argue, as living in the creative tension between these four zones and the differing principles of organization that they represent and embody.

In our conceptualization of the four-fold social-spatial organization of utopia we depend on the notion of boundary. Tellingly, the words 'yard' and 'garden' both owe their origin to the Old English word for 'wattle fence': a 'geard' (Schama, 1995:534). As such, it was to keep out wild animals. The term 'paradise' is said to come from 'pairidaeza' which is Old Persian, meaning an enclosure, and was taken into Old Testament Hebrew as 'pardes' to mean simply a park or garden enclosure and into Greek as 'paradeisos' which meant a sumptuous and extravagant park. From here it came to influence the later Hebrew sense of both the original Garden of Eden and the heavenly kingdom or 'celestial paradise'. Thus the common ground of garden and paradise is enclosure. Christian Norberg-Schulz (1980:52) informs us that:

> In the cultural landscape the natural forces are 'domesticated' and living reality is made manifest as an ordered process where man participates. The *garden* is hence a place where living nature is concretised as an organic totality. Man's image of Paradise was always in fact an enclosed garden. In the garden the known elements of nature are gathered; fruit trees, flowers and tamed water.'

Indeed, Norberg-Schulz goes on to suggest that '*the distinctive quality of any man-made place is enclosure*' (emphasis added) and this we see as highly pertinent to the organization of utopian spaces.

Throughout its history, the boundaries of the garden have been protected in diverse ways. These have been spiritual, as in the guardian angels that prevented Adam and Eve returning to the Garden of Eden, and with regard to *Terms* or statues evoking the god Terminus placed at the edges of the garden. Boundaries have frequently been the physical barriers of walls and fences. Both physically and symbolically, these landmarks protect boundaries from those outside and mark the limits of guaranteed safety for those within. But topiary has been the most fashionable boundary in various periods of history. The first recording of its existence was by Pliny the Elder in the time of Augustus when large villa gardens were becoming fashionable. The work in the ornamental garden (topia) was to be carried out by one of the slaves, who became known as a topiarius. The typical Roman topiarius sought to represent hunting scenes, fleets of ships and real objects. They were somewhat 'scissor-happy' (Clevely, 1988:11). This highly militaristic sculptural imagery is suggestive of an internal authoritarian regime, protecting that which is within the palisade from that which is without. Topiary is also found abundantly in a leisurely age of wealthy estate owners who employed large numbers of craftspeople to trim and train hedges as a part of garden decoration (Clevely, 1988:8). Topiary flourished therefore in the 17th century when the formal, architectural component of gardening reached its height. Espaliers, plants trained on a trellis or wire, are part of this tradition. In ways reminiscent of the picture in Foucault's *Discipline and Punish* (1977: plate 10) they evoke the training and dressage of the body involved in the disciplinary society. Carol Shields (1997:198) tells us that the espalier 'wants to grow in three dimensions, that's its impulse, but you can force it to occupy a two-dimensional plane, flattening it out so it nicely covers a fence or block wall'. *In toto*, topiary is an unnatural art since it seeks to control and bend nature and to make it represent forms of human production. Unsurprisingly, Walt Disney was a great fan of topiary and it was used throughout Disneyland. The typical plant for topiary was the box tree and it is no accident then that we speak in English of 'being boxed in'. In recent years, topiary has once again become fashionable.

Thus there is the suggestion in utopian spatial boundedness of a lack of free movement, free thought or free expression. More's *Utopia* was meant to be both no place and a happy place but at the cost of being a secure place – a semi-dictatorial hierarchical regime. More 'posits an ideal society based on social equality, where all but the most learned share both labour and its fruits' (Briggs, 1983:38). For the most learned then came the fruits without the labour! Lefebvre (1991) is resolutely opposed to this sort of traditional utopianism in relation to thinking about innovative spatial forms precisely because of their 'closed authoritarianism' (Harvey, 2000:182). And, before him, Marx had argued against the French utopian group, the Icarians, who were to go to America to set up their new life specifically because (as with Coleridge's abortive 'pantisocracy' scheme) they were fleeing the European cities in order to set up a closed sectarian society in the wilderness. Such utopianism ends up, Marx argued, by being politically neutralized because it is isolated and walled off. But they and the phalanxes of Fourierians went off to their phalansteries in the North American wilderness nevertheless. They left behind them the city.

Garden and city

First we deal with the rise of urban conurbations and the ways in which this forms the foil against which many utopias are developed as methods of obscuring urban blight. For the rest of the section we consider utopias of 'security'. We look at Absolutism and the attempt to fashion the new controllable capital city from within the garden. We move on to a bourgeois sense of the safe city with gardens in Victorian times and then at the ways in which the city becomes transformed into garden living under Edwardian thought. We look briefly at this basic idea in the first years of the 21st century.

It is important to note that, after industrialization, the utopiarian fence may well be seen as necessary to keep out the city rather than the wilderness. Indeed for some they become synonyms. The industrial city had come to be seen as the place of beastliness, of uncontrolled sybaritic and barbarian behaviour and the appalling exploitation of people, all unleashed by rapid industrialization, and epitomized by Engels' study of the working class in Manchester. The city was for work, pain and hard labour: a place from which one had to escape. Many if not all utopian images are of course 'class' or hierarchically based myths. Most envisage a controlled environment of a managed system, differentiated from the outside world that is characterized as dystopian. Clearly in certain important ways, the category of 'anti-urban' was legitimated in early and middle Victorian Britain. If we look at utopian imagery and the place of the rural idyll within it, we can find it strongly represented in the radical tradition. The Romantic movement of the 19th century spoke of a return to a pre-industrial world, of the magnificence of the countryside and of (non-urban) scenery. Marx's image of labour that is not alienated consists of hunting in the morning and fishing in the afternoon. This indicates a vision of post-socialist commune-ism based on rural lifestyles in which Manchester's slums do not exist and the Irwell, perhaps, is open once again to fish. In these anti-urban visions, the garden comes to occupy a significant place. William Morris, for example, advocated a return to vernacular skills and locally rooted traditions against industrial production (see Reedy, this volume). In his utopian *News from Nowhere*, (1890) Morris placed the Garden Tree purposively at the centre of his proletarian, arts and crafts based, Eden.

However, gardens are also about the securing of power, production, consumption and administration. And the ways in which these are organized, afresh, by the most powerful can be seen, by them, as utopian. At Versailles, Louis XIV commissioned Le Notre to design his Palace and estate in such a way as to be superior to that Le Notre had constructed for Nicholas Fouquet at Vaux-le-Vicomte. On the 17 August 1661, Fouquet had shown off his pride and joy to the King but such was the extravagance of the estate, Louis's envy and suspicion were immediately aroused. Three weeks later Fouquet was arrested for treason and spent the rest of his life in prison. Vaux was a monument to French rationalism and demonstrated human order and control over a landscape and over Nature in general. The Sun King decided that he too must have one. He sought to transform his father's tiny hunting lodge at Versailles into a palace that would reflect his potency and he would turn Versailles, not Paris, into the new capital of his kingdom. Before Le Notre began, the site was described as 'the saddest and most barren place with no view, no water and no woods' (van Zuylen, 1995:70). Huge hydraulic works were constructed and plant material was clipped into an outdoor architecture of walls, rooms and avenues. Every view was constructed so as to be best seen from the windows of the Grande Galerie. Versailles was designed to be viewed 'properly' from only one spot. And that was where Louis XIV would stand. For Versailles is derived from a Cartesian perspectivalist stance.

Van Zuylen (ibid) analyses the King's desire to have Versailles where and how it was:

> Versailles mirrors a period in French history during which the monarchy wielded absolute power over political, social and artistic life. The humiliation the young king had suffered during La Fronde – a series of uprisings aimed at limiting royal authority – made him wary of both the nobility and Paris.

Thus the palace and gardens at Versailles were a political device in which the capital of the state was moved from where it proved troublesome and into the countryside where, as Saint-Simon said, the king 'rode rough shod over nature' and kept courtiers amused and muzzled. The Gardens were conceived by Le Notre to be settings for vast outdoor fêtes and performances whereby the king could make spectacular entrances and exits through use of a whole set of phantasmagorical devices.

Turner (1994:23) argues that Baroque culture was very conservative and sought to manipulate the masses through fantastic images, colour and elaborate music. There was a very strong tradition, within this cultural period, of developing devices within the garden to fool the wanderer and the populace in general. Secret parts that are met with accidentally are a key part of the aristocratic garden, as are tricks to deceive the eye and the senses: allées with long views that give a false impression of depth, *trompes d'oeil* in the form of skilled paintings or mirrors, reflective pools and plantings to see the world differently from that which it is. Virtually all of these are to be found in Versailles. These subterfuges include many approaches to boundary maintenance and their aesthetic development. The control of water is a part too of the Baroque garden. *Giochi d'acqua* or hidden water jets offer the prospect of water being all around but subject to strict hydraulic management. At Versailles the system, though huge, was not enough to get every fountain to work simultaneously. As soon as Louis XIV was out of sight the pumps were switched off to the area that he had just left. Art and architecture were seen as central to the gardens with yew and box trees being planted on both sides of the 'parterres' in trained and clipped ways. Turner (ibid) describes devices, such as this, as being based on deception, complexity and artificiality with their aim being to bring about a culture of the spectacle by which and through which the commitment of the masses to absolute monarchy might be assured.

Vierhaus (1988:65) maintains that 'Baroque palaces, gardens, theatres and allées constituted extended spaces for the processions and receptions of sovereign authority as its symbols and decorations'. Gardens of the aristocracy also embraced mazes and labyrinths. Sennett (1994:179–80) argues that in Paris the labyrinth or maze offered a place of solitude from the masses prowling the overcrowded streets whilst the still, fountainless pools often placed there allowed self reflection of the valorized melancholic kind. In the grand homes and estates, however, several other features are noteworthy. Mazes could only be understood from the point of view of the superior – the one who looked down in the knowledge of its grand plan. They symbolically represented the long and arduous journey to Jerusalem and, on arrival, the likelihood of salvation. The concept of the Sun King itself is really an extended attempt at a *trompe d'oeil*. And the gardens at Versailles were meant to play a huge part in the realization of this monarchical utopia. And we should note that the close management of appearance within this space continues to this day. Even in the 21st century (which we might conceptualize stylistically perhaps as the Neo-Neo-Neo-Baroque, Burrell and Dale 2001) the paying visitor to Versailles is not allowed to walk on the grass and will be moved on by the mounted police who patrol the grounds.

From the garden as the utopian symbol of absolute power, separated off from lesser mortals, we move to consider the use of the garden to create spaces of power *within* the city: the garden as a bourgeois utopia. Nearly two centuries after Louis XIV, Napoleon III was a bourgeois King and no absolute ruler. But he saw that the protection of his position was made more difficult by the presence in Paris of the mob, over whom he had little opportunity to exercise administrative control outside of the musket and bayonet. If Louis XIV had governed the city from the Palace at Versailles, Napoleon III was to govern from within Paris itself. To make Paris fit to govern and as fit for Government, he called in the self styled 'artist of demolition', the remarkable Baron Georges-Eugene Haussmann. He was Prefect of the Seine and was empowered by the Emperor to change the face of the city. He drove wide boulevards through the poor areas of the city, the better to move troops into areas of insurrection when needed and the better to remove the homes of the offending populace at the same time. In their place came a huge programme of gentrification in which homes for the bourgeoisie were built in the newly destroyed, newly fashionable areas of Paris. And in order to bourgeoisify the districts, Haussmann created new tree lined public parks. Throughout the 1850s a major programme of building sewers and 40 public gardens was undertaken and the royal forest of the Bois de Boulogne became a public park (van Zuylan, 1995:113). Decorative horticulture was undertaken throughout the city using sub-tropical plants. Somewhat intriguingly, as part of the hygienization of the city, a ring of cemeteries was constructed around the newly bourgeoisifed centre that was, deliberately or not, to act as a green belt around the capital. This was to prove hugely popular with both the middle classes and the Court for it made the city safe and attractive, and brought garden life into the heart of Paris. This greening of the capital bought the Emperor political support – at least temporarily:

> Napoleon III knew full well that the oases of greenery he inserted in the restless city of Paris were much more than pleasure grounds; they were part of a political agenda. Public parks held out the prospect of social harmony, or the illusion of it. The aesthetic rationale of modern city parks harks back to the timeless theme of the Garden of Eden: in this brilliant variation, it was hoped that relaxation and diversion in a natural setting would act as a safety valve for the tensions of urban life and perhaps neutralize its harmful effects. Thus, to the extent that municipal parks were calculated to socialize the masses and therefore keep them under control, the 'Haussmannization' of Paris was part of a counter-revolutionary game-plan (van Zuylen, 1995:113).

Meanwhile, in the UK, the embourgeoisement of London and the (so-called) provincial cities was underway, but London had no Haussmann, and Prince Albert, who may just have had the will to force something like this through, by 1861 was dead. The middle classes were to be offered something else by way of gardens in an attempt to secure a rural triumph over the city that was to influence many others.

Garden cities, a concept that arose in the UK, had been expressed as early as 1827. Best known of its advocates, however, was Ebenezer Howard who articulated the concept diagrammatically in 1898. He had been converted to the possibility of a better life for the dweller of the filthy, overcrowded industrial city on a visit to the USA in the 1870s (Lampugnani, 1988:155). He was to take on board the anarchistic communism of Kropotkin and the Arts and Crafts approach of Ruskin and Morris, but it was Edward Bellamy's technologically driven utopian text *Looking Backward: 2000–1887*, published in 1888, which had the major impact on his designs (Curl, 1999:327). Bellamy's book foretold of an industrial society transformed by the development of co-operative endeavour. Howard's own vision of the future appeared first as *A Peaceful Path to Social Reform* (1898) but was renamed for the second edition *Garden Cities of Tomorrow* (1902). Howard 'rejected the suburb as a tolerable compromise: indeed he hardly considered it. . . . In rejecting the temporary, transitional form of the suburb he sought a stable marriage between city and country, not a weekend liaison' (Mumford, 1961:515). His utopian settlement was evocatively and provocatively named 'Rurisville'. It was to be a self-sufficient Garden City of some 32,000 people. Letchworth in 1903 saw the first real trial of this idea and consisted of English cottages set in an Arcadian environment of trees, winding roads and gardens. His original design, of which Letchworth and subsequently Welwyn Garden City are *not* close reflections (Fleming *et al.*, 1999:215), is of a design representing concentric rings with the aim partly being to prevent houses or industrial buildings entering 'green belts' around the city. The Garden City has at its core a large garden. Around this are placed important civic buildings with these being surrounded by a large park. Then come schools and road systems but outside of these are allotments. Outside this civically cultivated acreage lie houses and beyond this the small farms and then the large farms, that establish a return to the countryside. Lampugnani (1988:155) tells us of Howard that, 'with English pragmatism, he sought to find a middle ground on cooperative principles, with help from private initiatives, but assured against speculation'. In this way he attempted to steer between the 'utopian socialism' of Fourier and Owen on one hand and the corporate paternalism of Cadbury, Lever Brothers and Titus Salt. Not an easy path one might imagine but at the time this was not seen by all, especially Fabians, as impossible.

It is at the beginning of the 20th century then that ideas of utopian living come to be seen as being exemplified in the garden city of 30,000 population. Outside Britain the story is similar, for in Germany, Belgium and the USA at about this time the idea was taken up. In the USA, the Radburn experiment in New Jersey in 1929 was meant to develop a complete new town where pedestrians and moving vehicles were to be kept completely separate but the notion of a separate town soon disappeared into the maw of New Jersey City. And so too did the vast majority of the Howardian inspired designs. As Lampugnani (ibid) tells us, 'they remained isolated and weak palliatives against the explosion of city populations in the early 20th century'. In other words, the city took over both gardens and countryside. But Mumford (1961:519) from his temporal standpoint is particularly supportive of Howard and offers the testament that in 'the English Garden City, gardens actually abound, rich in fruit trees, flowers and vegetables'. But whilst they did represent a strand of utopian thinking with strong conceptual pedigrees, that saw gardens as the way forward against the rise of the city, it was to a liberal bourgeois conception of houses fit for employees of the corporate (and often Quaker dominated) firm that Sir Ebenezer moved in his later years.

A century later and it appears to be Florida where utopian plans for the new cities, like 'Centennial', are being concretized (Hollis, 1998:216–219). 'Seaside', conceived by Robert Davis is a resort stretching for miles along the beach at Boca Raton and controlled by a private company which offers Utopian lifestyles based on 'neo-traditional plans' of a central village green, few commercial buildings ringed around it and limited car access. The spirit of Ebenezer lives on. The next plan, of course, is to take the 'utopian' community permanently to sea in the world's most luxurious cruise liner – the 'ResidenSea' – with apartments starting at $2 million. Whilst based in Florida, built by Norwegians and 'flagged' in the Bahamas, this enormous ship, from January 2002 will roam the world's warmer seas seeking major cultural events, be free of crime and (in order to do so) will have a ratio of 1 security person per 12 passengers.

Also in the early 21st century, British consumers are offered 'utopian' holiday locations like CenterParcs and Oasis, whilst at home they are all exhorted and induced to create their own little bits of paradise (Hamilton, 1997) in an individualized and consumerized world. One of the paradoxes of the transgression and control found in gardens in present day times (Bhatti and Church, 2001) is the appropriation of 'nature' for consumption. Gardens, we might suggest, have become a form of soma, an 'opium of the people'. The back garden may represent a type of 'escape attempt' from the advancing front of corporate delayering and work intensification. Suburban utopia consists of shopping malls and out-of-town centres that provide garden material for those who wish to surround themselves with one particular 'take' on nature, thereby ensuring that a significant amount of GDP is spent per annum on gardens in the UK. A huge industry now exists for producing equipment, plants, and accessories but there is also the culture industry of the media, publishing, and information guides that have accompanied this centring of the garden. The sector has grown rapidly, aided and abetted by the insatiable desire for TV programmes on garden design. But as Rachel de Thame (July, 2001) has said, these programmes assume the garden is a featureless 'ground zero' of 'wilderness' to begin with and is completely finished (that is, put into stasis) when the make-over crew leaves. TV gardeners have become celebrities. One of them reveals the following 'I am a suburban boy, brought up in an environment devoid of risk or challenge, cocooned by a giant comfort zone' (Gavin, 2001:96). People such as this become responsible for the production of 'taste', design and forms of nature. Living spaces are conceptualized as moving to the outside. And the garden becomes the extra 'room' of the house thus symbolizing the domestication of the garden and rendering it fit as a place for consumption. We can compare this to the cottage garden where the family's need for a supplement to subsistence, for basic needs as well as pleasure, were typically satisfied. But this was a quite different sort of pleasure from that of conspicuous consumption. So, even within the halls of media gardening, we hear the tension between the need for immediate gratification which consumption brings and the gardener's pleasure in the gradual and uncontrollable aspects of nature (de Thame, 2001).

Garden and countryside

Thus, we have seen in utopian spaces the tension between the urban and the rural, between culture and nature. There is a long history of rural utopianism, well represented in poetic form in the works of Virgil, Sidney, Spenser and even to some degree in Shakespeare and Milton. In this section we will examine the conflicting rural utopias of Cockaygne and Arcadia (see also Reedy, this volume). Then we will turn to the practical playing out of the creation of utopian rural spaces – for some – through the enclosure of the English countryside and the advent of formal parkland estates and the contemporary consumption of the countryside in the form of utopian leisure worlds.

The 'Land of Cockaygne' is found in a medieval English ballad and forms an escape for the lower classes, particularly rural peasantry, from labour and serfdom. It stems from an ideal world with a 'happy confluence of man and nature in an earthly paradise with abundant resources and aesthetically pleasing surroundings' (Hollis, 1998:41), but is centrally associated with an excess of food, drink and sex: a utopia focused on the physical pleasures. The picture created is one of idle but healthy peasants in a classless and lawless society where private property rights do not govern. The tradition became associated with medieval festival and carnivals in the turning upside-down of the everyday world. In stark contrast, the Arcadian utopia is one in which 'the desire for satisfaction is tempered through moderation' (Hollis, 1998:14). Interestingly, the Arcadia of Virgil is a reinvention by the Greek lyric poet Theocritus in the third century BC of an earlier Arcadia, actually a part of Greece, represented as a wilderness (and to which we shall return in the next section) (Schama, 1995). In Virgil's reworking, the forests become fields, the cultivated replaces the wild, animals now conduct themselves like citizens and are grown full and fat on the land. Civilization is in its full refinement and it is man (*sic*) who lords it over the beastly. It is in the countryside that leisure might be taken in a tamed, controlled environment of security: quite a contrast to that of Cockaygne. Arcadia was re-popularized by Renaissance humanists who saw its images as an antidote to the greed of the rich, powerful upper classes. However, as we shall see, the rural utopia captured in the remodelling of the English countryside in the 18th century gives no ground to either the dreams of corporeal sensuality of the lower classes, nor those of social justice held by the humanists.

Wealthy English landowners began noticeably to reconceptualize the 'countryside' in the mid 18th century (Hill, 1969:146–8). A series of Parliamentary Acts had led to the enclosure of huge tracts of formerly common land. The Black Act of 1723 (Fox, 1985) had made 50 more offences against the property of the landowner possible, all punishable by death and these included deer stalking, the taking of hare and pheasants, rick lighting, the mutilation of cattle and so on. This suggests that the controlled expulsion of the peasantry as farm labourers was on the agenda but also that they were not going to go quietly. And why should they mutilate cattle? Because the landowners 'went as far as to import cattle not for any economic reason but purely to provide a "living land-scape"' (Hamilton, 1995:21). Thompson (1968:245) tells us that 'Game laws, with their paraphernalia of gamekeepers, spring guns, mantraps and (after 1816) sentences of transportation . . . all served directly or indirectly to tighten the screw upon the labourer'. Whilst the commons had been the 'poor man's her-itage for ages past' they became conceptualized as 'a dangerous centre of indis-cipline', as a 'breeding ground for barbarians, nursing up a mischievous race of people' (Thompson, 1968:242). In other words, the enclosure of the commons was needed not solely for purposes of greed but because of the threat of social indiscipline. The cow, the geese, the turf were all lost to the cottaged inhabitants of the countryside. So too was the cottage itself. The danger was, that it held out the possibility of self-sufficiency and survival after enclosure. The cottages and their gardens had to be demolished, as Sir Robert Walpole did at Houghton Hall in Norfolk, allowing the original erased village no further opportunity to block the view from the main house (Schama, 2001). Or, as a mark of the landowners' paternalism, estate workers were moved to highly visible sites at the edge of the enclosure such as model villages like Blaize Hamlet. The majority of previous inhabitants, however, were now free to enter vagabondage. It is worth noting that More's *Utopia* was written at a time of some of the first enclo-sures and sought to deal specifically with the social and economic problems thereby caused (Briggs, 1983).

This process of enclosure, by dispossessing the agricultural labourer, made significant acreage available for landscaped parks. Views stretched into the dis-tance as the wealthy wished to be able to see their new-found control of the countryside stretching beyond the house. The garden was extended well into the countryside. The 'artificiality' of the French formal garden was railed against by people like Alexander Pope because the 'picturesque', rather than the formal, was seen as in keeping with this new English country garden utopia. What Pope did like, however, was the 'ha-ha'. For the newly developing gentry and the old aristocracy, this particular form of deception was to become very popular. Ha-ha's were designed originally to provide a trench in which defenders could await the attackers of the property. In the new English country gardens they prevented local animals invading the lawns and floral areas, whilst still offering uninterrupted views of the landscape. In the novel *Mansfield Park*, Jane Austen (1813,1983:93) says 'that iron gate, that ha-ha give me a feeling of restraint and hardship'. Thus, it is made clear that the boundary of the gentlewoman's world is marked by this sunken 'fence'. Horace Walpole, son of Sir Robert, however, was to say 'the ha-ha permitted the gardener to leap the fence and find that nature is a garden' (in van Zuylen, 1995:85). Boundaries were to become heavily gendered as well as hierarchicalized.

The concept of the 'countryside' as the garden of the alliance of aristocracy, gentry and squirarchy in the face of those originating from the 'ag. labs' who once tilled the self same fields still remains in the UK today. 'Rural England' as conceived by the present day 'Countryside Alliance' represents the right wing utopianism of country estates and the squirarchy. The interests of the countryside, and for that read the interests of those who own much of the countryside, are seen as best served by treating the countryside as their garden. Permission to cross their land, permission to interfere with their rights to maim and kill anything that does roam across their land and permission to end their club in the House of Lords are all still seen as 'reforms' for the future (primarily by the Labour Government). In this utopian imagery, the countryside is property – to be defended against any *re*-colonization by the peasantry. Degrees are now offered in 'countryside management' which run the danger of an implicit con-servatism as the ideology underpinning their interest in conservation. Perhaps what is to be managed is maintenance of the status quo.

The utopian countryside is thus firmly intertwined with its organized nature: managed through boundary and artifice. Yet again it is the strategy of the *securing* of spatial orderings. The other side of this is the concurrent creation of disruption, misery, poverty, resistance and exclusion. These 'Other' organiz-ing principles are obscured. We not only have Walpole moving the village out of the line of sight of 'his' landscape but today's tourist guides and websites do not make any mention of this forcible removal and play upon the sanctity of private property. This interplay between the securing and obscuring processes of utopian organization can also be seen in the contemporary creation of spaces of leisure and consumption. For perhaps we all play 'tourists' in a form of capitalist utopian landscape. This landscape exhibits some elements of both Cockaygne and Arcadia, although much diluted and perverted. They are designed to enlist our sensual pleasure in the consumption of excess. They evoke or borrow from the (idealized) countryside to give visual beauty. They are also bounded and hierarchalized spaces managed through artifice and subterfuge.

The countryside in the form of the National Parks and various 'Heritage Sites' can be seen in this way. Areas like the Lake District are 'neat and tidy' parks (Urry, 1995:209), nicely themed for grandeur of vista and placed in the time warp of stasis just at the moment when National Park status was awarded. Urry (1995) shows how the construction of Cumbria as the concept of the 'Lake District' is attempted but at the cost of ignoring that part of Cumbria that does not fit this construction: the de-industrialized coast. Thus, a landscape held in stasis is the aim of those empowered with the defence of the countryside and its appearance. But the contradiction is that there is no original nature against which we can judge defence or offence. Organization is produced in the context of the vortex and there are many spatially structured 'Lake Districts' which are possible.

The countryside has also become the 'pleasure garden' in the likes of Busch Gardens, Disneyland and Disneyworld and their European equivalents. Let us look just at iconic Disney. The creation of fantasy worlds out of swamp land and orange groves is achieved by placing 'impossible' combinations of fauna and flora together in what J.M. Findlay (1992) calls 'magic lands'. Findlay reports that, within the Disney empire, plants are changed with some frequency to falsely suggest the movement of seasons in the parks. This also strongly hints, of course, at a very controlling approach to nature and the environment. Walt

Disney is reported to have said 'I don't want the public to see the world they live in while they're in the park' (quoted in Bryman, 1995:113) which, as Bryman points out, implies both the elimination of negative aspects of city life and the physical inability to see the outside world because of screening devices and, we might add, the use of trompes d'oeil. Utilities are placed underground and so on. But in Disneyland the corporation could not afford to buy enough real estate to prevent the explosion of use in surrounding land, creating the new, somewhat tawdry city around it. In Disneyworld, huge acreage was taken up from the swampland so preventing the encroachment of the city into the park in too obvious a way. But as Bryman (1995:114) reminds us, controlling the immediate environs of the Park also allows control over hotel accommodation on a massive scale and represents another business opportunity associated with the city not the countryside. The facilitator of this city, garden, countryside amalgam was to be the relatively unknown 'Reedy Creek Improvement District' which has huge control over what happens in and around Disney sites with regards to land drainage, pest control, road maintenance, public transport, police, as well as land use and planning. The parks are private cities located originally in the countryside. EPCOT (Experimental Prototype Community of Tomorrow) had a very strong utopian orientation in its early planning. Disney said, inter alia, 'there will be no slum areas because we won't let them develop' (cited in Mosley, 1986:275). It was to be a planned, controlled community, and a showcase for American industry. Disney's EPCOT, however, as has been pointed out many times, is a Panglossian celebration of what is, not what could be (Bryman, 1995:144–5). The utopianism of theme parks then, revolves around the superficial presentation of the carnivalesque and the tradition of Cockaygne but from within urban styled controlled cities in which people processing has reached new heights of sophistication and where the thrills are manufactured, not hard won.

Garden and wilderness

The garden as a utopian space is created on the very edge of the wilderness. Indeed, the wilderness seems the antithesis of the garden: untamed, uncontrolled, unbounded, unpredictable, even fundamentally unmanageable and disorganized. Sometimes it is a desert and is deserted. But the garden may be associated with the free play of nature, with all its violence and abundance that might, one day, be domesticated. The wilderness may also be associated with the non-human: monsters, beasts and chimeras. In this it will seem that the wilderness is the foil to the utopia. For utopia is ultimately based upon some form of humanism in its search for an ideal social organization. In this section we will explore how, despite the boundedness of the garden, the wild is often placed in its very centre, and we will also examine attempts to expel the wilderness, to create the perfect garden and the consequences this has for our conceptualizations of utopian social order.

As we have commented, the pastoral Arcadia turns out to be 'drastically reinvented' (Schama, 1995:528) from the original area of Arcadia in Greece. This was a pre-selenic wilderness, marked by beastliness and bestiality, inhabited by 'autochthons', original mankind sprung from the earth itself, whose divinity was Pan, half goat by form and animal-like in his nature. From the recreated Arcadia, 'this perfect pastoral state, all savage things have been banished' transformed by 'a sense of order which is the social invention of humanity rather than the pure work of nature' (Schama, 199:528). The wilderness seems to be completely Other than our 'man-made' utopias, yet we find in the garden a much greater ambivalence than this dichotomy would suggest.

The ambiguous relations between garden-utopia and natural wilderness can be symbolized in two strong medieval garden traditions. These are the *hortus conclusus*, the enclosed private space for contemplation which included hints of the wilderness but all under very firm control, or the more public and corporeal spaces of the *hortus deliciarum*, the garden of delights or the pleasure dome, as in for example the 'Valley of the Ladies' in Boccaccio's *Decameron* (van Zuylen, 1995:43). Thus, on the one side, we have the securing of the garden against nature, the wilderness, the beastly, perhaps particularly through the control of female sexuality as mythically symbolic of these forces. On the other we have the close association of the garden with the wild – fertility, phallocentric sexuality and Dionysian abandonment. Let us look at each in turn.

Historically, the times and spaces in which gardens have been seen as utopian locales have often displayed a compulsion to show 'mastery' over nature. Often represented here is the better control of women by men. Whereas the first woman, Eve, succumbed to temptation in the Biblical garden, the medieval cloister garden (the *'hortus conclusus'*), is the enclosed garden of Virgin Mary, the woman closest to the saving of humanity from its exclusion from paradise. In many representations Mary's closed garden was to emphasize that she could become pregnant without the involvement of any beasts or beastliness: it symbolizes fertility without penetration as a means to redemption.

Plumwood (1993:161) discusses the difficulties that the concept of wilderness proffers to two distinct approaches to nature. 'Accounts which base their analysis entirely on affirming human continuity with nature cannot recognize what seems to be the major distinguishing and value making characteristic of wilderness, its independence of the human'. However, this often leaves nature at the other end of spectrum as entirely alien and separate from humanity. As women have long been associated with nature (as opposed to the 'masculine' realms of culture, science or reason) this leaves the difficulty of excluding or controlling women. In *Mansfield Park*, Austen uses the desire of Miss Bertram to leave the part of the garden nearest to the house and enter the 'wilderness' (although this was an artificially created 'disorder') to symbolize her willingness to overstep accepted social and sexual mores: an implicit judgement in Austen's moral universe.

A more modern and sinister effort here is that of Nazi Germany, whose enthusiasm for eugenics targeted at the sterilization of woman is so aptly described by Bauman (1991:26–39) as part of 'the gardening state'. Bauman, of course, recognizes that eugenics was popular in many other places and he quotes H.G. Wells as summarising this metaphorical nightmare of organized effort against those who bred prolifically. For Wells, 'what makes all graciousness and beauty possible is the scheme and the persistent intention, the watching and the waiting, the digging and the burning, the weeder clips and the hoe' (Bauman, 1991:34). Uncontrolled fertility, with all its suggestions of the wilderness, becomes associated with women, but also with the proliferation of other undesirable elements in the garden state. Thus the control of women's fertility is also closely connected with the control of race: the garden is to be kept pure and not hybrid. Whilst it was men and women of all kinds who were to be weeded out, sterilization was usually targeted at 'the uncultivated foulness' of working class women.

For other classes, the better control of woman often became associated with employment and education in the enclosed, impenetrable garden. Against the massification of society represented by the toiling poor within the teeming unsewered city streets, the country garden came to represent for the bourgeoisie the fragrant and not the foul (Corbin, 1996). Control of the 'calls of nature' and their stench within the city streets was and is seen as part of the bodily disciplining of fellow human beings. Whilst the wealthy and the powerful could retreat from the hot summer days within the metropolis to their 'perfumed' gardens, these were walled enclosures in which nature was seen as female.

However, gardens are also phallocentric places of gentlemanly pleasure. It was Richard Burton of Victorian Britain who came back to a wide-eyed audience with fantastic tales of the pleasure gardens of the Sultanate harems. Interest was high in the *Tales of the Arabian Nights* where the garden plays such a major part in Scheherazade's tales. Although Victorian women might have been idealized as domesticated in their own cloistered garden paradises, Victorian men consumed the exotic and erotic gardens of the East. The link between the garden and male sexuality is, however, an old one. In ancient Greek mythology the only God with definite responsibility for the garden was Priapus who was portrayed as 'ugly, small in stature but with large genitals and carrying a sickle or pruning knife' (Thacker, 1979:12). At the same time, he symbolizes fertility, sexuality and the protection of the garden – indeed its control through the very threat of male potency and sexuality (ibid.). From the ancient Greeks onwards, gardens have been places of nature in all its fecundity, diversity, pleasure and sexuality. Even devices such as the mazes we have seen as symbolizing Louis XIV's absolute omniscience and omnipotence, have had somewhat different connections with male potency. Gardens have often guaranteed privacy of a less contemplative kind for 'mazes were bewildering outdoor theatres of choice and chance where tall hedges shielded lovers from view as they indulged in amorous pursuit' (van Zuylen, 1994:54).

If Priapus, by right, rules the garden, there are some dystopias that present a corresponding picture of the *impotence* of men within the garden. In this there are echoes both of fear of the impossibility of nature being controlled by humans but also of the fear of men of (women's and nature's) fertility. In *The Day of the Triffids*, where a discussion of male sexual 'privileges' in the post-Apocalyptic world certainly figures, we are presented with the end of civilization as being in the form of implanting in our gardens the very source of the end of humanity – the triffid. After the blinding of the vast majority of human beings, gardens become killing grounds where any human venturing into them is likely to be summarily despatched by deadly sting (Wyndham, 1999:160). Thus what we had thought as safe, protected and enclosed becomes within this novel the source of all woes. It almost leads to the end of humanity itself. Gardens are to be avoided at all costs. They have become, or returned to, the wilderness (Langford, 1999:xi–xii) in which (male) human beings are no longer in control.

Conclusions

This chapter has focused upon the spaces of utopia. However the utopian space is envisaged and however organization is produced within and around it, we suggest that 'utopia' is a relational concept. More often than not, utopia is constructed from the play of dyads involving four spatial zones: city, garden, countryside and wilderness. The particular pairings we chose to look at were garden – city, garden – countryside, and garden – wilderness, and whilst this threesome cannot exhaust the issue of utopian emplacement, we do suggest that it uncovers important themes for Organization Studies. To begin this analysis, we attempted to use the notion of 'securing and obscuring' that is partly based upon Burawoy (1985) who uses the term with regard to the relations of production. In his usage there is a clear idea that under capitalism (and unlike feudalism), there is a deliberate obscuring of those relations of production, carried out by capitalists, the state and the managerial agents of capitalism. When we talk of the 'obscuring of the production of organization' we mean this deliberate human activity too, especially with regard to forms of deception. In the practical attempt to create utopian spaces, many forms of 'trickery' may be employed to convince others that this is a 'better place'. We have shown that the garden uses many forms of deception, from *trompes d'oeil* to espaliers to the ha-ha, with the deliberate attempt being made to fool the eye and conceal power. But there are other attempts in re-organizing space to influence the human sensorium beyond sight. Today's prize-winning buildings, for example, pump 'white noise' into the administrative spaces, to suppress high and low notes so that decibel levels are reduced and workforce concentration might be maintained through this fooling of the ear (Dale and Burrell, 2001).

But also we wish to take the notion of 'obscuring' further than Burawoy does, in that we would argue that to be human is to suffer the deception that organization is formally fixed and ordered and constrained. We prefer the notion that organization is a vortex in which very little is secure. And we find when these notions of the untamed and vortices come together that we come close to some concepts of *dystopia*.

In this chapter we have argued that utopias are inextricably intertwined with multiple ways of 'producing organization'. It must follow then, perhaps contentiously, that we see the notion of dystopia as also concerned with organization. This may be in its horror of the lack of organization which we might call 'dis-organization', or may be to do with the dysfunctions of over-organization (see Grey and Garsten, this volume). Thus dystopias may focus, we might suggest, on hypo- or hyper-organization. The first root to dystopia might see the non-human wilderness as its ultimate repository. Here we might think of Wyndham as an example. Nature flowers, extends its tendrils, and protrudes into the world of order and harmony in ways that are not desired. The espalier breaks free from its confinement, the *trompe d'oeil* itself becomes masked and human-made organization ceases to be produced – what we might call hypo-organization. Thus, London either becomes a swamp (Jefferies, 1885) or, more famously:

> The gardens of the Parks and Squares were wildernesses creeping out across the bordering streets. Growing things seemed, indeed, to press out everywhere, rooting in the crevices between the paving stones, springing from cracks in the concrete, finding lodgements even in the seats of abandoned cars. On all sides they were encroaching to repossess themselves of the arid spaces that man had created (Wyndham, 1999:xii).

The second root to dystopia, very distinctive from the first, relies on an overly socialized conception of the human in hot pursuit of a 'madness of order' – an order without reason. And the madness of order can be seen as bringing a form of *human* wilderness: unpredictability, paranoia, alexithymia, fear. The imagined paranoia concerning regularity and regulation is what makes this distinctly dystopian. One might think of Kafka or Orwell or even Huxley as occupying this ground. It may be that this comes from a terror of profusion, confusion, intrusion and diffusion. Dystopias in some formulations may be about establishing over-regulated order within inappropriate boundaries: what we have called here 'hyper-organization'.

However, we are not arguing that utopia falls into some middle ground of ideal organization between hypo- and hyper-organization. Contemporary informed debates on idealized gardens suggest that the wilderness is often recognized as constantly within the garden. The search for complete order is usually (but not always) seen as totally inappropriate by those tending a garden. But this does not mean that the ideal garden is seen as a happy balance between neither under- nor over-organized horticultural arrangements. The garden thus conceived, is not seen as likely to contain 'organization' rather than either hypo-organization or hyper-organization. What we have played on in this chapter is the need to understand the tensions of obscuring and securing organization: the play of ambiguities. Utopian gardens are not perfectly organized. Rather, they contain the tensions between the disorganization of the hypo-organized and the dysfunctions of the hyper-organized and seek to live with them both. In utopiary, clearly a variant of hyper-organization, humans obscure the fact that no ordered security exists. So, no arboreal, utopiarian reading of utopias is ever likely to be enough. The hypo-organization of the wilderness has always to be included – in some way or another.

In contemporary Tasmania, the World Heritage area of the South West Wilderness contains a rhizome of 'Huon Pine' which has been recently uncovered. Located in Mount Reed National park it is estimated to be over 10,000 years old. Huon pine is generally thought to be a tree which produces a light coloured wood that has tremendous water absorbing properties. So this 'stand', which covers acres in area, represents to the untrained human eye little more than an arboreal group of competing pines. Yet it is one single, vegetating plant. In some senses then whilst the Tasmanian 'Huon pine' rhizome represents the oldest living thing on the planet it has hidden its single organizing longevity enough to survive the scientists' urge towards collection, for its under- and above-ground structures are very different. It is a rhizome masquerading as aborescent. It is as reflective of the arboreal as is the 'tree of knowledge' to those very few human eyes that have passed it by, yet below it struggles with its rhizomatic nature. It is not a DeluzeGuattarian dualism. It is both rhizome and arboreal simultaneously. And so too, by being rhizomatic and arboreal, is the concept of utopia.

Thus in their very ambiguity and multiple nature, utopian spaces offer us valuable security through which to produce organization differently. The constructive possibilities of the concept of utopia are both to undermine the status quo *and* to reinforce the notion that there is something that humans can do both to understand and to change their world in ways which are not fully determined.

Endnote

Thanks to Martin Parker for his astute and witty editing. We look forward to his semi-autobiographical paper on the organization of caravanning by the sea.

Bibliography

Adams, W. (1991) *Nature Perfected* NY: Abbeville Press Inc.
Austen, J. (1983) *Mansfield Park* London: Fontana.
Bauman, Z. (1991) *Modernity and Ambivalence* Cambridge: Polity.
Bhatti, M. and Church, A. (2001) 'Cultivating Nature: Homes and Gardens in Late Modernity', *Sociology*, 35, 2, 365–383.
Briggs, J. (1983) *This Stage-Play World* Oxford: Oxford University Press.
Brown, J. (1999) *The Pursuit of Paradise* London: Harper Collins.
Bryman, A. (1995) *Disney and His Worlds* London: Routledge.
Burawoy, M. (1985) *The Politics of Production* London: Verso.
Claeys, E. (ed.) (1997) *Modern British Utopias: 1700–1850* London: Pickering and Chatto.
Clevely, A. (1988) *Topiary* London: Collins.
Cooper, R. and Burrell, G. (1988) 'Modernism, Postmodernism and Organizational Analysis: An Introduction', *Organization Studies*, 9, 1, 91–112.
Corbin, A. (1996) *The Foul and the Fragrant* Basingstoke: Papermac.

Curl, J. (1999) *Oxford Dictionary of Architecture* Oxford: Oxford University Press.

Davis, J. (1993) 'Formal Utopia/Informal Millennium' in Kumar and Bann, 17–32.

de Thame, R. (2001) 'Interview' *Radio Times*, July.

Euripides (1973) *The Bacchae and Other Plays* ed. & trans. Philip Vellacott, Harmondsworth: Penguin.

Findlay, J. (1992) *Magic Lands* Berkeley, Calif.: University of California Press.

Fleming, J., Honour, H. and Pevsner, N. (1999) *Penguin Dictionary of Architecture and Landscape Architecture* Harmondsworth: Penguin.

Foucault, M. (1977) *Discipline and Punish* Harmondsworth: Penguin.

Foucault, M. (1974) *The Order of Things* London: Routledge.

Fox, A. (1985) *History and Heritage* London: Allen and Unwin.

Gavin, D. (2001) 'Take Two Garden Designers', *Gardeners' World*, March, London: BBC Publications, 96–7.

Hamilton, G. (1997) *Paradise Gardens* London: BBC Publications.

Hamilton, G. (1995) *Cottage Gardens* London: BBC Publications.

Harvey, D. (2000) *Spaces of Hope* Edinburgh: Edinburgh University Press.

Hill, C. (1969) *Reformation to Industrial Revolution: Volume 2 Penguin Economic History of Britain* Harmondsworth: Penguin.

Hollis III, D. (1998) *The ABC-Clio World History Companion to Utopian Movements*, Santa Barbara: ABC-Clio.

Jefferies, R. (1885) *After London, or Wild England.* London: Cassell.

Kumar, K. and Bann, S. (eds) (1993) *Utopias and the Millennium* London: Reaktion.

Kumar, K. (1987) *Utopia and Anti-Utopia in Modern Times* Oxford: Basil Blackwell.

Lampugnani, V. (1986) *Encyclopaedia of Twentieth Century Architecture* London: Thames and Hudson.

Langford, B. (2000) 'Introduction' to Wyndham J, vii–xvii.

Lefebvre, H. (1991) *The Production of Space* Oxford: Blackwell.

Lyotard, J.-F. (1977) *Libidinal Economy* London: Athlone.

Marin, L. (1984) *Utopics: Spatial Play* London.

Massey, D. (1984) *Spatial Divisions of Labour* Basingstoke: Macmillan.

More, T. (1969) *Utopia* Harmondsworth: Penguin.

Morris, W. (1993) *News from Nowhere* Harmondsworth: Penguin.

Mosely, L. (1986) *The Real Walt Disney* London: Grafton.

Mumford, L. (1970) *The Culture of Cities* London: Secker and Warburg.

Mumford, L. (1922) *The Story of Utopias* NY: Boni and Liveright.

Mumford, L. (1961) *The City in History* London: Secker and Warburg.

Norburg-Schulz, C. (1980) *Genius Loci: Towards a Phenomenology of Architecture* London: Academy Editions.

Plumwood, V. (1993) *Feminism and the Mastery of Nature* London: Routledge.

Schama, S. (1995) *Landscape and Memory* London: Fontana.

Schama, S. (2001) 'The History of Britain Part 2', BBC TV programme, first shown June 2001.

Sennett, R. (1994) *Flesh and Stone* London: Faber and Faber.

Shields, C. (1997) *Larry's Party* London: Fourth Estate.

Strong, R. (2000) *The Spirit of Britain* London: Pimlico.

Thacker, C. (1979) *The History of Gardens* London: Croom Helm.

Thomas, K. (ed.) (1999) *The Oxford Book of Work* Oxford: Oxford University Press.

Thompson, E.P. (1968) *The Making of the English Working Classes* Harmondsworth: Penguin.

Turner, B. (1994) 'Introduction' to Buci-Glucksmann C *Baroque Reason* London: Sage, 1–36.

Urry, J. (1995) *Consuming Spaces* London: Routledge.

Van Zuylen, G. (1995) *The Garden: Visions of Paradise* London: Thames and Hudson.

Vierhaus, R. (1988) *Germany in the Age of Absolutism* Cambridge: Cambridge University Press.

Wyndham, J. (2000) *The Day of the Triffids* Harmondsworth: Penguin.

The consumption of time and space: utopias and the English romantic garden

Rolland Munro

He who binds to himself a joy
Doth the winged life destroy:
But he who kisses the joy as it flies
Lives in eternity's sunrise.

(William Blake, Eternity)

Introduction

Utopia has a far-off feel. As a futuristic 'fixing' of politics, it hardly offers itself as a subject to submit for the UK Research Assessment Exercise, far less seems a project to justify to friends and neighbours. Answering an everyday enquiry with 'Yes, I'm finishing my chapter on Utopia', could get me a funny look, if not a slither down several places in the invisible Shropshire league tables of common-sense and practical worth.

Yet if we are not all working towards Utopia, what exactly *are* we working for? This is, after all, a 'culture of enhancement' (Strathern, 1995; Munro, 2000a), an age of vision and mission – well at least of statements of vision and mission – wherein our aims and goals are expected to be stated clearly and unambiguously. Surely, in line with standard definitions of utopia, the nub of the challenge is to articulate a 'clear set of values' that will help build the 'ideal community' (Burden, 1993)?

I'm unsure I'm up to this challenge. First, drawn to deferral more than decision, I eschew ideals of solidarity that anaesthetize community – 'purified of all that may convey a feeling of difference, let alone conflict, in who "we" are' (Sennett, 1996:36). Second, a self-relegated provincial, league tables away from circulation in the cool culture of city hot chat, I lack the requisite 'tele-vision' for utopian engineering, the far sight that sees ahead and knows how to generate those 'we are all alike' feelings. Third, unable to flee 'with terror' from the renewed demand for clarity (Lyotard, 1984), I find myself siding more with Strathern (1995) over the dangers of clarity becoming a goal.

Yet clarity and transparency seem to be where we are aimed. As a student of what I have begun to call, ironically, the 'sociology of relegation' (Munro, 2002), I'm fairly sure emancipatory agendas take a nose dive within league tables for institutions. The effect of all the current stress on accountability and audit seems precisely to install an aesthetics that focuses each of us on delivery – *now!* We can thus stop us jawing about ends (or whinging about a lack of the means to reach those ends). And of course, this is the point of empowerment and self-regulation, that no-one – even those with his and her televisions in the bedroom and the big flat one in the sitting room – is up to the challenge of deciding the future for others. We are (or should be) all too busy getting on with delivering (and consuming) the present.

In order to reflect on what this 'politics of the present' denies, I reflect not on the future, but on what is 'all about me' – in Hugo Letiche's (2000) fine phrase. In Hugo's case it is The Nude, paintings by Maria that hang everywhere on the walls of their home in The Hague. For Joanna and myself it is The Garden. Not the DIY plot of DoItAll, the frill to Everyman's castle, but the once-upon-a-time 'utopia' of the English Garden. So let me begin with the garden all about me in Shropshire. This will help explain why I think the 'natural' garden can help understand shifts in space and time and, hence, something of the current 'disorganisation' in contemporary institutional life.

Part I

The Classical and the Romantic

Hawkstone Park in Shropshire is now formally recognized as a 'Masterpiece of the School of Naturalistic Landscape'. The landscape has been recently designated Grade 1 in the Register of Historic Gardens and Parks, a distinction shared with Blenheim Palace, near Oxford, home to the Dukes of Marlborough. Strictly, both landscapes are *natural* (cf Keen, 1997:75). Otherwise, the contrast could not be more vivid.

Blenheim, famously the birthplace of Churchill, is a 'Classical' 18th century English parkland, variously recognized as 'one of Henry Wise's greatest achievements' (Hadfield, 1979:155) and the 'masterfiece' of Lancelot 'Capability' Brown (Hyams, 1971:39). Cedars of Lebanon straddle the sky, their spreading branches defining misty horizontals and elongated, curving paths meander towards a vast, elegantly bowed bridge, sitting astride the large peaceful lake. The overwhelming atmosphere is one of grace and calm, a gentility into which nature has been tamed and bent to order. The world appears to be 'standing in reserve', just waiting for its lords and masters to call upon it.

At Hawkstone, relations are reversed; the rock erupts from the earth, the lush vegetation is out of control and paths are invisible and hazardous. Although its origins are much earlier, the parkland is the epitome of the late 18th century 'Romantic' landscape. For example, in 1774, Dr Johnson commented on Hawkstone:

> ... it excells Dovedale, by the extent of its prospects, the awfulness of its shades, the horrors of its precipices, the verdure of its hollows and the loftiness of its rocks. The Ideas which it forces upon the mind, are the sublime, the dreadful, and the

vast. Above is inaccessible altitude, below, is horrible profundity.' (Johnson, 1995 [1774]:35).

At Hawkstone, the sense is of time passing, of our being close to the sublime – a cosmos that is still unfolding. Everywhere, nature seems in riot. Each view is partial and provisional, what is available to be seen is fleeting, becoming a matter of chance.

The Romantic glories in darkly mysterious grottoes and thinly wooded precipices of rock, with little more than a Gothic 'ruin', a Swiss Cottage, or a hidden Hermit hut to offer refuge. The Classical, in contrast, is marked by vast bland spaces anchoring its massive palatial building into the centre of miles of sedate green lawn. Where Hawkstone is 'temporal' in its mood, Vanbrugh's design for Blenheim, even with its later additions, is spatial in its architectural form – commanding huge horizons in a manner designed to evoke the spirit of Empire.

The formal and the natural

Gardens as an embodiment of the organization of time and space is a comparison that might be thought to embellish Goulder's (1973:323–66) depiction of the Classical and the Romantic as two 'deep structures in social science':

> Representing the perspective of order, Classicism sees the world in terms of clear-cut boundaries and neat categories of thought which privilege the unities of time and space, the transparency of meaning and the fixity of form. In contrast, Romanticism views reality as an 'intrinsic vagueness' in which objects and events blend into one another and thus lose their specific identities. (Cooper, 1986:300)

Gouldner's analysis acts like a dichotomy: against the universal and permanent, what he calls 'the contingent, the changing and local' are privileged; against the average, the special case is raised up; and the disorderly is prized over the orderly.

The contrast is striking and familiar. A caricature of the Romantic garden, prizing disorder and privileging the 'contingent, changing and local', is Stoppard's play *Arcadia*, in which 'Culpability' Noakes, the Emperor of Irregularity, is brought to 'improve' the 'green and gentle' slopes of Sidley Park. As Lady Croome complains:

> Where there is the familiar pastoral refinement of an Englishman's garden, here is an eruption of gloomy forest and towering crag, of ruins where there was never a house, of water dashing against rocks where there was neither spring nor a stone . . . (Stoppard, 1993)

In the Romantic, the special case is 'lifted up', the stricken oak left to stand alone as the embodiment of the power of lightning; object and event combining to re-mind us of contingency and hazard, highlighting the disorder integral to any appearance of order. Yet, in seeming to conflate the Classical with the *formal*, Gouldner's analysis is surely flawed. As a comparison, the contrast appears caught within Gouldner's (1959) earlier division between 'rational' and 'natural', if not also degenerating into Cooper's (1986) own comparison between formal and informal. As Cooper (300) remarks, Gouldner saw 'the "rational" model of organizations as an expression of Classic control and the modified "natural" model as a form of Romantic freedom'.

With regard to the English garden, however, neither the Classical, nor the Romantic, with their overlapping interests, should be confused with the formal. Differences between Classical and Romantic form a schism *within* the school of natural landscape. As forms of 'naturalistic' landscape, the Classical English garden and its Romantic counterpart, were both in revolt from the formal. The stilted emphasis of the formal garden was ridiculed in the verse of Alexander Pope:

> ... each Alley has a brother
> And half the plat form just reflects the other.
> (Epistle IV, Moral Essays, 1716)

Earlier, Temple (1685), drawing on letters from Jesuits in China, had suggested the Chinese scorned 'planting by rule and rote as favoured by the West, regarding this as fit only for children' (King, 1979:179).

The genealogy of any area of organization is thus important and the Romantic and the Classical were movements away from all that had become artificial and brittle about the formal garden. As Clifford (1966:161) suggests:

> The real enemy of both was uniformity, sameness that leads to boredom, which is a fault endemic in Utopias.

The claustrophobia of the formal garden, with its exquisite Euclidean topiary and symmetrical layout, is beautifully captured in films like *The Draughtsman's Contract* and *Last Year at Marienbad*. In contrast to Robbe-Grillet's play on the formality of repeating lines, and even scenes, over and over, to mock cinematic formulas, Greenaway's meticulously formal film is a dark comedy about power games between classes and is set in 1694, a time when wigs and topiary were never higher.

The emic and the phagic

The aims of the formal garden go back to the Arabian idea of paradise as an 'enclosed space'. The gardening manual of the day to be found in the libraries of early country houses was French, D'Argenville's *The Theory and Practice of Gardening* and focused on how formality could enhance the enclosed space. Thinking all its design precepts to be great and noble, this recommended parterres, groves and palisades to screen views of undesirable woods and mountains (D'Argenville, 1712).

The conception of the formal garden was intensely 'inward', creating a space in which the 'outside' was banished, particularly through the use of walls and high hedges. Here Bauman (2001:24), in a recent essay on uses and disuses of urban space, offers a different starting point to Gouldner's analysis. He draws on Levi-Strauss's analysis of two strategies for coping with the otherness of others, the anthropoemic and the anthropophagic. A first strategy, which Bauman calls 'emic', consists of:

> ... 'vomiting', spitting out the others seen as incurably strange and alien: barring physical contact, dialogue, social intercourse and all varieties of *commercium, commensality* or *connubium*.

I like the sound of this connubium! But it is not to be. The aim is either annihilation, or exile of the other. As Bauman adds, if the extreme variants of the emic strategy are now, as always, incarceration, deportation and murder, the upgraded and modern equivalents are spatial separation and urban ghettos. But of course separation was not always so physically distinct as one finds with modern zones or residential districts. One can easily recall grimy streets of the early city states, like Florence, where a door in the wall leads sometimes into a fine house, or even a palace. In line with the early meaning of the term paradise, the emphasis is on the inner perfection of the courtyard or the hallowed walks of a large enclosed garden, such as was made vivid in De Sica's 1971 film, *The Garden of the Finzi-Continis*.

The aim of the phagic (what Bauman calls the fagic) is also annihilation, but this time of *otherness*. So, rather than try to exile the other, this second strategy aims at assimilation, or suspension, of otherness and consists in:

> ... 'ingesting', 'devouring' foreign bodies and spirits so that they may be made, through metabolism, identical with, and no more distinguishable, from the 'ingesting' body. (Bauman, 2001:24)

An equally wide range of forms is available, from cannibalism to enforced assimilation. As Palli (2001) has pointed out, the resources of ethnography are prominent here, with a wide range of techniques and resources for incorporation of otherness at its disposal. In terms of the phagic, Bauman (2001:24) has in mind not only 'cultural crusades' and 'wars of attrition declared on local customs'. These encompass the effects of a benign colonization as well as US driven globalization. Indeed, the triumph of the English garden, and its overcoming of the formality of the French influence, Walpole (1995 [1770]:8) saw as 'the result of all the happy combinations of an Empire of Freemen, an Empire formed by Trade, not by a military and conquering spirit'.

Enhancing the threshold

The delights of enclosure were no doubt proving increasingly suspect in the face of the growing 'enlightenment' and Kent's contribution to the development of gardens was, in Walpole's famous phrase, to 'leap the fence'. In opening the garden up to its exterior – as if to 'ingest' the otherness of Nature – the English improvers, to all appearances, seem to have adopted a phagic strategy. But not everything is as it seems.

In doing away with the fence, what Kent actually created was the *illusion* of a much greater, harmonious space. While John Evelyn notes in his 1679 diary the terrace vista at Cliveden extending 'to the utmost verge of the horizon', the 'prospects' of the French vista gardens (cf Clifford, 1966:163) were not the same as giving a full sense of the garden being *in* nature, an effect gained by the innovation of 'borrowing' the landscape. I use this term borrowing, rather than incorporating, advisedly; Kent's actual achievement was to take the idea of a Concealment of Bounds to an 'excessive' scale. The technology which serves to do away with the fence and the balustrade is the ha-ha, a kind of walled ditch that literally 'drops' out of sight and so preserves the seamless 'join' of garden with the parkland beyond.

> But the capital stroke, the leading step to all that has followed, was [I believe the first thought was Bridgman's] the destruction of walls for boundaries, and the invention of fossès – an attempt so astonishing, that the common people called them Ha!Ha's! to express their surprize at finding a sudden and unperceived check to their walk. (Walpole, 1995 [1770]:42)

As it happens, the ha-ha was likely invented before Bridgeman, a 'lined ditch' at the end of walks to gain 'through views' being referred to in D'Argenville (1712) as the 'Ah Ah'.

In adapting this humble, literally low-level, technology to a Concealment of Bounds, Kent managed a radical transformation in its use. As Hyams (1964) comments, there was at the time:

> . . . enough influence and ultimately enough practical effect to carry the English garden further towards that natural composition of an artificially assembled plants in an artificial framework which was 'after' nature, towards the making, in short, of a paradise.

What Kent had found was a device which brought nature within the threshold. It enabled him to appear to adopt a phagic strategy of letting the outside in, and ingesting its otherness, without quite abandoning the emic strategy of the formal garden of repulsing certain aspects of the outside.

Kent's 'excess' in the Concealment of Bounds facilitated landscaping on a grand scale. Invisible from within, the ha ha allowed large pastoral areas containing cropping animals, deer, cattle and sheep, to make significant incursions into the garden of the park while keeping the animals themselves at bay. The effect is bucolic; one of God's creatures seeming to know their place in the order of things – so near and yet so far. As is now discussed, the key difference between the Classical and the Romantic can be defined in terms of how they approach the 'outside' and the naturalistic problem of how to 'let' this outside in.

Part II

Is there no change of death in paradise?
Does ripe fruit never fall? Or do the boughs

Hang always heavy in that perfect sky,
Unchanging, yet so like our perishing earth,

(Wallace Stevens, *Sunday Morning*)

Arguing out the formal

If gardening today is little associated with intellectual pursuits, or even concerned with taste, things were very different in the 18th century. Charles Bridgeman, for example, who succeeded Henry Wise as Royal Gardener in 1728, was described by Pope as 'another man of the virtuoso class as well as I, and in my notions of the higher kind of class, since Gardening is more antique and nearer God's own work than poetry' (quoted by Keen, 1997:64).

A collapse in the status of garden design from this early elevation might be related, among other matters, to a decline in the theological. From the beginning, the garden had been seen as God's work. As such, the early garden – to become a garden – had to 'exceed' the mundane concerns of the culture and cultivation of plants. Specifically, given the influence of Euclid (through Aristotle) on scholastics like Augustine, the design of the formal garden can be understood as 'revealing' God's plan and I hazard this explanation for much of the exacting grip of geometry on formal gardens.

With this in mind, the place of the intellectual at the heart of the evolution of the garden is less surprising. With its emphasis on symmetry and design, the formal garden had offered itself not only as a place for pleasure, but as a place for the contemplation of God's beneficence. Already learned and literary articles by Shaftsbury (1711) and Addison (1712) had begun to be published on differences between Nature and Art. For example, Lord Shaftsbury philosophized about 'Glorious Nature, supremely Fair and sovereignly Good' (quoted by Keen, 1997:67) and questioned the peace of mind a French grandee could derive from having a grand garden in the French style. Perversely as it might seem today, the need for argument and reason would have been particularly strong within the 'natural' movement. Only the best intellects of the day might hope to challenge something as marvellous as geometry and Charles Bridgeman's friends included Sir John Vanbrugh and William Kent, the former anticipating many tropes of the Romantics and the latter being the person most associated with the evolution of the 'Classical' garden.

Even so, it might also be supposed that the grip of geometry on gardens could be successfully challenged only at the point when reason was itself being usurped from the throne of the divine to become – as in the Enlightenment – the disposition of man. If so, we need to go beyond the separation of nature and art and appreciate a deeper rupture evolving here between reason, as man's territory, on the one hand and nature, as God's, on the other. Once reason had become the essential property of the human, God's likeness need no longer lie within geometry. A new 'excess' had to be found and it is this 'excess' which is striven for and is at the heart of the turn to the 'natural' style.

The eruption of Euclidean space

Thinking of the creation of the early city states, Lefebvre (1991:256) suggests the emerging dominance of a Euclidean sense of order abolished 'absolute space'. The 'broken lines and verticals' of the urban landscape of the Middle Ages – particularised in the rise of the great cathedrals – had 'leapt forth from the earth bristling with sculptures'. According to Lefebvre, this emerging city-space – 'developed from the Renaissance onwards on the basis of the Greek tradition (Euclid, logic)' – proclaimed its new landscape to be:

> a benevolent and luminous utopia where knowledge would be independent, and instead of serving an oppressive power would contribute to the strengthening of an authority grounded in reason. (256)

Lefebvre's emphasis is on a totalization of the *production* of Euclidean space. He sees Classical perspective and geometry as having been 'bodied forth in Western art and philosophy, as in the form of the city and the town' (25).

In creating this civil space of 'public man', it is unsurprising that the formal garden should also reflect the 'broken lines and verticals' of the urban landscape and create 'avenues' of pleached pears and apple trees as well as the 'axis' of gravel walks admired by Pepys. Or, indeed, that alongside the compulsory marble or lead statues, the formal garden should also be 'bristling with sculptures', in the form of a topiary of giant yews and regimented box hedges, a few surviving to this day at Powys Castle in Wales where the hanging terraces escaped the 18th century passion for landscaping.

Where Lefebvre (1991) misleads is in his repetition of the idea that this totalization of Euclidean space lasted till the beginning of the 20th century:

> The fact is that around 1910 a certain space was shattered. It was the space of common sense, of knowledge (savoir), of social practice, of political power, a space enshrined in everyday discourse, just as in abstract thought, as the environment and channel for communications. (Lefebvre, 1991:25)

The far-reaching consequence of this break with 'order' is something he sees as still having its repercussions around the world and singles out education establishments, in ever increasing isolation, as still clinging to their Euclidean heritage.

As the history of gardens testifies, a partial shattering of this space occurred almost two centuries earlier in the emergence of the English garden. As is now discussed, if a Euclidean colonization of space was already in retreat when Kent 'leapt the fence', its 'totalization' was finally broken when Repton and others began to step out of the picture frame. Utopian ideas, at least in its recreation of Arcadia and embrace of the sublime, had already moved outside the more European, and Euclidean, production of space.

The principles of the natural

A main source of inspiration for Bataille's principle of 'improductive expenditure' – an expenditure unrestricted by notions of efficiency – was his fascination with the sun and, in particular, with the appearance of sun spots. Different civilizations, especially Classical Greece and Rome, have long dwelt on relations between the sun and paradise. In wishing to rethink its variety of responses, providing shade as well as making suntraps, the English garden might well look back to these civilizations to understand how to organize the garden as a space 'in-between' the sun and the soil.

As Stevens reflects, in a poem on Western images of paradise, 'Sunday Morning', 'we live in an old chaos of the sun'. In the 17th century, the resurgence of painting in Italy seemed to offer itself as a kind of shrine to this, if forgotten, 'old dependency'. The fashionable dichotomy betwen Art and Nature, however, was not the main preoccupation of Kent, a painter who had lived in Italy where he studied the idealized landscapes of Poussin and Claude. Whereas these painters had used reason, not to 'copy' nature, but to help create idealized visions, Kent had the more ambitious plan for Nature to 'copy' painting, by producing Arcadia in the garden. Indeed, much of Kent's work anticipates a 'world conceived and grasped as picture' (Heidegger, 1977:129).

In making, as it were, nature copy art, Kent's ruling principle was that 'nature abhors a straight line' (Walpole, 1995 [1780]:49). However, Walpole records Kent as much influenced by Pope, thinking the poet's modest garden at Twickenham had inspired Rousham, 'the most engaging of all Kent's works'. For this reason it is worth enumerating Pope's own 'rules' for garden making. In addition to the Concealment of Bounds, discussed earlier, a matter in which Capability Brown was to later excel, Pope's precepts included, primarily, Contrast. Kent was a master in his use of different shades of green, having studied both perspective and chiaroscuro, and he 'applied the techniques of painting to bring light depth and shade to gardens that lacked variety, even though they relied on colours from flowers' (Keen, 1997:70).

Another of Pope's rules covered the Management of Surprises. As Keen suggests, the 'enchantment of a space, the poetry in a garden . . . was effortlessly stage-managed by Kent'. For example, his *trompe l'oeil* cascades at Rousham was dramatically different from anything else seen in England at that time (Keen, 1997:71). Against the 'forced elevation of cataracts', dramatically revived by Joseph Paxton at Chatsworth, Walpole (1995 [1780]:45) also saw Kent as having changed the nature of water: 'The gentle stream was taught to serpentine seemingly at its pleasure'. So too he seemed to change the nature of light: 'shades descending from the heights leaned towards its progress, and framed the distant point of light under which it was lost, as it turned side to either hand of the blue horizon' (45).

Independently of Kent, others were also at work in making nature copy art, this time 'literary' art. Thirty years before the banker Henry Hoare began his garden at Stourhead in Wiltshire, Addison had suggested there were three writers who excelled at opening a man's thoughts and enlarging his imagination. Of Homer, Virgil and Ovid, he wrote, 'the first strikes the imagination wonderfully with what is Great, the second with what is Beautiful and the last with what is Strange.' Hoare depicts these authors as follows:

> Reading the *Iliad* is like travelling through a Country uninhabited, where the Fancy is entertained with a thousand Savage Prospects of vast Desarts, wide uncultivated Marshes, huge Forests, mis-shapen Rocks and Precipices. On the contrary, the *Aeneid* is like a well ordered Garden, where it is impossible to find out any Part unadorned, or to cast our eyes upon a single Spot, that does not produce some beautiful Plant or Flower. But when we are in *Metamorphosis*, we are walking on enchanted ground, and see nothing but scenes of Magick lying round us'. (quoted by Keen, 1997:79).

In creating his own 'enchanted ground', including an idyllic 'circuit' of temples around a lake, Hoare, like Claude, favoured the 'well-ordered' garden of Virgil on a grand scale. But Homer, in offering visions of the sublime, was already knocking at the garden door.

Gathering the landscape

Both Classical and Romantic movements 'borrow' landscape to achieve their effects. Each *admits* the outside. The Classical perspective, as already mentioned, is one in which there is no apparent exterior to the Garden. Yet the Romantic would seem to want to go further and *install* the outside, to have it rush in – so to speak – unimpeded and untrammelled, in the manner of our falling headlong into a torrent or into a vast drop in altitude. Whereas the Classical wants only to install it *as* horizon, by admitting it just within the 'threshold' of sight.

I draw these terms 'admit' and 'install' from 'Building, dwelling, thinking', a late essay of Heidegger's (1993) that describes the way a bridge makes the region around it into a landscape. The key word is 'gather'. For Heidegger, the bridge '*gathers* the earth as landscape around a stream'. The bridge performs a 'forceful gathering' and Miller (239) translates accordingly:

> The bridge swings over the stream 'with ease and power'. It does not just connect banks that are already there. The banks emerge as banks only as the bridge crosses the stream. The bridge designedly causes them to lie across from each other. . . . It brings stream and bank and land into each other's neighborhood.

In making the bridge both admit and install the landscape, Heidegger's point is that 'spaces receive their being from locations and not from "space" '.

In his commentary in *Topographies*, Miller (1995) disturbs Heidegger's 'equivocation' between these tropes of admitting and installing. 'Which?', he asks. In sharpening my earlier distinction between borrowing and incorporating, some engagement with the landscape here is helpful. For example, to the extent the Classical admits the outside, it seems to 'gather' this to install the exterior *as* background, in ways that give depth to a contemplation of sculptures in the foreground. The distant hillside is thus an extension of the garden; a calm reflection of the interior – arranging, deepening, enchanting – in the manner of Claude and Poussin. The view – a 'frieze' of nymphs and satyrs – celebrates what is repeated in the background: the message is the world has been tamed and it is a better place for it. The impression is one of leisure and plenty, stretching out endlessly. With time thus banished, no change is possible. Even the Bacchanalias seem unhurried, languid under the limpid horizon.

The Classical trope is to colonize and order. Heidegger's particular image of a bridge – the old bridge at Heidelberg – fits well Vanbrugh's massive bridge at Blenheim. Particularly so after Capability Brown – in his 'most dramatic design' – dammed up the rather insignificant River Glyme to create a magnificent 'sheet of water whose source and termination seem remote' (Hadfield, 1979:213). It is building – whether of a bridge, or a house, or a temple – 'that creates locations'. As Miller adds, locations 'open space and make it into an organized field with boundaries' (241). Heidegger's analysis would equally do for Classic English gardens like Stowe, as well as precursors like Stourhead, which favour temples with Doric porticoes and the Palladian bridge for its 'gatherings'.

Heidegger's image of 'gathering', however, does not fit with the Swiss Bridge at Hawkstone. There, the rustic 'assemblage' – perched precariously on the pinnacles of two mountainous upsurges of rock – *scatters* as much it gathers. The long thin tree trunk which forms the main spar emphasizes the depth of the chasm falling away and dramatizes the distance between the bulging boulders on either side of the precipices, tilting the rocks towards the sky. There is no 'dwelling' here. The effect is to bring home the frailty of any crossing and engulf us in the immanent possibility of plunging – headlong – into 'horrible profundity' below.

Scattering the space

Two contrasting effects, then, one of scattering and another of gathering. In neither case is the boundary just what it seems. For Heidegger, in Miller's (241) translation, a boundary is 'not that at which something stops but, as the Greeks recognized, the boundary is that from which something begins its presencing'. Something is 'unconcealed', even at the moment when the boundary itself is being concealed.

So what is being presenced in the Romantic garden? The sublime, surely. Or, possibly, time itself, with all its accoutrements? In its unexpected and unpredictable variation, Hawkstone is a landscape that admits the sublime and installs time. It does so in ways that call upon *us*. But for what? There is almost nowhere to stand that does not compel the visitor to move – forward – onto the next view. Indeed, whereas the Classical seeks to elide time – and 'stay' its wreckage – it would not be hard to argue that the ideal of the Romantic garden is time embodied.

This effect of scattering things apart is vital for the Romantic. One recalls Marianne Dashwood, the heroine of *Sense and Sensibility*, for whom 'a tree, to be beautiful, had to be dead – preferably blasted by lightning' (Hyams, 1964:71). Time is made present through each 'horizon' of immanence, either in the landscape bringing into view the abyss immanently at our feet, or by emphasizing our proximity to death through a depth and length of shade and shadow. As Septimus, the Classically trained Tutor at Sidley Park replies to Thomasina's view that you 'cannot stir things apart':

> ... time must needs run backward, and since it will not, we must stir our way onward mixing as we go, disorder out of disorder into disorder. (Stoppard, 1993:5)

Yet Hawkstone offers something more than a mere analogy of disorder with time. Somehow Hawkstone 'exceeds' the landscape it both admits and installs:

> Hawkstone in Salop is another estate which shakes the reality of its surroundings, a landscaped park more completely in the spirit of Grotesque Architecture than any of the more rugged landscapes of the later eighteenth century; (Jones, 1974:78)

The sublime, yes. Time, also. But – in shaking the reality of its surroundings – the landscape also exceeds and surpasses itself. As Jones (83) goes on to comment about Hawkstone, 'the gloom and earthly terror are complete'. Although the metrical scale of the landscape is not so very large, the effect everywhere is that of excess: the shade is too deep, the verdure too rich, each precipice too huge.

Part III

> The maker's rage to order words of the sea,
> Words of the fragrant portals, dimly starred,
> And of ourselves and of our origins,
> In ghostlier demarcations, keener sounds.
>   (Wallace Stevens, *The Idea of Order at Key West*)

Stepping out of the painting

In understanding the aesthetics of the evolution of the natural garden, we can turn to Humphrey Repton, a late figure in the transition from Classical to Romantic. Like Addison, who went to Italy to 'compare the natural face of the country with the landskips that the rocks have given us', Kent had looked to the *Campagna* and brought the garden towards a 'production' of the ravishing languor and mystery of Claude and Poussin's landscapes. Repton, and to some extent others like Capability Brown and William Emes ahead of him, wanted to go that one jump further: to leap outside the framing of pictures altogether and immerse the garden into the landscape itself.

Repton's 'proper distinction between Painting and Gardening' has been summarized by Hadfield (1979:70) in three precepts:

1. the gardener surveys his [or her] scenery while in motion
2. the field of vision is much greater
3. the light . . . in nature varied from hour to hour.

Each precept seems to take on a life of its own, blurring the boundaries between the Romantic and the Classical garden as it was evolving between 1710 and 1770. First, in respect of gardens becoming places to 'survey . . . while in motion', the movement from one Classical *mis-en-scene* to the next would soon seem stilted. Travelling from one 'frieze' to the next, in an effort to be re-inspired by the scenes of Poussin and Claude brought to life, might become, if relied upon, as tiresome as the earlier 'prospects' of the formal garden.

The consequences of an expansion in the field of vision are also far-reaching. In contrast to paintings, where the viewer steps into place to view the picture, there are no fixed standpoints to view a landscape. Even armed with Claude glasses – darkened mirrors for inspecting the perfect view – the essential problem remains. Is the viewer to close her or his eyes while moving between the 'staging posts' of the circuit walk? Unlike paintings, which cannot be 'seen' unless one responds to its anamorphic demand to position oneself – usually in front – an actual landscape is all too 'demanding' (cf Munro, 2000b). Unpleasant or unfortunate views will be seen, whether intended or not.

In the 'roundness' of his landscaping, Capability Brown, while trained by Kent at Stowe, already seems to have had a more sculptural eye. What begins to collapse with his enhancement of the natural, is the 'hidden' geometry on which Kent and other Classical figures, trained in perspective, had relied. Although the natural landscapers had banished geometry from the *face* of the earth in their gardens, still a Euclidean order lingered through the use of perspective in the very 'sighting' of their prospects and the actual 'framing' of the views they sought to conjure up. Indeed, Kent's elaborate use of water at Stowe and the addition of the lake at Clermont (once owned by Vanbrugh) suggests he had also anticipated Repton's second precept about the absence of the 'frame' and thus had already, if implicitly, moved away from Poussin's idea of paintings being designed for 'contemplation' rather than immediate effect.

Repton's third precept, the 'variation' of the light with the hours – to say nothing of the seasons – counters the Classical need for time to be arrested. In 'Sunday Morning' Stevens, the American poet, captures this hankering for the eternal:

> She says, 'But in contentment I still feel
> The need of some imperishable bliss.'

Yet as it attempted to ingest more and more of the natural, the Classical production of space as 'imperishable' was also being undermined.

In its preoccupation with change, the Romantic garden became increasingly concerned with how to bring death to life:

> Death is the mother of beauty; hence from her,
> Alone, shall come fulfilment of our dreams.

Unless the Other was again to be banished, the only way forward was to go on and fully assimilate the otherness of the wilderness.

Picturing the picturesque

Noting how in many ways 'gardens turned to Romanticism before poetry or politics', Keen (1997:91) comments on the 'intense personal experience' offered by the Romantic garden:

> The landscape was no longer to suggest to the observer a series of framed images of a distant country, peopled by gods and goddesses; it was to be a place where a man could walk and think, preferably alone.

The Romantic garden was to offer the solitary figure 'repose', time for reflection and fallow of the social demands for civility.

Kent's installations were 'conversation pieces' for the day, *occasions* for the educated classes to demonstrate their mastery of Latin and appreciation of a Classical education. In contrast, the shade and edifice of gardens in the mould of Salvator Rosa gave the solitary soul, the hermit, an *opportunity* to 'commune' with Nature. Yet politics and poetry were not far behind. The simplicity of country life extolled by Rousseau (1760) in his novel *La Nouvelle Heloise*, focused on the idyllic innocence of the 'primitive', those unaffected by civilization and so rejected the earlier utopian emphasis on a 'shared' cultural knowledge. Unkindly it is said Voltaire stopped halfway through to laugh, before throwing the book out of the window.

The difficulty for Romantics in enunciating principles is mocked in Stoppard's comedy *Arcadia*, where the landscape improver, 'Culpability' Noakes, states 'Irregularity is one of the chiefest principles of the picturesque style' (1993:12). The anecdote of Voltaire is salutary, in that those on the side of Reason saw order itself being thrown out – in the destruction of the 'green and gentle' slopes of the garden outside their very windows.

> Here, look – Capability Brown doing Claude, who was doing Virgil. Arcadia! And here, superimposed by Richard Noakes, untamed nature in the style of Salvator Rosa. It's the Gothic novel expressed in landscape. Everything but vampires. (Stoppard, 1993:25)

This turn to the Gothic suggests Rousseau's image of utopia, while inverting ideas of order sufficiently to persuade a Queen to dress up as a milkmaid, was not to last. Shorn of civilization, his vision still centred on community as an emancipation of people.

By the late 1780s, the aim of the picturesque had moved on to become that of 'wilderness' (Jones, 1974:78). Price (1794) and Knight (1794) were advocates of what Hadfield (1979:71) calls the 'wild and rugged school' and a period began in which the Classical lakes were drained and massive rock landscapes installed – Joseph Paxton's imitation of the narrows at Wharfedale is still seen at Chatsworth – all at ruinous cost.

> Picturesque assumed, in the late eighties of the eighteenth century a new meaning. That was picturesque which was eminently 'paintable', and that was paintable was wild and rugged. (Hadfield, 1979:71)

141

Although the Romantic movement found its antecedents in painting, the construction of landscape was no longer dominated by painting. Rather painting and poetry was increasingly expected to be inspired *by* landscape, especially by what was taken to be the genuinely natural landscape – particularly the Lake District and the empty Scottish glens, conveniently made natural from being 'cleared' of their human inhabitants by landowners keen to make money from sheep.

By 1811, these ideas had become commonplace and, in *Sense and Sensibility*, Marianne Dashwood rails against the way dead leaves, without her, are seen 'only as a nuisance, swept hastily off'.

> . . . with what transporting sensations have I formerly seen them fall! How I have delighted, as I walked, to see them driven in showers about me by the wind! What feelings have they, the season, the air altogether inspired! (114)

To the Romantic, this 'transport' of the body is everything. Later, Marianne is gently teased by Edward, the admirer of her sister Elinor, on her Romantic attitude:

> I have no knowledge in the picturesque, and I shall offend you with my ignorance and want of taste if we come to particulars. I shall call hills steep, which ought to be bold; surfaces strange and uncouth, which ought to be irregular and rugged; and distant objects out of sight, which ought only to be indistinct through the medium of a hazy atmosphere. (121–2)

Evidently the language of the picturesque had its own 'correctness', something even Marianne – after her sister has rescued her from Edward's dry irony – recognizes when she accepts that 'admiration of landscape scenery is become a mere jargon'.

Proclaiming to 'detest jargon of any kind' Marianne goes on to claim 'sometimes I have kept my feelings to myself, because I could find no language to describe them in but what was worn and hackneyed out of all sense and meaning' (122). In suggesting here that 'sublime' experiences go beyond language, Marianne betrays a true Romantic spirit.

Between the song and the sublime

To consider this 'gap' between language and the sublime, I turn now to 'The Idea of Order at Key West', another major poem by Stevens. This involves shifting topographies, leaping – as it were – from gardens to the sea. As before, our guide is Miller (1995) and this involves our making a 'crossing' of but a few pages in *Topographies*, from chapter 9 on Heidegger to chapter 10 on Stevens.

As might be expected, the topography is not all the same. Whereas before we were *in* the garden, now we are *by* the sea. Stevens opens his poem – arguably one of the finest poems in the English language – with the line 'She sang beside the genius of the sea'. Pope spoke of 'the Genius of the Place', thinking of gardens; Stevens dwells on the genius of the sea, perhaps thinking of the sublime. Yet we are not about to fall 'headlong' into the sea. The song, while we listen, keeps the sea at a distance.

Otherwise much is similar. As with Repton, we 'survey . . . while in motion'. So we walk beside her, whoever she is; perhaps a friend, perhaps the Muse herself. And what we survey is truly vast. For in that part of the US, as Miller (260) remarks, Key West is 'as far as you can go'. We have stepped outside our horizons and, like Brown and Repton stepping out of the frame of the picture, we find 'the field of vision is much greater'. Except that, with Stevens, we are of course stepping from the visual into the vocal.

This is where topography begins to suggest how truly different the landscape has become. At Hawkstone, the Romantics might have been walking between the palette of the painting and the 'promontories' of the pastoral. At Key West, however, we walk between the pathos of the phonetic and the pounding of the ocean. Here is how Miller (273) captures the contrast:

> 'C' is only a letter in the human alphabet, comic and superficial, with the lightness and inconsequentiality of a pun . . . The sea, on the other hand, is terrifyingly inhuman, a body wholly body, fluttering its empty sleeves.

As Miller adds, 'Human speech names both with the same sound. No idea can reduce this dark monster to order'.

Between ideas of order and the sublime

Granted that the topologies of Hawkstone and Key West are different, is the effect not the same? Surely, in both cases, we are walking between 'ideas of order' and the 'sublime':

> A strong fear of the inhuman sea runs all through this poem. It is a tragic pity and terror for what *exceeds* the human. These emotions are properly tragic because they are pity and fear for what we may have been and what we might become, of what we still are, in our kinship with the sea-matter muttering meaningless gaspings and grindings. (Miller, 1995:273, emphasis added).

What we are after is this excess. But excess of which, song or sea? For surely our guide is misleading us in this last sentence?

Our kinship is not with the sea, much as we might sometimes be tempted to throw ourselves 'headlong' therein in the manner of Bruegal's mysterious figure (see Frayn, 1999). As Miller (264) comments on an earlier poem, 'The Comedian as the Letter C' opens by asserting 'man is the intelligence of his soil' only to revert, approvingly, to assert: 'his soil is man's intelligence'. It is not only the 'cry' of the sea, as Stevens captures it, which is inhuman; it is, as Miller transfers the epithet, the sea itself. We, who have so transferred our place to the soil, can have no kinship here.

Still the problems go deeper. As Heidegger might remind us, we dwell in language. So our kinship is here – in language, speech, song. Which is ours and ours alone. We live in a surfeit of words. So much so that, strangely, it is the sea that mimics us:

> . . . its mimic motion
> Made constant cry, caused constantly a cry,
> That was not ours although we understood,
> Inhuman, of the veritable ocean.

As Barthes remarked, there is no exit from language. Thus language, song, is supreme. The sea, the 'ever hooded, tragic-gestured sea', becomes 'merely a place by which she walked to sing'.

All this for Stevens to say it is the sea, or sky, that reminds us we are more than sound. For all the sea and the sky can attain – however 'clear' *they* could be – they remain:

> . . . deep air
> The heaving speech of air, a summer sound
> Repeated in a summer without end
> And sound alone.

Sound alone is 'empty', a body without gesture, a pathetic fallacy. This is why Stevens asks 'Whose spirit is this? For *this* is the spirit 'that we sought':

> It was her voice that made
> The sky acutest at its vanishing,
> She measured to the hour its solitude,
> She was the single artificer of the world
> In which she sang. And when she sang, the sea,
> Whatever self it had, became the self
> That was her song, for she was the maker.

This is the Romantic spirit, the indomitable spirit: a 'joy' unprepared to 'bend' to custom and tradition, but ready to re-make a world in which we can 'kiss joy as it flies'.

Passing on the Romantic

It is this Romantic spirit that is catching. Indeed, the experience excites Stevens 'so strongly' that he is moved to write a poem, 'a song about a song'. As Miller argues, this structure echoes another great poem in the Romantic tradition, Wordsworth's 'The Highland Reaper'. In this the poet hears a highland girl singing in Gaelic as she reaps:

> Wordsworth's poem passes the reaper's song on to us as readers, just as, in 'the Idea of Order at Key West', the reader is given no citation whatever from the woman's song. The reader is given Steven's poem instead, by a species of tropological transfer. It is description without place, since we are not given the original song on which this poem is a commentary, just as Wordsworth did not understand the Gaelic song of the highland reaper and had to imagine what it was about. (Miller, 1995:264)

Without meaning, we imagine there to be no possibility of knowledge and cannot think therefore of any transformation – transportation – taking place. Yet since time immemorial, it has been the task of the poet to 'exceed' this constraint. In stimulating someone else 'to imagine what it was about', there is a *passing* on of spirit, a transport that comes from an entanglement with the genius of the place.

But the catching of the Romantic spirit comes with a catch. There is no real community here, no companionable sharing of meanings, nothing to *dwell* within. For the Romantic spirit is singular, solitary. Standing back, this is what Stevens sees:

> Then we
> As we beheld her striding there alone,
> Knew there never was a world for her
> Except the one she sang and, singing, made.

If we take on the world, we do so alone. And a Romantic figure, such as Austen captures in Marianne in *Sense and Sensibility*, is for ever walking out alone and, to her sister's chagrin, can hardly be 'civil' even to those who extend to her their hospitality.

This experience, when reflected upon, suggests a limit of the Romantic, already noted above. Yet we should not despair from this failure of meaning. What remains possible is this passing on of 'excess'. The spirit, the cause of the poem, can be passed on even when meaning cannot. Not, abstractly, but made incarnate by virtue of an 'overpassing' (Miller, 1995:316), a kind of translation [*Übertragung*] in which the *marking* of experience within the body is 'carried over' from one flesh to another.

Order gives order. So much so, that even when the singing has ended and Stevens turns towards the town, to companionship and conversation, he still finds order:

> . . . tell why the glassy lights,
> The lights of the fishing boats at anchor there
> As the night descended, tilting in the air,
> Mastered the night and portioned out the sea,
> Fixing emblazoned zones and fiery poles,
> Arranging, deepening, enchanting night.

This experience of order, visual order, is asked as a question of Ramon Fernandez, his ghostly companion. For, far from experiencing chaos when the singing stops, another organization, this time the visual, comes to occupy him.

This use of direct speech ('Ramon Fernandez, tell me, if you know') signals a break in the 'song about a song', the passing on of song from the Muse to Stevens. Stevens's tone is now all male, all demanding of his friend. He is no longer 'lifted' by the Romantic spirit. Yet the 'maker's rage for order' persists. Why? The final few lines tell us. He finds himself returned to the *Classical* Muse, listening to 'words of the fragrant portals'. This is Stevens's opus, writing not singing. His communion is once again with the dead, a 'palm at the end of the mind', in which his will to knowledge is tacked onto his ear for 'keener sounds'.

Part IV

> there's that melody again
> where it's coming from I must have been
> drifting out of time, now I'm in
> underneath you'll find I'm just the same
> running wild – like you do
>
> (Bryan Ferry & Phil Manzanera, Running Wild)

The labour of the garden

Production, product, labour. In a series of reductionist moves, these three concepts emerge simultaneously as 'abstractions with a special status' and lay the foundation for political economy. To Marx and Engels, however, these are 'concrete' abstractions which make possible the relations of production. What they insist upon, Lefebvre (1991) argues in *The Production of Space*, is to treat the concept of production as purely abstract until questions about who, what, why and for whom are answered.

Lefebvre is attempting to recover production from the more 'banal' sense the term production has attracted, particularly for economists, and he returns to Hegel to clarify the idea of production.

> In its broad sense, humans are said to produce their own life, their own consciousness, their own world. There is nothing, in history, or in society, which does not have to be produced. 'Nature' itself, as apprehended in social life by the sense organs, has been modified and therefore in a sense produced. (68)

Lefebvre sees Marx and Engels as having narrowed down the concept of production so that 'works in this broad sense are no longer part of the picture'. As he adds, 'what they have in mind is things only: *products*' (68).

As for labour, the question of who does the producing, and how they do it, Lefebvre argues that the more restricted the notion of production becomes, 'the less it connotes creativity, inventiveness or imagination'. Indeed, production in this narrow sense tends to refer solely to labour' (69). Influenced by Ricardo, this further reductive step in the idea of production – to consider only labour – is enthusiastically endorsed by Marx (1973:104): 'It was an immense step forward for Adam Smith to throw out every limiting specification of wealth-creating activity'. Lefebvre's complaint is that Marx and Engels never did make these concepts concrete. He sees them as merely abusing a 'scientific' procedure whereby they, ingeniously, endowed the broad concept with 'a positivity properly belonging to the narrow or scientific (economic) sense' (70). He then disparages the narrowness of this thinking by considering Nature in terms of production.

A tree, a flower or a fruit is not a product – even if it is in a garden ... Nature cannot operate according to the same teleology as human beings. The 'beings' it creates are 'works' ... Nature's space is not staged. To ask why this is so is a strictly meaningless question: a flower does not know that it is a flower any more than death knows upon whom it is visited. (70)

Nature does not labour, Lefebvre insists; rather, 'it is even one of its defining characteristics that it creates' (70).

The creation of the 'natural' garden requires an 'excess' of labour, a labour that never could be justified by an abstract science that has lost all contact with the ground – home – that once bore its name oeconomy (Bay, 1998). Locked into precepts of efficiency rather than beauty, Utopia becomes the product of deciding everyone is to be the same.

The turn of consumption

The labour of discourse, the product of knowledge and the production of community. These are relentless demands in which the ultimate penalty for failing to 'keep up' a conversation is expulsion from the civic space. As Bauman (2001:31) quotes Sennett, 'maintaining community becomes an end in itself; the purge of those who don't really belong becomes the community's business'.

In seeking solidarity with Nature, it could be argued that what the Romantic longs for is a 'withdrawal' from this kind of production, particularly from their 'throwness' in language. Reaching towards the sublime, the Romantic attempts to liberate themselves from an endless production of civil space that has become the province of the petit bourgeoisie. The Romantic seeks a moment, momentous in being free from any 'spitting' out of speech. Yet only song, it seems, can vault the rhythms of speech and create an order – an idea of order – that approximates the sublime.

Alternatively, there is the garden. Within the Classical garden there is a 'suspension' of otherness, a phagic response in which time is expelled or stilled in order that conversation may be given its ample *occasions*. Whereas in the Romantic garden, the *opportunity* exists to allow oneself to be 'vomited' out of the production of space. Helped by the depth of the shade, or the immensity of the drop, or the sheer weight of water, the visitor turns from production and catapults her or himself into the passion of 'pure' consumption (Latimer, 2001).

Such Romantic experiences, on analogy with Lefebvre's (1991) reworking of production, would renew a broader, richer sense of consumption. Where Lefebvre sees time as confined to a sense of 'productive labour time' (404), it follows that much consumption will be equally caught within the experience of time as 'punctualized' in the *now!* Yet both Classical and Romantic gardens suggest that consumption need not be reduced to what it has become: an 'utterly, irredeemably individual pastime, a string of sensations which can be experienced – lived through – only subjectively (Bauman, 2001:21). The emptying out of consumption (in which no number of products will ever redeem the cost of 'dead labour') is particularly critical given the 'non-spaces' with which Bauman is concerned – airports, motorways, anonymous hotel rooms – where we experience time only in its abbreviated sense of being a kind of space simply to live through.

A rather different register in our consumption of time is the 'closure' of some opening. That is, we do not only have to experience the present as caught between the grammar of past present and future present. Occasionally, we register time at the point at which we realize an 'opening' is gone. For example, to the idea that 'we have time', Valentine, the computational mathematician in *Arcadia*, cryptically replies:

'. . till there's no time left. That's what time means.' (Stoppard, 1993:94)

As it appears on stage, this present day Valentine is replying to Septimus, the Tutor of Sidley Hall from 1809 to 1812. Thus, in his defining of time, Valentine is closing off an opening created almost two centuries before.

In visiting Hawkstone, we might recover a similar experience of time. The visitor, loaded down with picnic material for the four mile circuit, can just savour an ice-cream before stopping for lunch and trudging back by way of The Fox's Knoll, Indian Rock, The Hermitage and The Urn, taking photographs as they go. But if they stop for a moment and, like Marianne Dashwood, become *transported* by something like rapture, a bodily experience that scatters space and stops time, they are also closing off an opening created by an 'excess' of labour some centuries before.

Improductive expenditure

The land around Hawkstone was bought in 1556 by the first Protestant Lord Mayor of London (Hawkstone, 1993:4–5), whose descendant is attributed with inventing the postage stamp. The first Sir Rowland Hill, a noted philanthropist, is not thought to have visited his property, seemingly content to send money for its 'improvement'. Claiming views onto fifteen counties, his statue, placed in 1795 on top of the Monument (also known as The Obelisk), has been compensating for this omission ever since.

During the late 17th century the parkland began to be developed, a beneficiary of the 'lucrative arithmetick' of the Hon. Richard Hill – whose father is reported as saying 'My son Dick makes money very fast, God send that he gets it honestly' (Hawkstone, 1993:6). The first folly to be built was The Vineyard, a copy of a Roman vineyard, 'laid out in the manner of a fortification, with turrets, walls and bastions' (Bagshaw, 1851:288) and occupying the south-facing escarpment about half a mile to the south of the main house. Visited by royalty, The Vineyard was described in Philip Yorke's 1748 diary as 'a most warm spot'.

Attention then shifted, despite this massive expenditure, west of the escarpment. In 1750 the Hills purchased from the Audley family the remains of a 12th century castle, known as The Red Castle. This purchase helped to extend the deer park, giving views to the Welsh hills, and saw the beginnings of Hawkstone becoming a model of the Romantic garden. Later follies, including the White Tower, the Menagerie, the Hermitage, and the Citadel all mainly cluster around the Grand Valley in which the Red Castle is situated. The Red Castle also incorporates a feature known as The Giants' Well and much was made later by Emma and Jane Hill (1827) of the fate of Sir Lancelot at the hands of the infamous brothers Sir Tarquin and Sir Turquine. It is not known when the Grotto, a very impressive and extensive system of caves, was discovered but these were likely Roman copper mines possibly extended by the Hills for their own purposes of adding adventure and mystery to the park.

In 1850 a new drive and entrance to the Park was created to pass before the Red Castle by means of an arch being blown through the rock at the foot of Grotto Hill. The new drive thus joined up the Romantic landscape to the more 'Classical' parkland adjoining the house, Hawkstone Hall, an elegant Georgian edifice. This latter area also included the Hawk Lake, a man-made stretch of water of almost two miles length built at the end of the Napoleonic wars to give local employment and counter widespread famine.

The expense of the new entrance to the Park was ruinous and the finances of the Hill family appear never to have recovered from this last great extravagance. In his *Lives of the Poets* Dr Johnson wittily said of Shenstone, a poet dedicated to adorning his garden on an income of only £300 a year, 'He spent his estate in adorning it'. If obedience to the call of adornment, if not the principle of improductive expenditure, leads many owners of parkland towards financial ruin, Hawkstone is no exception. The expense of developing the parkland intermittently for over three centuries had been enormous and eventually took the Hill family into the bankruptcy court in 1911, ostensibly from slight being taken by a creditor overlooked in respect of invitations to a family birthday party.

A Garden of Eden

Hawkstone, long steeped in Arthurian legend, was once one of the most visited gardens in Britain. Boasting its own hotel for 'tourists' as early as 1780, the Park had begun to fall into disrepair around 1925 when the estate was broken up. Likely the gardens, with their mid-Victorian additions of fir-filled arboretums to the back of the Hall and around The Vineyard, had already lost appeal to a brash Edwardian fashion in horticulture.

The felicity of the 1925 sale can be judged by the fact that, over the next sixty years or so, the Romantic heart of the parkland remained intact, a facility loosely attached to the hotel which concentrated its efforts on that more modern of version of Elysian fields, the golf course. Jones (1974:79) describes the result as:

> a piece of picturesque landscaping in the naturalistic style that uses even its conversion into a golf course to advantage, for the great green sweeps are thus well cared for, and from the heights of Grotto Hill the little figures of the golfers with their tiny cries and red flags animate the scene without annoyance.

In between its closing as a family park in 1925 and its reopening as a 'visitor attraction' in 1993, the importance of Hawkstone seemed irretrievable. Much of the Park remained inaccessible, even to the curious hotel visitor. As an anonymous space, the parkland became instead a haven for a very diverse set of interests. Within the 'wilderness', and away from the golf links, were vast areas of rhododendron and woods within which local children ran wild (all around North Shropshire people recall endless days exploring the grottoes and the caves safe from interruption by their parents). Up to about twenty years ago, local farmers happily ran their 'shoots' inside the more abandoned areas of wood and organized such regular events as a 'hill climb' for their rally cars up the old driveway of the escarpment to the south of the main house.

Equally, peripheral areas of the former estate have developed in a number of heterotopian ways. Hawkstone Hall was first a Nunnery and is now a 'retreat', owned by the Order of the Redemptionists. Much surrounding land is divided into a number of independent arable and dairy farms. A caravan site now occupies the most northerly end of the Hawk Lake and all along its west bank fishermen could join the Wem Angling Society and enjoy a different kind of heaven. A thriving nudist colony attracting doctors and judges began on the rim of the more southerly escarpment, where Hawkstone is still host to several World Championships for trial and motor-cross bikes.

Archaeological excavations have begun further along on the southerly escarpment, half a mile to the south of The Vineyard for a different reason. Dismissed by earlier expeditions as having few Roman remains, the Bury Walls is now being recognized as a major Celtic settlement in Britain (Murdie *et al.*, 2000). Well over a mile in perimeter, the fort is almost inaccessible on three of its sides and boasts a double ditch and ramparts seventy feet tall to the north. However, the key feature that emphasizes its strategic importance is the spring that feeds fresh water into the pond in the centre of the fort. With its mild air and harmonious atmosphere, it is easy to imagine Camelot being here.

The visitor Renaissance

Gouldner's analysis of the Romantic, in Cooper's (1986:301) view, 'draws our attention to the role of the boundary as a complex, ambiguous structure'. It is not the normal case, but the *deviant* that attracts attention. As he suggests, referring to the work of the Chicago school, this matter of deviance can be turned to question the logic and structure of boundaries. Cooper goes on to add, it is this 'ordering of an intrinsic disorder' that constitutes organization and which prescribes the 'recuperation of the boundary concept from its present marginal position in social and organizational analysis' (301).

By the 1960s, boundaries were certainly shifting. England was on the move, sexually and morally. The countryside, somewhat neglected in post-war Britain, experienced renewed interest. Rather than admitting the inquisitive visitor, stately homes were opening their doors to the crowd. As with the contemporary bridge, a logic of efficiency was being 'gathered' and made present:

The highway bridge is tied into the network of long-distance traffic, paced and calculated to maximum yield. (Heidegger, 1993:354).

Consequently, many English gardens began to cater to popular culture in ways that added new 'attractions', such as the 'rides' at Alton Towers. Pop festivals were held at stately homes, with many visitors camping within the parkland. And members of top rock groups like the Beatles and the Rolling Stones each bought their country houses (Brian Jones bought Christopher Robin's House at Pooh Corner). For some, the civilization which had shot them to fame had become unpalatable and many lyric writers turned to Nature for inspiration and alternative lifestyles.

The contemporary 'utopia' making possible this renaissance was the small four-wheeled mobile box known as the car. But the 1960s motor, even with its radio, was not the hermetically sealed 'hot rod' of today's boy racer. Then its 'demanding relation' (Munro, 2000b) lay not in the speed of sailing its bubble of stereophonic sound around a series of tightly linked roundabouts, but in finding locations and places to visit. New Romantics like Bryan Ferry sang about the radio – and of parking their car to listen to 'the rhythm of rhyming guitars'.

If the English country house garden offered a popular venue in a country that kept its halls of consumption in village and town centres, rather than out-of-town shopping malls, a new kind of 'traveller' had also emerged. While some travelled to the Hindu Kush, looking for their Shangri La, others took to the road in Britain, often looking to stop at spaces like Stonehenge (Hetherington, 1997). For those seeking a sanctuary for their alternative lifestyle, Hawkstone became a favoured site: the English garden that once was Arcadia to one family metamorphosed into Utopia for itinerant bands of Hippies, attracted by the shelter of its caves and a supply of wood for their fires.

Reopened as a visitor attraction, Hawkstone now enters a culture of enhancement (Munro, 2001) in which it competes with English gardens like the nearby Hodnet Hall, an Edwardian venture, and world class venues like Tivoli in Copenhagen. It would be good to think that the very large grants offered by English Heritage to restore Hawkstone were raised to help restore this 'Lost Masterpiece'. But it is likely that the presence of unknown numbers of travellers and hippies galvanized law-makers and law-keepers alike into finding a solution that could help spit out this 'utopian' deviance.

Travel, transportation, the enigma of arrival. These three concepts summon up much of the contemporary mode of consumption and its entanglement with the spatiality of time. There are as yet no rides, although children travel by Landrover to visit Santa in his Grotto at Christmas. What remains is the 'Genius of the Place'. The result of several millennia of meddling with the thing-in-itself, its '*Ding an sich*', leaves Hawkstone relatively untouched. Or, rather, it remains sublime, adorned largely at the edges. Once rumoured to be home to the Holy Grail, perhaps the sleeping giant of Hawkstone will also, in time, set its sights on competing with the American utopia of Disneyland.

Conclusion

Clarity was never the goal of either the Romantic or the Classical. Nor need it be ours. Perspicuity is always the province of the *formal*, a prior system of logic whose self-sealed tests of validity banish truth to Nature, as if the empirical belongs to a separate domain. As discussed, it is not only within a Romantic sensibility that the boundary emerges as an 'intrinsically indeterminate medium'. Through a careful concealment of its bounds, the Classical also achieved a similar 'vagueness' in effect.

Yet cast adrift from reason by the break with geometry and formal logic, clarity is being returned to us today by way of its becoming a modern sublime. The problem is that this contemporary insistence on clarity installs an unreasonable division of labour, in which the burden of 'translation' is no longer left undecidable between speaker and hearer, but falls increasingly onto the speaker. Speaking, the call to reason, becomes subservient to the 'sight' of unseen auditors – a matter rapidly enclosed further within the fashionable dogma of transparency (Lyotard, 1984).

This asymmetry in power relations is being sustained within a society in which time has been confined to a sense of 'productive labour time'. When time pervades so persistently, our lives are punctualised into a series of insistent *nows!* There is no space left in which the Other can stand, no time to plumb the depths of the sublime in all its endless variation. Transparency turns out to be a 'fixing' of the present in which time for each of us is made *mine* and nothing is left to be given to the Other. It might even be said this abreviated form of time sets demands which are colonizing social relations into 'non-spaces'. As Benko (1997:24) indicates – perhaps wildly under-estimating – never before in the history of the world have non-places occupied so much space. Where everything is to be clear, there can be no building *for* dwelling; nothing is made 'present' apart from minimal cues to guide the minimal functions: eating, abluting, shopping.

Against the fetish for clarity, gardens embody the kind of concreteness to which we can submit ideas – an empiricism that isn't just good to think but actually *grounds* thinking. Thus I began work on this chapter with an idea I could distinguish the spatial concerns of the Classical garden from an embodiment of time in the Romantic garden. In so doing, I linked the displacement of formal knowledge with both a 'natural' consumption of space and the Classical project of learning – a project that still stands in some denial of time. I then contrasted this with an emerging Romantic conception of reality as transmittable only through the immediate and unmediated experience of the individual – a 'transportation' said to be unable to sustain any sense of theory at all.

My original aim was to transfer this concreteness to the analysis of contemporary institutions to help understand a current mood of 'disorganization' (Munro, 2002). This I saw as a shift from a formal concern with structure towards an on-going engagement with time; a current 'spitting' out of space and order, not to mention an abandonment of community and belonging (Munro,

1997). The agenda of institutions to withdraw structure, abandon ethos and then subject employees to the test of 'excess' (cf. Botting & Wilson, 2000) seem all the more Romantic – in a (mistaken) idea that managers and employees – once individuated – are more exposed to the market 'disciplines' of time.

Gardens, and their impact upon a consumption of time and space, proved too diverting to sustain this aim. What unrolled in the convolutions of Kent to Brown and then from Repton to Knight was the concrete insight that truth – a momentary revealing – is always 'rooted' in the spot. The Genius of the Place.

Beyond this, I want to register how it is that 'crossings' may be crucial here. At the height of the formal garden, the *transition* that mattered was stepping from wilderness into the enclosure – paradise. But in moving between town and country, the wild had to be re-ingested – if all nature was to become a garden. For the sake of civility, and coding the city, we could have geometry in town, but we didn't need Euclid to be also framing our conception of leisure. Indeed, as Clifford (1966:175) suggests, 'Repton and his successor wanted to have Arcis cake and eat' it: 'of prospect *and* seclusion, of geometry *and* nature, of arenas and belts, of streams and earnals of Burke *and* Price, of Brown *and* Le Nôtre'. Seclusion, as Repton (1806) argued, had to be admitted, as well as prospects' installed.

Today, I'm not sure where Utopia might be figured to live, other than in an array of perpetual crossings: between sun and soil, sand and sea, eye and hand, ear and spirit. Far from being two 'structures', as Gouldner suggests, the Classical and Romantic seem more two 'moods' we swing between. One moment we wallow in the production of civility and sociality. The next moment – blocked off by language from each other – we stand outside the arrest of time and no longer delight in 'making new' the repetition of entering, again and again, the same place, time and time again.

References

Addison, J. (1712) *The Spectator*, June 25 (No. 414).

Austen, J. (1969 [1811]) *Sense and Sensibility*. London: Penguin.

Bagshaw, S. (1851) *History, Gazatteer, and Directory of Shropshire*. Sheffield.

Bauman, Z. (2001) 'Uses and Disuses of Urban Space', in B. Czarniawska and R. Solli (eds) *Organizing Metropolitan Space and Discourse*, pp. 15–33. Malmo: Liber.

Bay. T. (1998) *And . . And . . And.* Doctoral Dissertation, University of Stockholm.

Benko, G. (1997) 'Introduction: modernity, postmodernity and social sciences'. In G. Benko and U. Strohmayer (eds) *Space and Social Theory: interpreting modernity and postmodernity.* Oxford: Blackwell.

Botting, F. & Wilson, S. (2000) 'Homoeconopoesis 1', paper presented at the ESRC Complexity Seminar, May, CSTT, Keele.

Burden, T. (1993) 'Utopia'. In W. Outhwaite and T. Bottomore (eds) *Twentieth-Century Social Thought*, pp. 691–2. Oxford: Blackwell.

Clifford D. (1966) *A History of Garden Design*, London: Faber & Faber.

Cooper, R. (1986) 'Organization/Disorganization'. *Social Science Information*, 25, 2: 299–335. [Reprinted in J. Hassard & D. Pym (eds) *The Theory and Philosophy of Organizations*, pp. 167–197. London: Routledge].

D'argenville (1712) *The Theory and Practice of Gardening*, translated by John James.

Gouldner, A. (1973) *For Sociology.* London: Allen Lane.

Hadfield M. (1979) *A History of British Gardening*, 3rd Edition. London: Hamlyn.

Hawkstone (1993) *Hawkstone: a short history and guide.*

Heidegger M. (1977) 'The Age of the World Picture', in *The Question Concerning Technology and Other Essays*, trans. W. Loveitt. New York: Harper & Row.

Heidegger, M. (1993) 'The Question Concerning Technology', in D.F. Krell (ed.) *Basic Writings*, London: Routledge.

Hetherington, K. (1997) 'In Place of Geometry: the materiality of place'. In R. Munro and K. Hetherington (eds) *Ideas of Difference: Social Spaces and the Labour of Division.* Sociological Review Monograph. pp. 183–199. Oxford: Blackwell.

Hill, J. and Hill, E. [attributed to] (1829) *The Antiquities of Hawkstone.* Shrewsbury.

Hyams E. (1964) *The English Garden.* . London: Thames & Hudson.

Johnson, S. (1995) 'A Journal into North Wales in the Year 1774'. In A. Briston (ed.) *Dr Johnson & Mrs Thrale's Tow in North Wales, 1774.* Wrexham: Bridge Books. Hyams, E. (1771) *Capability Broum & Plumphrey Repton,* London: J.M. Dent.

Hyams, E. (1971) *Capatility Brounn & Humbbrey Repiton,* London: J.M. Dent.

Jones (1974) *Follies & Grottoes.* London: Constable.

Keen, M. (1997) *The Glory of the English Garden.* London: Barrie & Jenkins.

King, R. (1979) *The Quest for Paradise: a history of the world's gardens.* New York: Mayflower.

Latimer, J. (2001) 'All Consuming Passions: materials and subjectivity in the age of enhancement'. In N. Lee and R. Munro (eds) *The Consumption of Mass*, Sociological Review Monograph, Blackwell, pp. 158–173.

Lefebvre, H. (1991) *The Production of Space*, translated by D. Nicholson-Smith. Oxford: Blackwell.

Letiche, H. (2000) 'Situating Complexity'. In J. Hassard, R. Holliday and H. Willmott (eds) *Body and Organisation*, London: Sage, 87–107.

Lyotard, J.-F. (1984) *The Postmodern Condition: a report on knowledge*, translated by G. Bennington & B. Massumi. Manchester: Manchester University Press.

Miller, J.H. (1995) *Topographies.* Stanford: Stanford University Press.

Munro, R. (1998) 'Belonging on the Move: market rhetoric and the future as obligatory passage', *The Sociological Review*, 46, 2: 208–243.

Munro, R. (2000a) 'The Culture of Enhancement: performance measurement and the new managerialism'. In A. Neely (ed.) *Performance Measurement: past, present and future.*

Munro, R. (2000b) 'Punctualising Identity: Time and the demanding relationship', paper presented at the British Sociological Association, York.

Munro, R. (2002) 'Disorganisation'. In R. Westwood & S. Clegg (eds) *Point/Counterpoint: Central Debates in Organisation Theory.* Oxford: Blackwell.

Murdie, R.E. *et al.* (2000) *Geographical Surveys at Bury Walls, 1999–2000: results from the Earthwatch campaigns.* Keele: University of Keele.

Palli, C. (2001) 'Ordering Others and Othering Orders: the consumption and disposal of otherness'. In N. Lee and R. Munro (eds) *The Consumption of Mass*, Sociological Review Monograph, Blackwell, pp. 189–204.

A. Pope, *Moral Essays, Epistle IV, To Richard Boyle, Earl,* Burlington, Edition 1716.

Price, U. (1794) *An Essay on the Picturesque.* London: Robson.

Repton, H. (1806) An Enquiry into the *Changes of Taste in Landscape Gardening.* London: Taylor.

Sennett, R. 1996. *The Uses of Disorder: personal identity and city life.* London: Faber & Faber.

Stevens, W. (1972) *The Palm at the End of the Mind: selected poems and a play*, edited by H. Stevens. New York: Vintage.

Stoppard, T. (1993) *Arcadia.* London: Faber & Faber.

Strathern, M. (1995) *The Relation: issues in complexity and scale*, Cambridge: Prickly Pear Pamphlet No. 6.

Temple, Sir Wm. (1685) *Upon the Gardens of Epicurus.* London.

Walpole, H. (1995 [1780]) *The History of Modern Taste in Gardening*, edited by John Dixon Hunt. New York: Ursus Press.

Writing utopia

Geoff Lightfoot and Simon Lilley

Did you know that the first Matrix was designed to be a perfect human world? Where none suffered, where everyone would be happy. It was a disaster. No one would accept the program. Entire crops were lost. Some believed we lacked the programming language to describe your perfect world. But I believe that, as a species, human beings define their reality through suffering and misery. The perfect world was a dream that your primitive cerebrum kept trying to wake up from. (AGENT SMITH, computer simulacrum: Wachowski & Wachowski, 1999)[1]

To begin: happiness

Where should *we* begin[2]? At the beginning would be nice, but that spoils our ending, for our contribution here is, in part at least, about the importance of beginnings and their absence in utopian writings. So we shall begin by writing, and with writing, with a problem that Orwell identifies in writing about happiness:

> Dickens is remarkable, indeed almost unique, among modern writers in being able to give a convincing picture of happiness. [. . .] To begin with, however thick Dickens may lay on the paint, however disgusting the 'pathos' of Tiny Tim may be, the Cratchit family give the impression of enjoying themselves. They sound happy as, for instance, the citizens of William Morris's *News from Nowhere* don't sound happy. Moreover, and Dickens's understanding of this is one of the secrets of his power their happiness derives mainly from contrast. . . . Their happiness is convincing just because it is described as incomplete (Orwell, 1943/1998)

Orwell is certainly correct to remind us of the importance of contrast in our considerations of happiness, or indeed anything else. However, his conception of the ways in which contrast may operate seems too limited to capture Dickens' bathetic achievements. We glimpse happiness not only against the foil of the hardships of 'normal' Cratchitian existence but also through our identification with and against the outsider who can only witness the light within, from outside. Scrooge, in his journeys through time and space, is reduced to a cipher for both the causes and consequences of unhappiness. But the window scene remains an alchemic moment. In *A Christmas Carol* Scrooge begins to regain his humanity at precisely the point when his gaze through the window renders him as empty outsider. And repetition has so sensitized us to the image of the warm light spilling out into the cold winter night, that we now see Christmas as a synonym for happiness, despite our myriad experiences of the actual tawdriness of the lived celebration. The festival can stand for happiness precisely because it is not 'normal' (Bakhtin, in Morris, 1994) because it parades an inversion of the drudgery of everyday existence.

Accounts of permanent happiness are mercifully rare. Only the mad, bad and dangerous to know construct such totalities.

> It would seem that human beings are not able to describe, nor perhaps to imagine, happiness except in terms of contrast. That is why the conception of heaven or Utopia varies from age to age. In pre-industrial society Heaven was described as a place of endless rest, and as being paved with gold, because the experience of the average human being was overwork and poverty. The houris of the Muslim paradise reflected a polygamous society where most of the women disappeared into the harems of the rich. But these pictures of 'eternal bliss' always failed because as the bliss became eternal (eternity being thought of as endless time), the contrast ceased to operate ... All efforts to describe permanent happiness [. . .] have been failures. (Orwell, 1943/1998)

Indeed, as our editor reminded us, satirists from Dave Allen to Julian Barnes (1989; see also, Belk, 1996) have pointed out just what a dull place these 'heavens' would be. However, accounts of happiness, both in utopian totalities and literary contrast, do share a form, that of writing. And it is to the relation of writing and utopia, of beginnings and ends, that this chapter is devoted. We explore these themes primarily because recent changes in the nature of the connectivity of society's constituents have highlighted literary mechanisms as resources both for constructing new worlds and critiquing them. The most virulent forms of both these beasts are to be found in the genre of Science Fiction (Parker *et al.*, 1999; Smith *et al.*, 2001), a resource that has become increasingly fashionable in the social sciences (see also Turkle, 1995; Stone, 1996 and Featherstone and Burrows, 1996, for example). So it is to the centrality of Fiction to Science Fiction that we now turn our attention.

Beginning science, fiction and organization

Although science fiction may currently be mediated by video, film, or static graphics with directing text, to give but few examples, its primary form as literary genre is the novel[3]. And as Said (1997:82–3) notes, echoing Harry Levin, 'the novel is an institution, wholly differentiated from the more generalized idea of "fiction," to which even the most unusual and *novel* experiences are admitted as functions' (original emphasis). It is thus not novelty *per se* that is likely to be of interest in the body of work that we term science fiction.

Novelty is nevertheless important in explaining the current wave of popularity of SF amongst the social and organizational theory community. Indeed, it seems that SF's popularity in this field is itself an epiphenoma of generalized acceptance of the seemingly endless, breathless talk of unmitigated levels of change at and between all recognizable levels of analysis. To be fair there are other, related, sympathetic resonances between literatures here: the emotiveness of the reaction to technology in general, be it philic or phobic, and more particularly, the (pseudo)problematization of the source and persistence of 'interests' which systems of technology are 'intended' to serve. Of course we can and do flip this coin, problematizing 'human' 'identity' and the origins and maintenance of 'human' 'interests' and 'intentions' in a deluge of scare quotes in our commentaries and reflections. All are bound and unbound in SF's utopian and dystopian (Kumar, 1987) futures and pasts.

But whether the future is good or bad, bright or bleak, or indeed, Orange, is not our central interest here. There is nothing potentially so dull as writing caught in the glimmer of glamour (see McHugh, 2001, for similar reservations). For the cynical, SF may appear merely as a collection of novels whose subject matter happens to combine flesh, code and chrome in order to weave its web. And it is the attachments of these resources in other networks of meaning, particularly those of destructive, hypersexualized masculinities that are seen as responsible for the worst of SF's excesses.

Boys and their toys, maybe. But in their attraction to the glitter of the new, new things, SF throws into sharp relief a feature of all novelistic work: the necessity of constructing the seemingly new from the rubble of the old. It is thus much more the beginning act of the work that seeks to make new from old that is of interest. In SF this occurs within the opportunities and constraints offered by the genre of the novel, the maintenance and unravellings of prior deferrals (in Derrida's sense) of its form. And if SF achieves its interesting effects *vis-à-vis* central contemporary social theoretics such as 'identity'[4], 'intention', 'material, 'prosthesis', 'cyborganization' and the rest, primarily through its capacity as novel to generate a *beginning* (Said, 1997), then it is to this facet of the novel more generally that we turn our attention. We do this via a mobilization and interrogation of the dialectic of 'authority and molestation' that Said (1997:83) sees as the heart of the *authorship* which provides the material for his investigation of human *beginnings*.

Beginning writing

SF's most interesting productions problematize the bases of both organization, and the identities and differences that are both cause and consequence of organization. Boundaries, particularly of bodies (see for example, Featherstone & Burrows: 1995), and thus necessarily also of the things that abut, penetrate and mediate them, are artfully weakened as 'new' connections and perpetuations are similarly stabilized. The subjection of the body (and the other forms of identities seemingly associated with it) to consideration as artificial construction is, however, certainly not a strategic gambit unfamiliar to social theory (ST), as the work of Heidegger, Foucault, Derrida and Deleuze and Guatarri, to name but the most obvious examples, reminds us. And as even this brief tour of the field makes clear, there is no necessity within such moves to draw upon the vernacular, stylistics or tropes of SF in order to produce them. Indeed, from such a perspective one may venture to suggest that it is precisely the newness of SF worlds, their degree of distance from our own, which robs the genre of much of the power that we see in other forms of de/reconnective literary moves. For such newness, often (wildly) extrapolated from the current everyday, however inadvertently, advertises itself as either warning or celebration, by highlighting how particular extrapolations of the present may be more or less attractive than that from which they derive.

ST offers us instead, histories of the present (Foucault), strange connections and connections of the strange, that derive their grasp from cunning and nuanced accounts not of what may be, but of what has become. These 'fictions' reside *in* and are organized through the facticity of the present. Its weavings in the here and now are shown *in* the here and now, there being no necessity (but nevertheless often sufficient reason) to utilize a device like 'the future' to extract these unusual aspects and align them through invocation of a time when that fiction may become the facts. And it is, as a result, that much more powerful in its purchase upon us. For it challenges our common-sensical understandings of ourselves in the here and now within the same space in which we make and sustain these truisms. Now good SF can do this too (and when it does, it does it to a wider audience), but ST shows us that we don't need the tricks of SF in order to do it.

As it goes about its work, this form of ST mimics, indeed often self avowedly adopts, the tools and techniques of 'new' (or perhaps 'new new', see preface to Said, 1997, particularly p. xviii) literary criticism. But works such as Said's *Beginnings*, whilst taking literature as their point of departure, are keen to distance themselves from such limited starts. Mimicking their more interesting sources, such texts treat texts and the divisions between them, *both* as a body of particular 'things' to be studied in themselves and in their relations, *and* as a metonym providing conceptual purchase upon a more broadly conceived 'human' work. And whilst the creativity that we glimpse in such work may certainly be seen to conspire with the divine (see Said, 1997, on Kierkegaard) it is not limited in either its inspiration or its conceptualization of metrics of 'originality', to such a source. In short, it provides ever-newer ways of seeing the connections and disconnections of our world, but crucially it explicitly does so within the confines that currently pertain to that world. This immanent criticism reflects upon the possibility of construction of particular texts, indeed of text *per se*, but does so in textual form. It reflects upon the beginnings of a textual account whilst being itself a textual account with a beginning (and end) of its own. It is a practice in which future unfolds in the text, rather than being invoked in advance, in which a 'not now' functions as enfolded sediment, rather than *deus ex machina*. A conscious connection. For as Said (1997:XX) notes:

... if there is some especially urgent claim to be made for criticism ... it is in that constant re-experiencing of beginning and beginning-again whose force is neither to give rise to authority nor to promote orthodoxy but to stimulate self-conscious and situated activity, activity with aims non-coercive and communal.

Sales of SF literature are declining both in absolute and relative terms[5] . What has taken its place on the bookshelves is Fantasy: endless recreations of the Dark Ages complete with witches and warlocks. And except for a few exceptional exceptions (Holdstock, 1986; Martin, 1998; Pratchett, 2001, for example) these are works bereft of *beginning* in Said's sense. And we posit two reasons for this shift. The first is perhaps the most obvious: the technocratic dystopia of the present calls for ever purer visions of what the world could be (or could have been) as 'science' becomes seen as (part of) the problem rather than the solution. The second is that SF's former audience no longer has time to read – it is too busy writing.

The fact that someone like Archie was responsible, at least in part, for decisions with enormous economic implication, is testament to the notion that anoraks are now running the world. The hooded playground loners who brought sandwiches in for lunch are the new gods – the gods of technology. Who could have imagined that the non-communicators would be the kings of communications, that the trainspotters would be the new trendspotters, that the bedroom castaways would now be the boardroom castigators? (McCabe, 1998:9)

New beginnings I: society as code

Organizations of space and time may be conceived as texts or scripts: for they 'talk about' or evoke certain states of affairs as appropriate readings. Indeed, Ricoeur (1978) suggests that the notion of text is a good paradigm for understanding a great many aspects of human action (see also, Brown, 1987; Burke, 1966; Said, 1997).

[H]uman action is in many ways a quasi-text. In becoming detached from its agent, the action acquires an autonomy similar to the semantic autonomy of a text; it leaves a trace, a mark. It is inscribed in the course of things and becomes an archive and document. Even more like a text, of which the meaning has been freed from the initial conditions of its production, human action has a stature that is not limited to its importance for the situation in which it initially occurs, but allows it to be re-inscribed in new social contexts. Finally, action, like a text, is an open work, addressed to an indefinite series of possible 'readers' (Ricoeur, 1978:160–161).

For those who seek to render actions as predictable, the better to manage them, those 'meta-actions' that form key frameworks of interpretation for other actions must be somehow insulated from the semantic slide that Ricoeur identifies. In short, other actions are required to buttress these frames in order to ensure that 'appropriate' readings persist. For those who merely read these texts, however, the authoritative 'reading' must seem natural, not imposed, if hegemony is to be achieved and power is to remain invisible.

The form of writing to which Ricoeur refers is perhaps better conceptualized as scripting following a theatrical metaphor. The virtue we detect in ST, SF and indeed Said's literary criticism is certainly not explicitly of this sort. Rather, its descriptions invite us onto Ricoeur's semantic slide. It refuses to surrender all authority to the script. Which is not to say that it does not recognize the authority of the script but merely does so to utilize its power for other purposes, to interpenetrate its commands with interpretations that are the reader's own.

We interrogate this latter critical commentary first. In deference to our reflections on science fiction, we turn to a writer who has been claimed by SF enthusiasts as an early luminary. We utilize Kafka's 'Josephine the Singer, or the Mouse People': one of the later short stories that, like many of K's 'artist' tales, clearly reflects upon the author's own artistic activity and his sceptical view of its value[6] . The story concerns a *prima donna* who is a mouse, a curious *prima donna*, for her singing is virtually indistinguishable from the squeaking of her fellows or, indeed, is an even weaker form of this mode of expression. K explores the significance of her conduct for the mouse people via an analogy of cracking nuts:

> Cracking open a nut can hardly be called art; consequently no-one is going to assemble an audience, stand up in front of it, and seek to entertain it by cracking nuts. If he does so nonetheless, and if he succeeds in his purpose, there has to be more involved than mere nutcracking. Or it is only nutcracking that is involved but it turns out that we have been overlooking this art, being past masters of it, and that it has taken this new nutcracker to show us what it is really about, the point being that the effect might even be enhanced if the person concerned were a marginally less competent cracker of nuts than most of us.
>
> Perhaps it is like that with Josephine's singing; we admire in her what we would not dream of admiring in ourselves . . . (Kafka, 1924/1995:255)

From this vantage point, we recognize that the critical purchase of 'art' is, in part at least, a product of the inadequacy of its producer as well as the inevitable impoverishment of all representation. 'Good art', like good acting for Brecht, derives its goodness from the ability to throw into relief the commonplace, to open it up for reflection. 'That factor in a work of art which enables it to transcend reality . . . is to be found in those features in which discrepancy appears: in the necessary failure of the passionate striving for identity.' (Horkheimer and Adorno, 1986:131). When art is completely 'mastered' it becomes as empty as past utopian visions. The actor in showing their acting, the artist in struggling with the mundane: both shed light upon the penetralia of the everyday, the taken for granted that *must* be taken for granted to perform normal membership (Garfinkel, 1967).

New beginnings II: revenge of the nerds

(Science) Fiction, at its best, illuminates the present precisely via this mechanism. Hence the representations of its afficionados as socially inadequate, as 'anoraks . . . , hooded playground loners who brought sandwiches in for lunch . . . , non-communicators . . . , trainspotters . . . [and] bedroom castaways' (McCabe, 1998:9). In these accounts, the audience of SF is not like the critical audiences we encountered above. Fans of SF are rendered as like the authors of their preferred text, rather than as different. They share the dislocation from normal membership, not as mere technique nor as slight maladaption, but as the essence of their being and the reason behind their literary predilections. They 'could' have been in the texts themselves. Well, not exactly. For the heroes of SF tend, in their valorization of their distance from the normal, to romanticize using fairly standard heroic tropes. The Matrix's 'Neo' *is* a dissociated bedroom castaway, but crucially, he is also Keanu Reeves *and* he gets the girl! But if they could not really have been there, maybe they could have written the script.

Indeed, there is superficial evidence that this may be the case, there being almost as much overlap between SF writers and SF readers as there is between the writers and readers of ST. However, even the most crude SF novel does display a certain literacy but, with audiences falling, there was more money to be made by deploying these writerly skills elsewhere. If no one would listen to their critiques of society and reflect upon them to bring about change, another avenue of attack was opened up, one which could cut out the middleman. Writers of SF who lacked the sexy artistry that bestsellers demand could give up on fantasy and, rather than critique the scripts of the everyday, they could write the scripts that write the scripts of the everyday. In short, they were ideally suited to supply the labour required to actualize the potential of information and communication technologies. Their meat becomes our poison.

> . . . [I]t was precisely the self-imposed solitary confinement that eighties anoraks had thrived on that predisposed them to the nineties computer workplace. Companies composed entirely of loners, so much so that the word 'company' became incongruous, and gave way to Corporation (McCabe, 1998:9)

Whilst there are of course many literary counter examples, such as Neo and indeed, Gibson's 'Case', who continue to draw upon an Eastwoodian outsiderliness to the world they create, for those who could see on which side their bread was buttered, a curious miscagenation occurred. The new heroes of the SF fraternity became indistinguishable from the entrepreneurs of the information age. Their musical taste was the same, they dressed the same, and they both wrote dystopias disguised as utopias.

> All 'favourable' Utopias seem to be alike in postulating perfection while being unable to suggest happiness (Orwell, 1943/1998)

Perhaps the hero's hero of this new valorization of (information/social?) engineering is Jim Clark, founder and Chief Executive Officer of Silicon Graphics, Netscape and Healtheon: 'the world's most important technology entrepreneur, the man who embodies the spirit of the coming age' (Lewis, 1999, frontispiece). Lewis follows the maelstrom of Clark's life as he finishes his founding of Healtheon, whilst continuing his quest to 'reinvent the old social order' (*ibid.*:

24). The author utilizes a central metaphor to explore Clark's insatiable search for the 'new new thing', his attempt to construct not only the world's largest single mast yacht, *Hyperion*, but also to computerize every element of its controls[7]. Lewis's account of this endeavour exemplifies Clark's adoption of the 'outsider' position that we witnessed above:

> *Hyperion* was not merely a technologist's utopia or a budding new new thing. It was both of those things. It was also a place where Clark could remain apart from the environment he was constantly reinventing. He could never become one of those ordinary people – a venture capitalist or a chief executive or a member of a museum board or anything else that required him to behave in the way important businessmen are meant to behave. Circumstance had made him an insider, but temperament kept him forever an outsider. He was like the man who threw the world's biggest bash and failed to show up for it. This outsiderliness was what gave him his unusual view of the world. His talent for groping the future was generally viewed as a supernatural gift, but it was as much a measure of his limitations as of his strengths. He could see human society in ways that most businessmen could not, because he was not very much part of it. And consciously or not, by retiring to his floating island, he preserved this precious limitation. (Lewis, 1999:133)

Clark remains 'outside' in order to maintain *his* freedom to move, and indeed to move others. This is no mystery to Lewis, an ex-derivatives trader (one of the Masters of the Universe that populate Wolfe's *Bonfire of the Vanities*). For Lewis and his erstwhile colleagues, everything was seen as moveable and tradable, at least by those traders that could place themselves above and beyond any earthly ties that might hamper their ability to move and trade (Lewis, 1989; Lightfoot and Lilley, 1999, forthcoming). But what of those who are not so fortunately placed? How do they react to the scripts written for them by the playwrights of the information age?

Beginnings and ends

Said's account of the virtue of (critical) writing may usefully be exemplified via consideration of the work of two contemporary novelists, Don DeLillo and Greg Egan.[8] In DeLillo's (1997) *Underworld*, an account of the latter half of the 20th century is connected by the passage of a baseball that was hit for a homer in the 'Shot Heard Round the World' that won the World Series for the Giants on the same day that the Soviet Union successfully tested its first atomic bomb. The novel, like much of DeLillo's work, can be seen as an extended reflection upon the bases of connection, the extensions that reach to, into and from, people and things. But the Minerva view offered is not that of system, of an order whose totality may, however theoretically, be conceived. Rather we enter a world of fractal imagery, of ever-imperfect self-similarity, of mutual production, but not determination, of scale. Of partial connection (Strathern, 1991). And it is a world that we recognize, however obliquely, because it is a world that we (have) inhabit(ed). This is how it begins:

He speaks in your voice, American, and there's a shine in his eye that's halfway hopeful.

It's a school day, sure, but he's nowhere near the classroom. He wants to be here instead, standing in the shadow of this old rust-hulk of a structure, and it's hard to blame him – the metropolis of steel and concrete and flaky paint and cropped grass and enormous Chesterfield packs aslant on the scoreboards, a coupe of cigarettes jutting from each.

Longing on a large scale is what makes history. This is just a kid with a local yearning but he is part of an assembling crowd, anonymous thousands off the buses and trains, people in narrow columns tramping over the swing bridge above the river, and even if they are not a migration or a revolution, some vast shaking of the soul, they bring with them the body heat of a great city and their own small reveries and desparations, the unseen something that haunts the day – men in fedoras and sailors on shore leave, the stray stumble of their thoughts, going to a game.

Michel de Certeau (1984) provides us with another appropriate way of using the metaphor of people moving through the city. For de Certeau, the space of the city itself, like history, is constructed by the lines of movement traced by myriad footsteps. It is (re)marked and produced by the intertwining of paths created by footsteps which weave places together, the daily activities and movements that allow the space to endure. *Underworld* finishes in 'Peace', as a word spreads through the web of the world in which 'Everthing is connected in the end' (1991:826). But like the subject of one of De Lillo's previous works (*Libra*), the story does not end here, for it cannot be contained in the covers of the book. Its connections roll on, beginning again and again. For even when the baseball seems to have stopped, those who have touched it may still move, and thus move it as they do so, just as we have passed it to you.

But for our authors, exemplified by Clark, the view of the creation and maintenance of the pattern of connection is different. In (t)his a-social world:

> Clark had no past, only a future. That's when he really came alive: when you got him on the subject of what was going to happen *next*. (Lewis, 1999:31)
>
> Clark's inability to live without motion and change had gotten him to where he was. In his world change and motion begat money, which begat even more change and more motion, and so on. (Lewis, 1999:30)

Indeed, for some of Clark's team on the *Hyperion* project, this asociality reaches its logical conclusion not only with the elimination of flesh from consideration but with a final step in which connection to all matters material are severed.

> 'The great thing about this project,' said Tim, 'is that it's software that talks to physical things rather than software that just talks to other software. You can *see* the effect of what you are doing.' Lance disagreed. He thought Tim's need to *see* his work manifested in the physical world outside the computer betrayed a weakness of spirit. 'Real nerds,' Lance said, 'get just as excited when they're talking to other software.' (Lewis, 1999:142)

Clark has to move on to escape the stasis, the repetition he creates for others. For not to do so would condemn *him* to the part of cipher in a pseudo-social engineered system.

Such a future is fine for others, but the hero author must turn to a new page, to leave the script once more in order to construct a new one. Egan's novel, *Permutation City*, provides an account of just such a scripted, putative future, one in which the processing powers of information technology have advanced to a stage where the complexity that can be accommodated by such systems is sufficient to create a virtual space, peopled by 'living' constructs that are replications of their 'real' selves. In a world where anything is possible, one way that some fill their endless nano-seconds is by creating a new, computer-modelled, universe (the Autoverse), generated from a series of initial equations. In time, the Autoverse develops to the stage where it is peopled by a new 'race' – nicknamed the Lambertians. Self-aware, the Lambertians start to explain, through their own science, their beginnings. These new beginnings are a shock for those who thought of themselves as creating these models: their position as creator is usurped by novel regularities appearing 'spontaneously' in that which they see themselves as having created. Durham and Maria, the anti-heroes of Egan's account and joint 'authors' of the 'new world', greet this crisis with the following exchange in which Durham tries to mobilize the reason that constructed the new world in a vain attempt to reverse its immanent secession from their rule (as embodied in the seemingly rational base from which it was constructed).

> Durham leant forward urgently. 'We have to win back the laws. We have to go into the Autoverse and convince the Lambertians to accept our explanation of their history – before they have a clear alternative. 'We have to persuade them that *we created them*, before that's no longer the truth.'
>
> [. . .]
>
> He said, 'Whose side are you on? *You* designed the primordial cloud! *You* sketched the original topography! You *made* the ancestor of the whole Lambertian biosphere! All I want to do is tell them that. It's the truth and they have to face it.'
>
> Maria looked about, at a loss for words. It seemed clearer than ever that this [Auto-verse] world was not her creation; it existed on its own terms.
>
> [. . .]
>
> 'Now the Autoverse is sloughing us off like dead skin.' Maria gazed at the Lambertian field equations; they were far more complex than the Autoverse rules, but they had a strange elegance all their own. She could never have invented them herself; she was sure of that.
>
> She said, 'It's not just a matter of the Lambertians out-explaining us. *The whole idea of a creator* tears itself apart. A universe with conscious beings either finds itself in the dust . . . or it doesn't. It makes sense of itself on its own terms, as a self contained whole . . . or not at all. There never can, and never will be, *Gods*. (Egan, 1994, italics in original)

Just as Clark himself can never be a God, despite his mythologising by Lewis and hordes of adoring hackers, so Durham cannot retain his Godspot in the face of the richness of that which has been created. Again and again, Clark leaves, or is forced to leave, his creations just at the point when he can no longer control their totality. The total order, that he seeks to impose upon others but will not accept himself, masquerades as the utopic but the rejection of his order that others seek reveals its dystopic core.

> A Catholic writer said recently that Utopias are now technically feasible and that in consequence how to avoid Utopia had become a serious problem. We cannot write this off as merely a silly remark. For one of the sources of the Fascist movement is the desire to avoid a too-rational and too-comfortable world (Orwell, 1943/1998)

This *is* an increasingly clear and present danger, to be sure. But not one we should perhaps be unduly worried by. For even Kafka's mice, just like Clark's erstwhile colleagues and Durham's Lambertians, seem inherently predisposed to resist the closure that utopia would bring.

> ... unconditional devotion is virtually unknown among us; a people that loves above all else a harmless enough cunning, goes in for childish whispering, and practises an innocent enough sort of gossip involving no more than the lips – a people like that is quite incapable of devoting itself unconditionally ... (Kafka, 1924/1995:258)

Conclusions or, at least, the beginning of the end

Each of the literary examples introduced above does a very nice job of creating a strange world out of re-arranged artefacts and suggestions that surround us. And each does so by taking leave of and returning to a tradition that is governed by the idea of the novel. The novel is *the* exemplar of the infinite limits of individualised *authority* in a world *molested* by the seeming coherencies and discontinuities of what has come before and what must come after. It mimes its status as such as its protagonists – author, character and reader – jostle to join the authentic through the ever-swirling fogs of fiction. It speaks the truth, but only by lying. Truth, wisely rejected by the Lambertians, can be a very dangerous thing!

From Cervantes on, we have been tempted by flights of fancy that culminate in the fulminations we glimpsed above. Glimmers that allow us to see the denseness of our worldly interweavings in ways that encircle any SWOT analysis of our times in which we may be tempted to wallow. Works such as these show us the fate of character in a world of colliding technic planes and discursive rationalities, just as SF shows us the fate of the 'human'. Character cannot play itself out meaningfully in such conditions, being too multi-mediated to act as centre, although in recognizing itself as such it can regain strategic space. It is precisely in such a move that the utopian*ism* Fournier (this volume) delightfully describes and justifiably celebrates is enabled. But the grander aims of utopian system builders are the enemies of even this limited room for manoeuvre, for with their emphasis on the endless (and thus on repetition rather than beginning) they excise even this space. 'Utopias *can't* be achieved because a utopia achieved is no longer a utopia' (Brown and Maclaran, 1996:274).

This tension is at the heart of More's (1516/1965) neologism, which conflates the Greek term for no place (*outopia*) with that for good place (*eutopia*) (Brown and Maclaran, 1996:261) and is reflected in the discontinuities and difficulties which beset both anthologies of writing on utopias (see the beginnings and endings by Parker in this volume) and the innumerable classificatory schemes that have attempted to delineate different forms of the utopic beast (eg, Kumar, 1987; 1991; Carey, 1999; Manuel, 1973; Manuel and Manuel, 1971; 1979) Writing, of ink on page, pixels on screen or indeed directly of the connectivity of society, carries with it a weighty responsibility, for nothing so enables and ensures the 'killing of . . . utopias' as *'their absolute realization'* (Baudrillard, 1994:104, emphasis added). One must of course *begin*, but one's work cannot *end* the lives of characters and readers. Such a view is just the one to give us an excuse to avoid (a happy) ending. Instead we choose to finish where we started, in celebrating beginning as that which . . .

> . . . methodologically unites a practical need with a theory, an intention with a method. For the scholar or researcher, a beginning develops when the conditions of his reality become equal to the generosity of his, of everyman's, intellectual potential. To call this a *radical* beginning is to risk repeating a hackneyed expression. Yet a root is always one among many, never *the* radical method or intention. Thus beginnings for the critic restructure and animate knowledge, not as already-achieved result, but 'as something to be done, as a task and a search'. Such radicalism – to continue the quotation from Pierre Thevenaz [1962:96] – 'aims at fusing together the moral will and the grasping of evidence' (Said, 1991:380).

With all this at stake can you resist our invitation, not to end (Kermode, 1967; 1995; Kumar, 1993; Baudrillard, 1994), but to begin again?

Notes

1 Our thanks go to Victoria Taylor for pointing out this apposite beginning.

2 The paper has benefited from comments provided by the editor of this monograph; participants at the SCOS conference on 'Institutions, Organizations and Violence', Dublin, July 2001; and those who attended the 'Practices of Meaning Workshop' at the University of Humanistics in Utrecht, September 2001. Inadequacies that remain are all our own work.

3 To be pedantic, the primary form of science fiction as literature is probably the short story. Indeed, many of the novels from the 'Golden Age' of science fiction were re-workings and amalgamations of earlier short stories (eg Van Vogt, Simak).

4 Or, perhaps better for our purposes here, given its Burkean lineage (Burke, 1966, 1969), the idea of *processes of identification*.

5 Science Fiction films have, however, retained some of their popularity although the flop of the latest Star Wars and the success of the first Harry Potter may mark the same shift here. And although Star Trek derivatives and a host of imitators remain schedulers' staples, Xena may be the presage of television's New World.

6 We are grateful to Dave Horrocks of the Department of Modern Languages at the University of Keele for providing this source and its interpretation.

7 To hammer home his point here, Lewis romantices contrast in a very Dickensian fashion. The yacht was commisioned from the Huisman Shipyard in Holland, a shipyard that was proud of its 'long and glorious family tradition'. The craftsmen of this yard apparently 'resisted change. They did not cling to the past mindlessly. But they were as immune as people can be to the allure of a new way of doing things. Traditional in a word.' (Lewis, 1999, pp. 8–9). Whilst Clark . . . ' . . . had

seen a yacht, Wolter [Huisman] had just finished building, he said, and wanted one like it. Only bigger. And faster. And newer. He wanted his mast to be the biggest mast ever built. And he wanted to control the whole boat with his computers. Specifically, he wanted to be able to dial into his boat over the internet from his desk in Silicon Valley and sail it across the San Francisco bay. It was as if someone had distilled manic late twentieth-century American capitalism into a vial of liquid and poured it down Wolter's throat' (Lewis, 1999, p. 9).

8 Egan is certainly writing to an SF tradition and thus his inclusion as exemplar here needs little explanation. DeLillo may seem an odder choice, however, many of the tropes employed in his novels, particularly *Underworld* are avowedly science fictive. Indeed, DeLillo's novels even find a place in the 'slipstream' section of The Forbidden Planet bookshop chain.

References

Barnes, J. (1989) *A History of the World in 10¹/₂ Chapters*, London: Jonathan Cape.

Baudrillard, J. (1994) *The Illusion of the End*, trans. C. Turner, Cambridge: Polity Press.

Belk, R. (1996) 'On Aura, Illusion, Escape, and Hope in Apocalyptic Consumption', in S. Brown *et al.* (eds), *Marketing Apocalypse*.

Brown, R. H. (1987) *Society as Text: Essays on Rhetoric, Reason and Reality*, Chicago: University of Chicago Press.

Brown, S., Bell, J. and Carson, D. (1996) *Marketing Apocalypse: Eschatology, Escapology and the Illusion of the End*, London: Routledge.

Brown, S. and Maclaran, P. (1996) 'The Future is Past: Marketing, apocalypse and the retreat from utopia', in S. Brown *et al.* (eds), *Marketing Apocalypse*.

Burke, K. (1966) *Language as Symbolic Action: Essays on Life, Literature and Method*, Berkeley: University of California Press.

Burke, K. (1969) *A Grammar of Motives*, Berkeley: University of California Press.

Carey, J. (1999) (ed.) *The Faber Book of Utopias*, London: Faber and Faber.

de Certeau, M. (1984) *The practice of everyday life*, Berkeley: University of California Press.

Egan, G. (1994) *Permutation City*, London: Millennium.

Featherstone, M. and Burrows, R. (1995) (eds) *Cyberspace/cyberbodies/cyberpunk: cultures of technological embodiment*, London: Sage.

Garfinkel, H. (1967) *Studies in ethnomethodology*, Englewood Cliffs, NJ: Prentice-Hall.

Holdstock, R. (1986) *Ancient Echoes*, London: Collins.

Horkheimer, M. and Adorno, T. W. (1944/1986) *Dialectic of Enlightenment*. London: Verso.

Kafka, F. (1924/1995) "Josefine, die Sängerin"/'Josephine the singer, or The mouse people' in J. A. Underwood (trans.) *Franz Kafka: Stories 1904–1924*, London: Abacus.

Kermode, F. (1967) *The Sense of an Ending: Studies in the Theory of Fiction*, New York: Oxford University Press.

Kermode, F. (1995) 'Waiting for the End', in M. Bull (ed.), *Apocalypse Theory and the Ends of the World*, Oxford: Blackwell.

Kumar, K. (1987) *Utopia and Anti-Utopia in Modern Times*, Oxford: Blackwell.

Kumar, K. (1991) *Utopianism*, Milton Keynes: Open University Press.

Kumar, K. (1993) 'The end of Socialism? The end of Utopia? The end of History?', in K. Kumar and S. Bann (eds), *Utopias and the Millennium*, London: Reaktion.

Lewis, M. (1989) *Liar's Poker*, London: Corgi.

Lewis, M. (1999) *The New New Thing*, London: Hodder and Stoughton.

Lightfoot, G. and Lilley, S. (1999) 'Fixing Futures?' *Emergence* Vol 1:3 pp. 37–50.

Lightfoot, G. and Lilley, S. (forthcoming) 'Trading Narratives?' *Organization*.

Manuel, F. E. (1973) *Utopias and Utopian Thought*, London: Souvenir Press.

Manuel, F. E. and Manuel, F. P. (1971) (eds) *French Utopias: An Anthology of Ideal Societies*, New York: Schoken.

Manuel, F. E. and Manuel, F. P. (1979) *Utopian Thought in the Western World*, Cambridge, MA: Harvard University Press.

Martin, G. R. R. (1998) *A Clash of Kings*, London: Voyager.

McCabe, J. (1998) *Stickleback*, London: Granta.

McHugh, D. (2001) ' "Give me your mirrorshades": science fiction "methodology" meets the social and organizational sciences', in Smith *et al.* (eds) *Science Fiction and Organization*.

More, T. (1516/1965) *Utopia*, trans. P. Turner, Harmondsworth: Penguin.

Morris, P. (1994) (ed.) *The Bakhtin reader: selected writings of Bakhtin, Medvedev and Voloshinov*, London: Edward Arnold.

Orwell, G. (1943/1998) 'Can Socialists be Happy?', originally attributed to John Freeman, *Tribune* (Christmas Issue)/first published as Orwell's work, within P. Davison, 'My Problem with George', *The Observer*, 28th June.

Parker, M., Higgins, M., Lightfoot, G. and Smith, W. (1999) (eds) 'Thematic issue on Organization as Science Fiction' *Organization*, 6 (4).

Pratchett, T. (2001) *Thief of Time*, London: Doubleday.

Ricoeur, P. (1978) 'Explanation and Understanding: On Some Remarkable Connections Among the Theory of the Text, Theory of Action and Theory of History', pp. 149–166 of *The Philosophy of Paul Ricoeur: An Anthology of His Work*, trans. C. E. Reagan and D. Stewart, Boston: Beacon.

Said, E. (1997) *Beginnings: Intention and Method*, London: Granta.

Smith, W., Higgins, M., Parker, M. and Lightfoot, G. (2001) (eds) *Science Fiction and Organization*, London: Routledge.

Stone, R. A. (1995) *The War of Desire and Technology at the Close of the Mechanical Age*, Cambridge: MIT.

Strathern, M. (1991) *Partial Connections*, Savage, MA: Rowman & Littlefield.

Thevenaz, P. (1962) *'What is Phenomenology?' and Other Essays*, trans. J. M. Eadie, Chicago: Quadrangle Books.

Turkle, S. (1995) *Life on the Screen*, London: Weidenfield and Nicholson.

Wachowski, L. and Wachowski, A. (1999) *The Matrix*. Script at http://www.geocities.com/Area51/Capsule/8448/Matrix.txt

Keeping the Black Flag flying: anarchy, utopia and the politics of nostalgia

Patrick Reedy

Introduction

In this chapter I make a case for the rescuing of utopian thinking and writing from its neglect by critics of managerialism. I argue that utopianism provides a stimulus to both critical thinking and practice by its interrogation of the 'good life'. In particular I draw attention to the distinctive features of anarchist utopianism as being worthy of further attention. The chapter begins with an account of the development of utopian thinking, identifying a number of common strands running through the fabric of utopianism. It goes on to apply this framework, firstly to an analysis of the claims made for managerial utopias and then, by way of contrast, to anarchist utopias, where I argue that there are some potentially fruitful points of contact between anarchist and post-structuralist theory. I then discuss William Morris's *News from Nowhere* as an example of the critical value of utopian writing, and as an important influence on anarchist utopianism. Finally some conclusions are drawn regarding the possibilities for the development of utopian thinking by critical organizational theorists.

The good life and how we can achieve it have been central concerns of philosophy and religion from ancient civilizations through to modernity (or even post-modernity). Plato's *Republic* (c.428–347BC/1966), Christ's Sermon on the Mount, Thomas More's *Utopia* (1515–1516/1951), Campanella's *La Citta del Sole* (1623/1962) or Thoreau's *Walden* (1834/1983) are all classic examples, counterbalanced by cautionary dystopias such as Butler's ironic *Erewhon* (1923/1932), Huxley's *Brave New World* (1932), Orwell's *Nineteen Eighty-four* (1948/1954), or Golding's *Lord of the Flies* (1954/1962). This art, of formulating possible answers to what the good life should be through the medium of literature, is the genre of 'Utopia'. This chapter argues that the imaginary and creative construction of utopias can make a contribution to critical thinking about the implicit conception of the 'good life' within managerialist approaches to organization. After all, as Martin Parker suggests in the introduction, an utopian vision of the organization also seems to underlie the 'excellent' company (Peters and Waterman, 1982) or the 'learning organization' (Senge, 1993) and why should the Devil have all the best tunes? What counter-visions can more critical voices offer?

The Left has found utopian narratives of immense importance throughout its history, athough this has faltered in more recent years. The articulation of the good life involves both implicit and explicit critique of prevailing social arrangements (Mannheim, 1936; Levitas, 1990; Bloch, 2000), and this utopian current has not only been of critical value, but has provided models for practical (if usually inglorious) attempts at the communal realization of utopias (Hardy, 2000). Utopianism survived the hostility of Marx; and even Marx and Engels, though critical of what they saw as the neglect of fundamental theoretical analysis within the utopian leanings of Proudhon and Saint-Simon, believed it had the important function of relativizing social reality (Engels, 1908; Wheen, 1999). In other words, utopianism possesses the capacity to de-naturalize the dominant reality by imaginatively transcending what are seen as current material limitations, a trait also evident in more socially aware science fiction (LeGuin, 1974). Critical theory has also deployed utopianism as critique (Benhabib, 1986) and Habermas's 'ideal communication community' is not intended as a fully realizable goal, but rather a counter-reality by which our existing ideologically distorted communication may be evaluated (Habermas, 1984).

Utopia and dystopia may also function critically in their imaginative extrapolation of current conceptions of the good into more fully developed social forms, thus exposing the dangers lurking in our desires. The technocratic, instrumental and rationalistic aspirations of much management theory can thus be held up to critical attention by a comparison with *Brave New World* or *Nineteen Eighty-four* (Willmott, 1993). The remainder of this chapter develops some of these initial thoughts in more depth and attempts to demonstrate the potential of utopian thinking in a critique of a managerial vision of the good life. In particular it explores another neglected strand of social and political thought – anarchist theory. Firstly, because anarchists have demonstrated an incurable fascination with attempts to both delineate and live out the good life (Woodcock, 1963). Secondly, anarchism, with its rejection of hierarchy and authority, has struggled with the problem of how communities may be organized and maintained without these usually ubiquitous features (Kropotkin, 1974; Marshall, 1993). As such, anarchism can be claimed to be a powerful counter-discourse to the managerial vision of the good life – ordered by a benign hierarchy of authorities (Ward, 1974, 1991).

Anarchistic utopias are also distinctive in their defence of the principles of diversity, difference and voluntarism over collective norms and orthodoxies. This suggests potential linkages between post-structuralist thought and anarchistic conceptions of the good life. The fruitful cross-fertilization of post-structuralist and anarchist thinking presents some intriguing possibilities, and suggests a form of political practice suited to the post-modern world (May, 1994). In addition, anarchist utopianism can be powerfully nostalgic, frequently displaying a longing for a past that never was but that should have been. This contrasts a desirable mythical past with the technologically fetishistic narratives of progress associated with recent political projects of both Right and Left, and

170

critiqued by postmodernist theory as demonstrating the inherently oppressive nature of such grand narratives. Such nostalgic longing, far from being an enervating melancholy, has precipitated many practical attempts to rediscover the mythic past in the present. Such attempts may be detected in Spartacus' slave revolt, the Cathar communities of Occitan, the English Peasants' Revolt and the Paris Commune. In more recent times, the environmental and anti-capitalist protests of our own day seem to be at least partly motivated by a desire to return to a pre-Globalized, pre-industrialized Golden Age (Woodcock, 1963; Marshall, 1993).

In the light of the possibilities outlined above I shall next discuss the emergence of utopian thinking in general, and then go on to explore anarchistic utopianism in particular. One such anarchist utopia, *News from Nowhere* by William Morris (1986), is analysed in more detail in order to illustrate some of the characteristic features of utopian anarchist thought. Finally some conclusions are drawn regarding how anarchistic utopianism may help conceive of how 'good' organizations and communities may be unmanaged, constantly renegotiated, and exist solely to meet the needs of their members; providing a counter-attraction to the seductive technocratic paradise being marketed to us by late managerialism.

The founding of Utopia

Utopianism has a long history and was central to the thinking of the Left before Marxism became its dominant theoretical view. Following the long hegemony of 'scientific' socialism, anarchism has largely inherited the utopian mantle. Retracing the history of utopian thinking in order to bridge this discontinuity reveals that many aspects of utopian theory and practice have their roots in the ancient world and have proved themselves surprisingly robust. They have continually returned in different ages in different forms to haunt us with the dream of an ideal world. Kumar (1987) provides a very useful discussion of the nature and origins of utopian thought, beginning by making a distinction between utopianism and the practice of utopia proper. The distinction drawn rests on the difference between thinking and practice motivated by a longing for a better future, and the literary genre of creating fully realized ideal (or cautionary) narrative portraits of the desired future life, partly through the everyday existence of its inhabitants. Thus the reader is invited imaginatively to participate in the life of a fictional community.

The inclusion of dystopian thinking within this definition may seem perverse. However, dystopianism may be considered as another expression of the same impulse as utopianism rather than being an opposing principle. The practice of dystopia is the expression of utopian longing in times which give little hope of its realization. This is another way of saying that pessimism is hope deferred. Dystopian despair is still fuelled by the desire that things should be otherwise, even though the possibility that change could occur seems remote. This is in itself a call to arms, at the least to avoid the worst that could happen. Foucault (1977) is rarely accused of utopianism, but the Panopticon is hardly presented for our amusement or approval, rather there seems an admittedly ambivalent attempt to produce an ethical rejection of disciplinary power on the part of the reader (Griffiths, 1995).

Kumar (1987) and Levitas (1990) argue that utopianism appears to be a universal urge, at least within the Judeo-Christian tradition. As Orwell wrote 'It is the dream of a just society which seems to haunt the human imagination ineradicably and in all ages' (1944:274). Kumar traces the origins of this universal urge to explore the 'good' life through its imaginative reconstruction and identifies several fundamental strands of utopian thought developing from the ancient world. These are worth considering in some detail (see also Burrell and Dale, this volume) as they are still a significant influence on recent utopian thinking and the juxtaposition of these strands appears to affect whether utopias become a stabilizing influence on a given social order or a transformative one.

The first of these strands is that of 'Arcadia', 'a time and place of rustic simplicity and felicity' (Kumar, 1987:3). Arcadian utopias are characterized by harmony between mankind and nature, and the innocence of human society uncorrupted by 'civilization'. Part of this innocence is a natural restraint in the demands made upon Arcadia. Life is simple, uncomplicated and needs are kept as basic as possible as in Thoreau's *Walden* (1834/1983). The most powerful expression of Arcadia within the Western tradition is perhaps the Garden of Eden. More recently eco-utopias have illustrate the enduring appeal of this strand and many anarchist conceptions of the good life also suggest that natural restraint and simplicity are ends that directly contribute to the sum of human happiness. After all, there are two routes to the satisfaction of our desires, one being to seek further means of satisfaction, which might be said to be the path of modernity, but the Arcadian route is essentially to have fewer desires to satisfy.

In contrast with Arcadia is our second strand, exemplified by Plato's 'Republic' in which the city is proposed as the ideal society, a machine for living in where nature, far from being a nurturing womb, is a hostile wilderness to be kept at bay outside the city walls:

> The Hellenic ideal city represented human mastery over nature, the triumph of reason and artifice over the amoral and chaotic realm of nature. Hence the importance, in the ideal city tradition of founders and framers of cities and constitutions, the philosopher-kings, the architect-planners. (Kumar, 1987:4)

It was the Spartan version of the ideal city-state (authoritarian, ascetic, communistic) rather than the Athenian (democratic, tolerant, hedonistic) that became the dominant influence on later European utopias, via Plato's *Republic* and its influence on Thomas More. One might see in this the origins of the managed organization as the ideal social institution. There is an emphasis in city utopias on an authoritarian and regulated communal order, founded by a mythical figure such as Solon of Athens or Lycurgus of Sparta. Moses the law-giver founds the principles on which the Land of Milk and Honey is to be settled. As well as these founding charismatic entrepreneurial philosopher-kings, a subordinate aristocratic caste, trained and disciplined in the techniques of government, figure strongly in the management of these utopias.

> The best society would be the society ruled by the best, those most fitted by training and temperament for the most difficult of all the arts, the art of government. (Plato's *Republic* cited in Kumar, 1987:5)

The third strand of utopian thinking, originating again in the classical world, is that of 'Cockaygne', 'a land of abundance, idleness and instant and unrestrained gratification. . . . found in practically all folk cultures.' (Kumar, 1987:7). Cockaygne has often been used ironically to parody Arcadia, but there is an important distinction between Arcadia and its assumption of scarcity requiring restraint in consumption and Cockaygne's abundance where all needs and desires are satisfied.

> Brueghal painted it in a picture which shows roofs made of cake, a roast pig running round with a knife in its side, a mountain of dumplings, and citizens lying back at their ease waiting for all the good things to drop into their mouths. (Kumar, 1987:9)

Most modern utopias including anarchistic ones are constructed from these three strands in various combinations, but before I discuss this further it is worthwhile introducing the dimensions of time and space into the consideration of the origins of utopian thought. The degree to which utopianism might be considered a force for change or for the maintenance of the status quo is bound up with these dimensions. Utopia may be positioned in the past as a Golden Age from which we have degenerated or, as in Eden, from which we have been cast out because of our folly. Alternatively, utopia may be positioned in the future, the Kingdom of Heaven or the fully communist society, both of which are dependant on various historical events preceding the final revelation. The third temporal alternative is that utopia may be realized or at least instigated in the here and now by political action or simply by the setting up of utopian communities. This is an important plane of cleavage between Marxist and anarchist thought, as communism can only come about at its appointed historical epoch, whereas for anarchists 'an anarchist society, a society which organises itself without authority, is always in existence, like a seed beneath the snow, buried under the weight of the state' (Ward, 1973:11). As Ackroyd's chapter in this volume shows, Mannheim (1936) points out that conservatism attempts to position Utopia firmly in the present as always-already existing, 'you have never had it so good'. The status quo must be preserved, as it is already the best of all possible worlds where history comes to an end (Fukuyama, 1992).

In addition to the temporal positioning of the 'beginning' of utopia, the powerful sense of nostalgic longing integral to the Golden Age in many ways contradicts the common assumption that it is only progress driven by the rejection of the past that is a radical force. According to this view, nostalgia arises from a sense of hopeless defeat and is simultaneously a comforting but also an eviscerating reverie. But as Mannheim (1936) asserts, the utopian mentality always threatens to 'break the bonds of the existing order' and it is its containment in an eternal present that saps the desire for change rather than the longing to return home to where home never was.

By this containment of utopia in the present, societies have been able to incorporate conceptions of completely contradictory and highly desirable ways of life without destabilization as long as they are positioned outside of normal temporal and physical space. For example, medieval society could safely promote the idea of Paradise but only as long as it was outside of society, positioned in the future, beyond the grave. As soon as Paradise became something certain groups attempted actually to construct within that society, as did millenarian heretics such as the Cathars, with their notion of human perfectibility before death, then a violent and repressive response utilizing the full military and ideological resources of Christendom was mobilized. During the Albigensian Crusades from 1208 to 1226 the papacy, aided by the northern French, sent army after army to the region around Albi, in the south of France, to crush the heretics and punish their supporters. Even by the often brutal standards of the times (theirs and ours), the putting to the sword of every inhabitant of substantial towns and cities, simply for the tacit support of heresy, is still shocking (Strayer, 1971).

The same utopian conception positioned within rather than outside the social system took on entirely different implications for the maintenance of the status quo. This example also illustrates the potential for seemingly the most socially stabilizing of nostalgic utopian conceptions to be developed in a radical and transformative direction. For example, The Peasant's Revolt, in the 14th Century, was at least partly inspired by a mythical lost Golden Age of ancient liberties guaranteed by the King. (Bennett, 1987). The Revolt radicalized nostalgia for the paradise of Eden with the slogan 'When Adam delved and Eve span, who was then the gentleman?' In this case the utopia was removed in time but was seen to be the normal state of current society with the actual conditions experienced being aberrant. This ability of utopianism to turn 'official' myths designed to maintain the *status quo* into myths that threaten the social order is often overlooked by those who characterize utopianism as a form of melancholic passivity. It also presents the possibility that the utopian pretensions of managerialism can not only be used as a critique according to their own criteria but also re-framed as a demand for the reality behind the sham (Parker, 1998).

The 19th century saw some profound shifts in Utopian thinking, including a shift in the temporal positioning of utopias. With the Enlightenment's emphasis on the individual, utopias now have to be able to provide for the development and differentiation of individuality as well as a stable communal order. Advances in science and technology seem to promise abundance to satisfy a more extended and diverse set of human needs and desires, re-introducing an element of Cockaygne into utopian thought. More's *Utopia*, written in the 15th century, was based on a static and limited conception of human needs, those it is possible to satisfy by six hours communal labour per day. By the 19th century, Rousseau believed that the purpose of utopia was to lead to the optimum state of human consciousness (Kumar, 1987; Marshall, 1993). As the desires of differentiated individuals must now be satisfied, so too must Utopia accommodate them by being open-ended and dynamic.

> Human nature was now seen to be in a process of constant and continuous formation and growth, as protean and changeable as human society itself. It had to be conceived as potentiality, as a striving for fulfilment in a mental and material world that had no limits. (Kumar, 1987:47)

The Golden Age was now firmly positioned in the future. According to Marx, the historical process unfolds towards a communist utopia through a series of stages of development. Thus utopia is still possibly distant in time but guaranteed by a scientifically determined process of historical materialism (Mannheim, 1936; Wheen, 1999). Anarchist conceptions of utopia, however, have continued to display a more complex temporal character with the amalgam of past, present and future strategically deployed in their critique of current arrangements, a characteristic evident in Morris, as I will demonstrate later in the chapter.

The high optimism of European revolutionary movements in the mid-19th century, whose members hoped for the imminent collapse of the imperial and capitalist order, left little time for the reflective construction of fully realized fictional utopias, but by the end of the century, this hope was fading and the literary utopia begins to re-emerge, suggesting that the genre of utopias may provide a way of remembering and redefining emancipatory projects in those times least propitious to their realization. The period spanning the first and second world wars and their aftermath, not surprisingly, gave rise to more dystopias than otherwise and the only seemingly historically realized utopias of the United States and the Soviet Union gave little encouragement for utopian thinking. The 1960s' counter culture, however, gave rise to a new flowering of utopian experiments and thinking, with the anarchist tradition the clear inheritor of utopian practice. Indeed, since the 1960s, anarchist influence has been growing and a plausible argument can be constructed for it having more relevance to post-industrial radicalism than more traditional forms of Marxism. One striking example of this trend is the growth in environmentalism and green political theory which have re-introduced a note of the restrained, harmonious Arcadia as the various drawbacks of Cockaygnian hedonism have made themselves felt (see Fournier, this volume).

It is not only those who long for fundamental changes to society who have been rediscovering the lost shores of Utopia. Management gurus have also unearthed the deep-seated appeal of utopian conceptions and have begun to present their own visions of the ideal society, usually closely identified with the business organization. In the next few paragraphs, I attempt to evaluate one such vision and use the utopian vocabulary developed above in order to position and critique Managerialist utopias within the wider genre of utopian writing.

Managerialist utopias

Increasingly, mainstream management writing has shifted in its delineation of the ideal organization from the Taylorist efficient machine, in which all know their place and proper function (which in itself has elements of the ideal City State), to one which far more explicitly suggests that the complete immersion of the individual in the organization leads directly to personal fulfilment. These strongly utopian claims can and should be subjected to critique within their own terms and as an example of the utopian genre. For by their utopias shall ye know them.

In order to illustrate my argument I shall examine the claims of one particular expression of this strongly managerial utopian current, as found in *The Fifth Discipline* (Senge, 1999). Senge recounts something of a conversion from seeing the public sector as the agent for the development of a progressive society to seeing the business organization as the driving force, and in particular the emergence of the 'learning organization', where 'people continually expand their capacity to create the results they truly desire, where new and expansive patterns of thinking are nurtured, where collective aspirations are set free, and where people are continually learning how to learn together' (1999:3). The emergence of the learning organization is seen as part of a natural historical process in the developed world where affluence for the 'majority' has brought about a rejection of an instrumental attitude to work. Instead, we are all seeking to build organizations 'that are more consistent with man's higher aspirations' (1999:5). Such aspirations appear to include righting social injustice through the development of a broader sense of corporate responsibility. Strangely there is a strong reminder of Marxist utopian thought here, at least in its rhetorical appeal to a historical process leading to the realization of a new and better society. However, the implicit conservatism of the temporal positioning of this realization not as something to be hoped for but as something already achieved has already been discussed.

Senge makes a great play of the fulfilment of humanity's higher aspirations through the learning organization but is a little coy about spelling out what these aspirations are, so the reader is left to infer them from the prescriptions suggested by the book. These prescriptions turn out to be the main subject matter as they are the eponymous five disciplines. An examination of them seems to imply that our highest aspirations involve the complete identification of our own selves with that of our work, and in this case the only 'work' that counts is that done in an organization. Essentially, Senge appears to adopt the same idea of humanity's highest aspiration as that proposed by Peters and Waterman, which is 'to be a conforming member of a winning team and to be a star in his own right' (Peters and Waterman, 1982:*xxiii*).

Senge claims that, so powerful are his disciplines, that the problem of the work/life balance is to be solved by the annihilation of the distinction. For example, 'personal mastery' will make us better parents and in turn better managers because 'the real skills of leadership . . . are the skills of effective parenting.' (1999:310). The various 'disciplines' all reinforce the centrality of this concept. The 'discipline of personal mastery' (1999:8) is explicitly linked to a complete commitment to one's work. That of working with 'mental models' requires 'turning the mirror inward' (1999:9) in order to adjust ones attitudes and thoughts to conformity with the learning organization. 'Building a shared vision' requires a collective understanding that fosters 'genuine commitment and enrolment rather than compliance' (1999:9).

Utilizing a critical utopian analysis, it appears that the means and ends have been fully integrated but, in this case, the means of being a fully committed member of the organization are also the aspirational end within which every individual will find fulfilment. For example, Senge suggests that the experience of being a member of a 'great team' will 'stand out as singular periods of life lived to the fullest. Some spend the rest of their lives looking for ways to recapture that spirit.' (1999:13). We are, in fact, to be so intoxicated by the process of 'doing' work that its effects and purposes disappear entirely from view. Yet these techniques are to be the preserve of those fitted for government, and may only be entrusted to the rigorously trained few, those selected for Senge's 'leadership and mastery workshops' aimed at those 'in leadership positions of importance' (1999:16).

So what sort of Utopia are we being invited to embrace? We have elements of a hierarchical Spartan city-state in the ideal business organization, ruled over by a beneficent managerial elite. The individual finds total fulfilment in their allotted job. The conservatism of this utopia is startling. We have already arrived at the ideal community, all that is needed is to refine and extend it to the four corners of the Earth. Despite the rhetoric of change, development and learning, the static conception of the needs and desires of humanity is also striking. Work itself is not to be transformed but the individual will be, through learning 'commitment'. Not only this, but all work is to be considered worthy of this total commitment, whether it is that of managing or of flipping burgers, and there is no ethical/aesthetic evaluation of what kinds of work are socially necessary or give opportunity for the exercise of artistry. When contrasted with the expansive, dynamic, and aesthetically sensitive utopia of Morris, the managerial vision is revealed in all its insipid vulgarity and mean-spiritedness.

If the Learning Organization is the most inspirational utopian vision that managerialism can construct, then its influence can only be attributed to the lack of more attractive alternative visions. Now is perhaps not the time to leave this genre to management consultants, for recent history makes it quite clear what sort of institutions have the words '*Arbeit Macht Frei*' above their gates. In order to support my admittedly sweeping criticism, I shall turn to anarchist utopian thinking in order to contrast the poverty of the managerial conception of utopia with an altogether more complex and attractive one.

Anarchism and utopia

How then does anarchist thought relate to utopianism? The first point to note is that there is a wide variety of anarchist thinking from the extreme individualism of Stirner to the patriarchal anarchist communism of Proudhon. The following remarks attempt to sketch out basic principles that most, but certainly not all, anarchists would generally accede to. A fairly typical and sympathetic definition of anarchism is that:

> All anarchists reject the legitimacy of external government and of the State, and condemn imposed political authority, hierarchy and domination. They seek to establish the condition of anarchy, that is to say, a decentralized and self-regulating society consisting of a federation of voluntary associations of free and equal individuals. The ultimate goal of anarchism is to create a free society which allows all human beings to realize their full potential. (Marshall, 1993:3)

Alternatively, anarchism is 'a system of social thought, aiming at fundamental changes in the structure of society and particularly. . . . at the replacement of the authoritarian state by some form of non-governmental cooperation between free individuals' (Woodcock, 1963:11). In other words, utopianism is at the centre of anarchism.

Anarchists regard a lack of authority and hierarchy as a natural state of affairs for human society and as having been the lived experience for most people most of the time in the commonest form of human institution – the small community. Despite the obvious restrictions of many traditional communities from a modern perspective,

> they show that the Hobbesian nightmare of universal war in a 'state of nature' is a myth. A society without hierarchy in the form of rulers and leaders is not a utopian dream but an integral part of collective human experience. Anarchists wish to combine the ancient patterns of co-operation and mutual aid of these organic societies with a modern sense of individuality and personal autonomy.' (Marshall, 1993:13)

Although anarchism as a distinctive political philosophy traces its history back to William Godwin's *Enquiry Concerning Political Justice* (Marshall, 1986), it emerges as distinct from other forms of radicalism and particularly Marxism in the 19th century. Indeed, this separation was accelerated by the expulsion of Bakunin and fellow anarchists from the First International at the instigation of Marx (Woodcock, 1963; Marshall, 1993; Wheen, 1999). Despite this, anarchism does share a significant common inheritance with Marxist Socialism, in particular its belief in the perfectibility of human society and the rejection of the oppression, inequality and suffering caused by Capitalism.

Anarchism has not had a good press, and a variety of elected political leaders have recently been queuing up to denounce 'anarchist extremists' following recent large-scale protests against global Capitalism, but nevertheless I believe that anarchism is worth the serious consideration of critical organizational thinkers for a number of reasons. Firstly anarchism may be regarded as something of a submerged discourse within radical intellectual currents. It is perhaps not surprising that capitalist governments have been hostile to it, but anarchist movements have also been savagely suppressed by Marxist political parties. Orwell's (1986) account of the elimination of the anarchist militia 'POUM' in the Spanish Civil War provides an example of what was a wholesale suppression of anarchism by the Soviet Union. Politically incorporated left-wing parties and Trade Unions have also been hostile, not least because of the fundamental difference on the issue of representation. This hostility from both wings of political orthodoxy raises the question of whether anarchism might provide a more credible radical 'third way' than the one currently in vogue. The very vehemence with which it is dismissed suggests that there might be something worth considering.

Secondly, anarchism is a failed movement that refuses to lie down and accept the fact. Indeed, there has been a convergence with anarchist thinking on the part of the activist Left following disillusionment with the aftermath of the Russian and Chinese Revolutions. Anarchist critique from Bakunin onwards warned that new forms of authoritarianism would arise from the vanguard tactics of Marx and, sadly, this now appears to be widely confirmed by history. That anarchism was able to predict this when other radical traditions were not, implies that its theoretical foundations are worthy of more serious analysis. Thirdly, Anarchism's rich history and the re-emergence of its thinking and forms of organization make it arguably the one radical tradition that appears to be flourishing in the post-modern era. Anarchist praxis seems to provide the motive force for a number of diverse but dynamic protest movements and other forms of resistance to late Capitalism. From the activities of the Situationists in 1968 to the current anti-capitalist protests, or political movements such as the Zapatistas, a resurgent anarchist sensibility is evident. (Marshall, 1993; Klein, 2000). Finally, anarchism deserves to receive more serious academic attention as a political and social philosophy. It has a number of distinctive features that attracted the scorn and ridicule of 'scientific' socialism. These very features, however, following the perceived failures of the 'scientific' route, seem to make it worth reconsideration, particularly as anarchism appears to provide a more fruitful approach to linking radical ethical and political projects to post-structuralist theory. (May, 1994; Call, 1999)

In order to offer support for at least some of the above assertions, I shall outline several key features of anarchist thought, emphasizing an intriguing compatibility between anarchism and post-modernism. To start with the obvious, anarchists reject the State and ascribe many of the ills of humanity to this institution.

> To be governed is to be watched over, inspected, spied on, directed, legislated, regimented, closed in, indoctrinated, preached at, controlled, assessed, evaluated, censored, commanded; all by creatures that have neither the right, nor wisdom, nor virtue ... To be governed means that at every move, operation or transaction one is noted,

registered, entered in a census, taxed, stamped, priced, assessed, patented, licensed, authorized, recommended, admonished, prevented, reformed, set right, corrected. Government means to be subjected to tribute, trained, ransomed, exploited, monopolized, extorted, pressured, mystified, robbed; all in the name of public utility and the general good. Then at the first sign of resistance or word of complaint, one is repressed, fined, despised, vexed, pursued, hustled, beaten up, garrotted, imprisoned, shot, machine-gunned, judged, sentenced, deported, sacrificed, sold, betrayed, and to cap it all, ridiculed, mocked, outraged, and dishonoured. That is government, that is its justice and morality. (Proudhon, 1851 cited in Marshall, 1993:20)

This rejection of the State is far from being a naïve ascription of all evil to a single source, at its root lies a more subtle and wholesale rejection of the notion of representation (May, 1994). Godwin originated the idea that no individual can legitimately represent another. This includes any idea of a universal consent given to a body of laws or rules on the basis of election or taxation. This principle was also at the heart of the dispute between Bakunin and Marx, the idea of even a temporary 'dictatorship of the proletariat' was anathema to the anarchists. The claim that a vanguard party would better know the 'true' interests of the working-class than they did themselves was regarded as a direct route to new forms of tyranny and oppression. (Marshall, 1993)

Equally significantly, the rejection of representation extends to the level of the micro-political. Kropotkin wrote that 'we refuse to assume a right which moralists have always taken upon themselves of mutilating the individual in the name of some ideal' (Kroptokin, 1970 cited in May, 1994:48). To provide people with images of who they are, or who they should be, is to damage their ability to decide this for themselves. (May, 1994). Likewise the rejection of the principle of hierarchy in anarchism goes beyond the obvious and extends into looking beyond a top-down, centralized understanding of the operation of power and recognizes the need to 'widen the field of politics' (May, 1994:50). 'The picture of power and struggle that emerges in the anarchist perspective is one of intersecting networks of power rather than of hierarchy' (Ward, 1973:26). Thus resistance should occur at multiple sites in diverse ways for local results, rather than seeking to sever the head of the body politic and replace it with another. 'There is no final struggle, only a series of partisan struggles on a variety of fronts.' (Ward, 1973:26).

Anarchist thinkers have also taken a distinctive position on means and ends. Whereas for Marx the means of the dictatorship of the proletariat was justified by the end of full communism, anarchists have been much more distrustful of the oppressive potential of using power in this way. In fact anarchists tend not to make a distinction between ends and means. Thus means are always 'ends in the making' (Ward, 1973; Marshall, 1993). Whilst the typical anarchist tactics of community experiments, civil disobedience, protest, passive resistance and so on frequently appear not to achieve an ultimate end, they are nevertheless in themselves anarchic and are a challenge to dominant ways of thinking. They are a way of nurturing the submerged anarchist society that is always there under the surface.

Without leadership, hierarchy and representation, how can anarchists organize beyond small groups? The answer has usually been federalism. 'Federation . . . is an agreement by which one or several communes, one or several groups of communes or states, find themselves by mutual and equal agreements for one or several determinate aims.' (Proudhon, 1863 cited in Edwards, 1970). The distinctive feature of federalism is that diverse types of community voluntarily combine where necessary into a federation and may select delegates to attend on their behalf. However all authority remains within the community which is in no way bound to the decisions of the federation but can leave it at anytime. In Kropotkin's words, federations would be 'an interwoven network, composed of an infinite variety of groups and federations of all sizes and degrees, local, regional, national and international – temporary or more or less permanent – for all possible purposes' (Marshall, 1993:326). The other basic unit of organization is the commune. Kropotkin, Bakunin, Tolstoy, and Ghandi all drew inspiration from peasant or craft communes as already possessing many of the features of anarchist communes linked to others by loose federations. For example, Kropotkin writes admiringly of the peasant '*obshchina*' as a utopian model. (Kropotkin, 1873). Kropotkin develops this idea further, however, so that the commune is no longer a geographically bounded traditional ascriptive community but 'a generic name, a synonym for the grouping of equals, knowing neither frontiers nor walls. The social commune will soon cease to be a clearly defined whole. Each group of the commune will necessarily be drawn towards other similar groups in other communes; it will be grouped and federated with them by links as solid as those which attach it to its fellow citizens, and will constitute a commune of interests whose members are scattered in a thousand towns and villages.' (cited in Marshall, 1993:326)

The overriding principles of these communities are voluntarism and diversity. Membership is not exclusive and individuals may leave and seek membership of alternative ways of living and constructing their selves through different forms of community. Arcadia, Cockaynge and the Ideal City may all be present and flourishing in an anarchist utopia. It is no coincidence that feminists often display an affinity for anarchist ideas both because of a shared recognition that power is more than simply a question of economics and class (patriarchy is both more than these questions and different to them) and because of the potential for the recognition of diverse ways of living with and relating to each other. Emma Goldman, who gave anarchism an explicitly feminist analysis, first stressed that the personal is the political in the 1940s and feminist communitarians have since drawn on anarchist utopianism (for example see Brown, 1991; Friedman, 1992) .

Finally anarchism has struggled more openly than most utopian mentalities with the problem of regulation of behaviour. In a society where no individual can be bound by rules, how does one deal with individuals whose choices result in harm to others or whose behaviour limits the choices that others can make? Anarchists tend to assume that with the distorting effects of the Law and inequality removed there will be much less cause of such behaviour, but recognize that conflict and unruly passions are an ineradicable element of the human condition. However, prescriptive or institutionalized means of deterring or punishing violence, abuse, and other forms of anti-social behaviour are seen to make the effects of such behaviour more damaging than doing nothing. Despite this, various ways of dealing with problems have been suggested, including 'leaving alone', community juries, ejection from the community, or the influence of community norms and disapproval. The problems with all of these are frequently discussed within anarchist debates and perhaps appropriately, any suggested solutions are never presented as a final answer. Nevertheless what may from one perspective seem a fatal flaw, a failure to produce a coherent system of ethics, from another can be perceived as a vindication of the anarchist principle. If social practices never become institutionalized then they are always debatable, provisional and can be re-negotiated. The ideal anarchist community is a dynamic one, where groups and individuals can extend the realm of freedom to include the determination of needs and desires within consensual social relations.

Rather than develop anarchist theory further in the abstract, and in the utopian spirit of this chapter, the following pages attempt to outline what such principles might lead to in terms of the lived experience of an idealized anarchist society. In the spirit of the radical deployment of nostalgia I shall employ an unfashionable artefact of high Victorian romanticism as my example.

An anarchist utopia: going Nowhere

William Morris's *News from Nowhere* was first published in 1887, according to the author as a way of imaginatively resolving debates within the circle of the 'Socialist League'. I would be reluctant to suggest that Morris was an anarchist, as it was something he himself denied. Nevertheless Morris both knew and liked Kropotkin, had regular contact with anarchists through the Socialist League and, in his seeking inspiration for the ideal community in the medieval peasant and artisan's communes, shows a strong affinity for anarchist thinking rather than Marx's 'scientific' socialism. Because of this anarchists have often taken Morris to be one of their own and *News from Nowhere* is frequently discussed as an archetypal anarchist utopia. (Woodcock, 1963; Marshall, 1993)

The book is probably best read alongside Morris's *A Dream of John Ball* which describes how the author finds himself in a Kentish medieval village on the eve of the peasants' march to London to demand an end of villainage. Morris's rejection of the 19th century notion of progress is reflected in his unfavourable comparison of the oppressed but relatively free and wholesome life of the 14th century medieval peasant with that of the industrial worker, particularly through his aesthetic preference for medieval craftsmanship over the vulgar perfectionism of mass-produced factory goods. A similar narrative device is used in 'Nowhere' where the narrator finds himself transported into a utopian future. He awakes in his bed but soon realizes that all has changed about him.

Morris attempts to describe his new world in its social relations, the natural and constructed environment and the effects of the new social arrangements on the identity, character, and physical appearance of its inhabitants. It has to be said that his delineation of character and attempts at dialogue grate in their mawkishness, and despite his obvious intention of describing equality between the sexes, his female characters are presented in a way that many would now find horribly trivial and patronizing. However, in other respects, his vision of the new world is one of the few pieces of utopian writing to display a high degree of artistic merit. There are also some good jokes, such as the defunct Houses of Parliament being used by the new society as a dung store.

The plot, such as it is, consists of the narrator's befriending some citizens of Nowhere in the communal house he wakes up in. He is taken by his new friends to visit 'Old Hammond' who is both something of a historian and old enough to personally remember the transition to the new society in the 20th century. The journey into London enables Morris to describe how the ugliness of industrial civilization has been cleared away both from the physical city and from the appearance and behaviour of its inhabitants. Morris's aesthetic sense enables him to make a proto-environmentalist critique of the destructiveness of industrialization. The conversation between the narrator and Hammond is a device to describe the revolutionary events which have lead to the new society; these events follow broadly Marxist historical doctrine. After this conversation, the narrator is taken by his friends up the course of the Thames on a 'hay-making' holiday. This is once more a plot device which enables Morris to describe his beloved upper Thames as far as his own house above Oxford, 'Kelmscott'. This device also enables him to describe the life of the country, having already described the life of the city, through a series of conversations, incidents and observations which occur as part of the journey. Finally, having reached journey's end, the narrator finds himself transported back to the squalor and degradation of the 19th century, which seem all the more appalling and unnecessary by comparison with the world he has been forced to leave.

It is an act of vandalism to treat the story as a source of anarchist social theory, particularly as part of the point of utopian writing is for the reader to engage and imaginatively participate in the everyday life of an artistic creation. As such Morris's lovingly described buildings, clothes, scenery, and work are themselves a seduction to accept the possible reality of Nowhere and to regard the contemporary scene as irrational, temporary and insubstantial. Readers need to immerse themselves in the original before the following observations will seem much more than trite and banal. This is in itself an indication of the limitations of academic writing in exploring alternative realities. Nevertheless, doomed though it is, I shall plough on regardless.

Morris partly uses Nowhere to describe an ideal future society, but he also uses this future society as a vantage point for evaluating 19th century industrial Britain. The narrator's own assumptions about society frequently cause confusion in Nowhere, as, for example, when he tries to pay for goods offered freely to him. His stock objections to the absence of laws, punishment, compulsory education, extrinsic motivation for work, a division of labour, the absence of money and so on simply appear ridiculous to the inhabitants of Nowhere. He rather finds himself eventually embarrassed into reticence about the nonsensical arrangements of his own time. What would appear as serious constraints to a free, harmonious and fulfilled existence simply disappear within this new reality.

In terms of the earlier typology of utopias, Morris manages to incorporate elements of all three strands and to position Nowhere out of a realistic sense of temporal sequence by combining idealized features of medieval society with those of a future world. One of the striking features of this relativization of the 'reality' of the capitalist order is the way in which the Nowherians regard the Middle Ages as more relevant, admirable and closer to them than Victorian Britain. Woodcock remarks that Nowhere creates a sense in the reader that they have 'passed into a continuum where ordinary time relationships have ceased: The Middle Ages are in fact more real to the inhabitants of Nowhere than the chronologically much nearer nineteenth century. The idea of progress as a necessary good has vanished, and all happens, not in the harsh white light of perfection, which Morris denies, but in the mellow stillness of a long summer afternoon.' (1963:21). The inhabitants of Nowhere find their fulfilment in the simple acts of everyday life, functional and creative work have fused so that the building of houses or boats, the making of clothing or simple household objects enable the expression of artistry and individuality and are freely exchanged. Nowhere is a very beautiful place where natural landscapes, buildings, agriculture and the inhabitants mutually adorn each other. 'Property' is not so much held in common as it is completely defunct.

Most machinery has been abandoned as being a source of destruction of pleasurable and beautiful work. However, Nowhere is technologically sophisticated where it needs to be. Automated barges carrying heavy goods ply the canals, powered by a system the narrator is not knowledgeable enough to understand. Manual labour is looked on as a communal holiday or a chance to engage in pleasurable physical skills and exercise. Although there is very little crime (none, given the complete absence of laws), impulsive violence does sometimes still break out, usually as a result of the complexities of human relationships. One conversation the narrator becomes involved in centres on how a community is to deal with a killing resulting from a fight caused by romantic jealousy. The solution seems to be that the killer, full of remorse, will be provided with solitude at his own request. The main concern of his friends is the welfare of the killer and the third member of the triangle, there are no thoughts of vengeance or of punishment. Nevertheless there are dangers in this Heaven on Earth. There are grumblers who look with nostalgia on the industrial age without an awareness of its accompanying evils. The study of history is dying out with so many more pleasurable activities and some of the narrator's older conversationalists worry that old evils may return as a result. There is also a worry that eventually work will run out, but the remedy for this appears to be that the fusion of work with artistry makes work itself as inexhaustible as the human imagination. Even this 'fear' serves to invert our usual reaction to work as something irksome to be avoided. These fears also strengthen the sense that this new society is a dynamic one and still developing, along with the individuals who occupy it.

What is the significance of Morris's vision for a discussion of the place of utopia in any radical approach to organization? Morris combines both high Victorian Romanticism with Marxist theory and manages to create a utopia for anarchists, albeit at times lurching into cloying sentimentality. There seems to be both an attempt to strengthen the desire for a new order, but also to educate that desire with an aesthetic and social sensibility, partly in response to what he saw as Edward Bellamy's vulgarized 'Cockney Paradise' of *Looking Backwards*, to which Nowhere was partly published as a response. (Kumar, 1987; Levitas, 1990). In doing this, Nowhere tries to stimulate action in the here and now that will lead to this desirable state rather than a new tyranny. However, Morris is concerned in anarchistic fashion that the action that is taken leads to the sort of ends that can truly result in the good life. For Morris this means the full development of the aesthetic capability.

By imaginatively transcending the limitations of his own time Morris tries to demonstrate that the seemingly unarguable objections to the practicality of such a political project are simply the result of thinking limited by current rather than possible social conditions. There is, of course, a danger that such a 'dream' invites a retreat from dealing with current problems into quietism, a passive longing for a far off future beyond our reach. This danger Morris tries to head off with his dialogue with 'Old Hammond', historically linking the new with the old through the political action required to transform society. Perhaps the key point is that such a utopia makes order and organization work to fulfil the needs and desires of individuals, without hierarchy and authority seeming 'real'. Whether the form it takes in Nowhere is one we find seductive is not the point, although the rediscovery of Morris by the Green Movement implies that this is not simply a Victorian literary museum piece. If power and knowledge are inextricably interwoven, so that thinking and practices are also intersecting threads on a web, then flights of imagination may stimulate both counter-knowledges and counter-praxis. The challenge is to write new utopias that will aid this project in our own times for Nowhere, as with all Utopias, was written as a response to its own times and conditions, and new expressions of utopia are needed for our own times.

Some conclusions

Those of us who identity ourselves with critical intellectual currents or emancipatory politics inhabit a world which is imbued with a sense of the defeat of radicalism. There seem to be few indications of a turn in the tide of a triumphant managerial capitalism, and there are few political projects, following the critiques of post-modernism, to which intellectuals can lend unequivocal support.

In some respects radical academic activity in recent years mirrors that of another utopian institution; the monasteries in the dark ages. We have retreated into closed orders where we generate arcane theory and use our comfortable positions to point out the theoretical shortcomings of the more risky efforts of others to bring about change, but more positively we also preserve a mode of thinking and critique which has all but disappeared from more public spaces.

Utopianism is a challenge to this comfortable intellectual quietism. It enables the most remote possibility to be considered as an experienced reality through the power of narrative. When combined with anarchism it enables a resurgent political philosophy and praxis to be considered as a way of thinking about organization. Anarchists have struggled both practically and theoretically to construct a way of thinking about organization that does not rely on either bureaucratic authority or on the hidden hand of cultural self-disciplinary control. Our conceptions of the 'good' organization are then no longer restricted by the 'possible' organization and to envisage the utopian organization makes it seem more possible. However, to take utopianism seriously removes the defence of 'realism' from us. We cannot refuse the question 'Well what would you replace it with?' Anarchists have sometimes blamed the refusal of Marxism to answer this question for the failure of communist revolutions. Without any clear sense of where such revolutions were headed, it is argued, it was inevitable that they would revert to existing models of authoritarian organization. If this is the case, it may be that there is an ethical imperative on the part of intellectuals to do more than critique, and the imaginative construction of utopias is one possible avenue to answer the question.

The serious consideration of counter-realities is not just a way of speculating about the 'good life'. It is also a powerful technique of critique in its own right. By rendering current reality as both undesirable and absurd, attempts to bring about change are stimulated and are likely to be more sustained and to expand the existing spheres of autonomy and authenticity. As anarchists insist on the integration of ends and means then practice, including the production of knowledge, is also an end in itself. Anarchist utopianism, because of its affinity with areas of post-structuralist thought, may also offer a more fruitful rapprochement of ethics, practice and theory than existing debates between post-structuralists and critical theorists. Post-structuralism can provide the theoretical case for a non-essentialist anarchist philosophy whilst anarchism can provide a compatible form of praxis. Because of this possibility anarchist theory deserves much more serious consideration by critical organization scholars. Even though we are supposedly far too sophisticated to swallow 19th century Marxism whole, as an infallible orthodoxy, yet we still seem to retain an unreflective contempt for utopian and anarchist thinking.

To end this chapter of a wildly utopian note, the genre of utopianism may provide an escape from the sometimes stultifying cul-de-sac of academic writing. It invites the use of imagination, emotion, wit and artistry in our work and frees us from the medieval practice of needing to endlessly quote the authority of acknowledged 'masters' before we dare to state an opinion. It is a genre capable of integrating rigorous critique with an aesthetic sensibility which in turn enables judgements concerning the validity of what we write from the viewpoint of everyday experience. It suggests one way of opening up our writing to a wider audience and enabling the re-engagement of academic endeavour with the desire for an ideal society.

Bibliography

Benhabib, S. (1986) *Critique, norm and utopia: a study of the foundations of critical theory*. New York: Columbia University Press.

Bennett, H. (1987) *Life on the English Manor. A Study of Peasant Conditions 1150–1400*. Gloucester: Alan Sutton.

Bloch, E. (2000) *The Spirit of Utopia*, Stanford University Press.

Brown, H. (1991) *Women Organising*. London: Taylor & Francis Books Ltd.

Butler, S. (1932) *Erewhon*. London: Dent.

Call, L. (1999) 'Anarchy in the Matrix: Postmodern Anarchism in the Novels of William Gibson and Bruce Sterling.' *Anarchist Studies* 7: 99–117.

Campanella, T. (1981) *Città del Sole*. Berkeley and los Angeles: University of California Press.

Edwards, S., Ed. (1970) *Selected Writings of Proudhon*. London: MacMillan.

Engels, F. (1908) *Development of Socialism from Utopia to Science*. Eclin Gargh: Socialist Labour Press.

Foucault, M. (1977) *Discipline and Punish: The Birth of the Prison*. London: Allen Lane.

Friedman, M. (1992) Feminism and Modern Friendship: Dislocating the Community. *Communitarianism and Individualism*. S. Avineri and A. Avner de-Shalit. Oxford: Oxford University Press: 101–119.

Fukuyama, F. (1992) *The End of History and the Last Man*. Harmondsworth: Penguin.

Golding, W. (1962) *Lord of the Flies*. London: Faber.

Habermas, J. (1984) *The Theory of Communicative Action Volume 1: Reason and the Rationalization of Society*. Boston: Beacon Press.

Hardy, D. (2000) *Utopian England: Community Experiments 1900–1945*, E & FN Spon.

Huxley, A. (1932) *Brave New World*. London: Chatto & Windus.

Kropotkin, P. (1873) Must we occupy ourselves with an examination of the ideal of a future system? *Peter Kropotkin: Fugitive Writings: The Collected Works of Peter Kropotkin*. G. Woodcock. London: Black Rose Books. 10: 13–69.

Kropotkin, P. (1974) *Fields, Factories and Workshops Tomorrow*. London: Allen & Unwin.

Kumar, K. (1987) *Utopia and Anti-Utopia in Modern Times*. Oxford: Blackwell.

LeGuin (1974) *The Dispossessed*. London: Gollancz.

Levitas, R. (1990) *The Concept of Utopia*. New York: Philip Allan.

Mannheim, K. (1936) *Ideology and Utopia*. London: Routledge & Regan Paul.

Marshall, P., Ed. (1986) *The Anarchist Writings of William Godwin*. London: Freedom Press.

Marshall, P. (1993) *Demanding the Impossible: a History of Anarchism*. London: Fontana.

May, T. (1994) *The Political Philosophy of Poststructuralist Anarchism*. Pennsylvania: Pennsylvania State University Press.

More, T. (1951) *Utopia and a dialogue of comfort*. London: Dent.

Morris, W. (1986) News from Nowhere. *Three Works by William Morris*. London: Lawrence and Wishart.

Orwell, G. (1944) Arthur Koestler. *The Collected Essays, Journalism and Letters of George Orwell, Volume III As I Please, 1943–1945*. S. Orwell and I. Angus. Harmondsworth: Penguin: 267–282.

Orwell, G. (1954) *Nineteen eighty-four*. London: Penguin.

Parker, M. (1998) 'Organisation, Community and Utopia.' *Studies in Cultures, Organisations and Societies* 4: 71–91.

Peters, T. and Waterman, R. (1982) *In Search of Excellence: lessons from America's best-run companies.* New York: Harper Collins.

Plato (1966) *Plato's Republic.*

Senge, P. (1993) *The Fifth Discipline: the art and practice of the learning organization.* London: Century Business.

Strayer, J. (1971) *The Albigensian Crusades.* New York: The Dial P.

Thoreau, H. (1983) *Walden and Civil Disobedience.* London: Harmondsworth, Penguin.

Ward, C. (1973) *Anarchy in Action.* London: Allen & Unwin.

Ward, C. (1974) *Utopia.*, London: Allen & Unwin.

Ward, C. (1991) *Influences, Voices of Creative Consent.* Bideford: Green Books.

Wheen, F. (1999) *Karl Marx.* London: Fourth Estate.

Wilmott, H. (1993) 'Strength is Ignorance; Slavery is Freedom: Managing Culture in Modern Organisations.' *Journal of Management Studies* 30: 515–552.

Woodcock, G. (1963) *Anarchism: A History of Libertarian Ideas and Movements.* London: Penguin.

Utopianism and the cultivation of possibilities: grassroots movements of hope

Valérie Fournier

On endings and openings

Following the anti-capitalist demonstrations at Seattle, representatives of the most powerful Western states and corporations – Tony Blair, Bill Clinton and corporate executives such as Bill Gates and Nike CEO Phil Knight – met in Davos, Switzerland, to outline a 'Third Way' that was to give global capitalism a new conscience. The 'third way' went something like: 'Globalization is the wave of the future. But globalization is leaving the majority behind. Those voices spoke out in Seattle. It's time to bring the fruits of globalization and free trade to the many' (Bello, 2000:6). So if we are to believe our state and corporate leaders, the answer to the devastating effects of globalization on the most disenfranchised is to throw in more globalization and free trade (Korten, 1995). It is as if no amount of protest about the wreckage caused by market liberalism can shake off the faith in its promise, or at least in its inevitability. We, or at least some of us, seem to have become unable to conceive of anything other than global capitalism as the solution to everything, including the problems it itself creates. This sense of closure is maybe best captured by Fukuyama's (1992) end of history thesis. According to Fukuyama, the collapse of the Berlin Wall has shown us the true path and paved the way for the triumph of capitalism and liberal democracy, 'We cannot picture to ourselves a world that is essentially different from the present one, and at the same time better' (Fukuyama, 1992:46, see also Grey and Garsten, this volume).

This inability to conceive of anything different seems indeed to be spreading like a disease among the political class, the media and intellectuals (Derrida, 1994). And if one looks at the field of organization studies specifically, one may be forgiven for thinking that there aren't many alternatives to capitalist corporations. Thus even the 'radical' visions of self-declared 'management revolutionaries' reveal a rather atrophied imagination in breaking away from the historically contingent principles underpinning modern organizations (eg waged labour, corporations, hierarchism) (Blaug, 1998; Jacques, 1996, Reedy, this volume). The deployment of the vocabulary of radicalism by corporate executives and proponents of neoliberalism seems to have sucked up from under our feet all grounds for oppositional practice, any 'alternative' being inexorably drawn into reproducing what is was meant 'to overthrow. When for example, environmentalism, feminism, anarchism, anti-corporate movements get 'incorporated' as 'fair trade branding', 'diversity management', the heralding of Codes of Ethics, the development of the 'Seattle look' by clothes retailing companies, or employee empowerment programmes, it may be tempting to abandon all hope for alternative futures. But why worry? Corporations and neoliberalism will make it their mission to take care of everything, from providing coffee to delivering hope to the under-privileged:

> When I looked at [illiterate] fifth-grade children, it kind of broke my heart . . . I grew up in a blue-collar family, with not many privileges, so I know first-hand what happens when hope and opportunity is not available . . . If we can reach kids at a young age and provide some inspiration, I think we've done our job. (Howard Schultz, chairman of Starbucks, quoted in Burkeman, 2000:4).

The resigned silence, despair, or cautious critiques with which visions of Starbuckstopia have been met in radical social science have done little to counter the flattening of organizational possibilities (Blaug, 1998; Gabriel, 2001; Harvey, 2000). Thus at the 'critical end' of organization studies, we may find numerous studies highlighting the disciplinary effects of modern organizational practices, but we will find little attempt to radically shift the terms in which organizing is conceived. For example, we are warned that whilst critical management research should seek to give voice to the marginalized, it should remain sensitive to the economic and organizational constraints within which management operates, and should not embark on a programme of 'naïve' anti-capitalism (Alvesson and Deetz, 2000:16).

Yet in a world of escalating poverty, inequality, environmental devastation and thriving corporate power, can we become so easily persuaded that 'there is no alternative' to market liberalism (Harvey, 2000)? Have we become so powerless, so indifferent, so blinded by the 'tyranny of the visible' (Blaug, 1998) that we accept this unprecedented suffering as some inevitable consequence of the otherwise benevolent unrolling of the free market? Are we reduced to joining the 'Howard's way' (Burkeman, 2000), the mission to bring Starbuckstopia to those previously deprived of hope?

My aim here is to argue against such vision of doom (or glory for those embracing the 'good news' of the triumph of neoliberalism) by suggesting that many have sought to escape from its shackles. These triumphalist or pessimistic visions of 'the end of history' are problematic on several counts. Firstly, the pronouncement of the end of history assumes not only that the power of Marxist critique has died with the collapse of the Berlin Wall, a position that has been challenged by many (eg Derrida, 1993; Harvey, 2000; Kumar, 1993), but also that Marxism is the only form of opposition to liberalism and capitalism. It ignores other radical traditions (eg feminism, environmentalism, or anarchism) which, as recent anti-corporate protests have demonstrated, are still very much alive (Starr, 2000).

Secondly, and more importantly for the purpose of this chapter, if the 'we' of Fukuyama refers to those with the 'power to change the world', world politicians, political scientists, multinational corporations executives or organizational scientists, it is maybe not surprising that they are not able to think of something 'better' (for them). Nor is their lack of imagination an indication that nothing better is left to be imagined, or indeed is being imagined by some. Furthermore, for some at least, thinking up 'better' or at least bearable alternatives may not be an optional exercise of imagination but driven by necessity. For those whose means of survival (eg use of land on which to grow food for domestic consumption, clean air and water, safe food) have been hijacked by precisely those allegedly benevolent forces of global capitalism and liberal democracy, it may make little sense to believe in the promise of global capitalism, or to wait until its *promesse de bonheur* finally materializes.

Fukuyama's statement above about what WE can conceive seems to be flying in the face of myriad of grassroots movements which seek to cultivate new possibilities (eg Bennholdt-Thomsen and Mies, 1999; Ekins, 1992; Starr, 2000). Could it be that if we loosened the 'we' of Fukuyama to include those on the margins, and toned down the ambition to 'change the world' to 'changing our lives', we might recover some sense of possibility? After all, as Lefebvre (1971:36) put it 'people do not revolt to change governments . . . but to change their lives'. Out of necessity or hope, some have dared to believe that there are alternatives, to make a wager that there *must* be alternatives (Young, 1996). It is to refer to this cultivation of possibilities by grassroots movements, this daring to imagine alternatives, that I use the term utopianism.

Before I say more about utopianism, I should maybe explain what I mean by grassroots movements. The grassroots movements I am talking about here are born out of and embody a wide range of concerns.[1] Some may start as women's movements, simply because women often happen to be at the points where the material and environmental effects of global capitalism are most urgently felt (Agarwal, 1992; Bennholdt-Thomsen and Mies, 1999; Rocheleau *et al.*, 1996). Others may be about small farmers or landless people reclaiming the right to use common land to meet their subsistence needs, as in for example the Zapatista movement in Mexico (Holloway and Pelaez, 1998), or local people reclaiming their rights over traditional knowledge of life forms from corporate biopiracy (Shiva, 1997). These movements are not moved by a common vision or political agenda but by a common enemy (Starr, 2000): the 'force' of neoliberalism. True this common enemy may occasionally bring them together in some temporal tactical alliances (as we have seen in anti-capitalist protests), but this does not extend into the establishment of some general system of equivalence (Guattari, 2000) that would point to another 'stultifying consensus'. My aim here is not to offer a comprehensive or even representative overview of grassroots movements[2], but rather to capture something of their 'movement'; and it is this idea of 'movement', the movement of hope, that I want to discuss in relation to utopianism. By reading these movements in terms of utopianism, my interest is less in the organizational alternatives they represent than in the very possibility of alternatives. They stand as 'emblems of the possible' (Guttenplan, 2001:5). By seeking to reclaim control over the conditions of their existence from the 'inevitable force of neoliberalism', they are living examples that history has not reached its end, that 'there are alternatives'.

The chapter starts by discussing the moving nature of utopianism and distinguishing it from 'utopia' as a static blueprint. The following four sections discuss the processes of critique and transformation through which utopianism opens up possibilities, and illustrate these through the practices of grassroots movements. In the final section, I rather uncomfortably bring the idea of utopianism to academic practice, and in particular the academic practice of writing a chapter like this one.

Utopianism and movement

I use the term utopianism rather than 'utopia' to emphasize movement over static visions of a better order. Thus I follow several writers in defining utopianism in terms of its critical, transgressive and transformative functions rather than in terms of its form or content (Harvey, 2000; Levitas, 1990; Sargisson, 1996). From this perspective, utopianism is not a blueprint for a 'perfect society', but may be better conceptualized as a movement of hope. It undermines dominant understanding of what is possible and opens up new conceptual spaces for imaging and practising possible futures. Utopianism is about movement and processes rather than 'better states'; about journeys rather than destinations; it is about opening up visions of alternatives, rather than closing down on 'a' vision of 'a' better society; it is about what moves us to hope for, and to cultivate, alternative possibilities; and it is about establishing the conditions for the development of alternatives. This 'moving' nature of utopianism is well captured by the ambivalence inherent in More's (1516/1965) discussion of utopia as a 'good place' and a 'no place', and hence the structure of Parker's beginning and ending to this volume. This ambivalence opens up a space for a continuous process of deferral, for perpetual movement; or as Marin (1984) suggests, it creates 'tension zones' that prevent movement from ever reaching an end. Thus utopianism cannot end with a critique of the present, nor even with the construction of a better future; it cannot end at all. It has to resist the temptation of closure around another 'best' alternative (Sargisson, 1996), it lives off 'tension zones', disruption mechanisms that will stop it settling.

So what of the utopianism of grassroots movements? As I said earlier, by proposing to read grassroots movements in terms of utopianism, I want to emphasize their 'moving' nature, and explore what gets them and keeps them moving. And this starts with a critique and rejection of the present, a critique that makes the all too familiar 'promise of neoliberalism' look absurd, outrageous, but also 'resistible'. As I will argue below, by exposing the choices and decisions behind the supposedly faceless and irresistible force of the market, grassroots protest movements open up spaces for making different choices, for the possibility of alternatives. Grassroots movements also embody the transformative function of utopianism through their collective attempts to organize themselves differently. Their very grassroots nature leads these movements towards small scale, self-governing, self-reliant organization. However, what is interesting, and utopian, about the organizational principles underlying these movements is not only that they present alternatives to 'modern' organizing (and its emphasis on hierarchism, Blaug, 1998), but also that they create the conditions under which possibilities remain open. As I shall suggest in a later section, the small scale, decentralized and disjointed nature of grassroots movements provides for points of disruption that stop the development of a general system of equivalence swallowing up alternatives into a 'third way'. So, the point is not to herald these alternatives as providing better organizational blueprints, but rather to explore the conditions they offer for the cultivation of alternatives.

In what follows, I try to capture the utopian movement of grassroots alternatives by discussing their critical and transformative functions in terms of four themes highlighted in the short account above: cultivating outrage, challenging inevitability, inventing organizational alternatives, and creating permanent disruption.

Estrangement and the cultivation of outrage

Let's start with some facts:

> PASAR [Philippine Associated Smelting and Refining Corporation] operates a Japanese financed and constructed copper smelting plant in the Philippine province of Leyte to produce high grade copper cathodes for shipment to Japan. The plant occupies 400 acres of land expropriated by the Philippine government from local residents at give-away prices. Gas and wastewater emissions from the plant contain high concentrations of boron, arsenic, heavy metals, and sulphur compounds that have contaminated local water supplies, reduced fishing and rice yields, damaged the forests, and increased the occurrence of upper-respiratory diseases among local residents. Local people whose homes, livelihoods, and health have been sacrificed to PASAR are now largely dependent on the occasional part-time or contractual employment they are offered to do the plant's most dangerous and dirtiest jobs. The company has prospered, the local economy has grown. The Japanese people have a supply of copper at no environmental cost to themselves. The local poor – the project's professed beneficiaries- have lost their means of livelihood and suffered impaired health. The Philippine government is repaying the foreign aid loan from Japan that financed the construction of supporting infrastructure for the plant. And the Japanese are congratulating themselves for the cleanliness of their domestic environment and their generous assistance to the poor of the Philippines. . . . There are thousands of such stories illustrating the realities of corporate colonialism that economic globalization is advancing around the world. The *Economist*, an ardent globalization proponent, has argued that those who criticize such toxic dumping practices would deprive the poor of needed economic opportunities. (Korten, 1995:31–32).

As Korten makes plain, there is nothing 'exceptional' about the case of PASAR, this is just a corporation going about its business of maximizing value to shareholders, using all means and resources 'legally available', including the 'right' guaranteed by 'free trade' to export pollution, and to 'buy' land and labour at 'market rates', in order to achieve its purpose. And it is precisely the normality of this case that calls for attention. How can we have reached a state where the 'normality of corporate behaviour' has come to efface the grotesque and devastating nature of its consequences?

Although the harrowing, indeed dystopic, depiction of the effects of corporate actions above may seem a paradoxical point of departure for utopianism, it is, I would argue, essential to shake us off our 'normal' course. Exposing the 'normal' as outrageous, 'nothing less than an act of collective, suicidal insanity' (Korten, 1995:247) may make us move, or at least disrupt the grounds on which we stand. The opening up of the conceptual space within which alternatives can be imagined relies on establishing a sense of estrangement, on making the 'normal', the currently possible, look strange, absurd, grotesque. Indeed, estrangement has been used very powerfully in science fiction where futuristic dystopian / utopian societies are built on the garbage of old ones, holding up a mirror to the insanity of the past or present, its grotesque wastefulness, and suffering (Moylan, 1986).[3] But looking at the devastating effects of contemporary corporate actions from the perspectives of the margins, the disenfranchised, is equally unsettling. There have been many recent publications piling up facts about the outrageous effects of our ways of organizing, seeking to expose the insanity and brutality of an economic system based on 'free trade', where 'free trade' effectively means that Northern based multinational corporations get to pollute developing countries for free, to use their labour and natural resources from for next to nothing (eg Bello *et al.*, 2000; Bennholdt-Thomsen and Mies, 1999; Klein, 2000; Korten, 1995; Monbiot, 2000). We may of course point a finger at the hypocrisy of the largely comfortably middle class writers who have built their fame and careers (as well as their corporate publishers' profits) on the pile of excess and devastation of global capitalism (a point to which I return in conclusion). But it remains that they have provided a far more moving critique of corporate actions and neoliberalism than we can find in 'critical' organization studies (Parker, 2002a).

For, oddly, we see little of this excess in organization studies. Of course, there is a long tradition of 'critique' in the discipline, drawing upon various intellectual traditions ranging from Marxism to poststructuralism, feminism and so on (eg Fournier and Grey, 2000). There is even talk about 'unnecessary suffering', waste, injustice, and the use of 'defamiliarization' as a technique for 'critical research' (Alvesson and Deetz, 2000). However there is a sense in which this 'unnecessary suffering' once called up gets little attention for itself. Thus, reading critical organization studies, one learns little about whole population being made sick, starved, left with no other ways of surviving than selling themselves as slave labour to the corporations that have appropriated their land. It seems that we cannot just point to 'facts of devastation', we have to legitimize our critique by wrapping them up in layers of 'theory', adding Foucault, Derrida, Marx or whatever intellectual heavyweight we want to claim allegiance to.[4] Suffering and devastation get diluted into rather feeble and tame critiques: an empowerment programme that does not really empower; a group of workers reappropriating corporate culture and subverting it in the process. I am not suggesting that such 'critiques' are invalid, or have no place in organization studies; but simply that they do little to evoke the brutality and insanity of corporate practices, or to move us towards demanding alternatives. After all, the 'intellectual heavy weights' do not encumber themselves with 'theory' to denounce the effects of global capitalism and liberal democracy. Marx's graphic depiction of labour conditions in Victorian workshops was a poignant illustration, and so is Derrida's (1994:85) forthright denunciation of the 'obvious macroscopic fact[s]' of violence, starvation, subjugation, and extermination.[5]

Ironically, the proponents of neo-liberalism have been more successful at pointing to the absurdity of an economic system run on 'free trade' than critical organization theorists. According to the neoliberal view, it is only by expanding 'free trade' that the poor will prosper; and international institutions such as the World Bank (WB), the World Trade Organization (WTO), and the International Monetary Fund (IMF) are there to ensure that trade runs 'free', uninhibited by the 'irrational demands' of 'special interest groups', such as environmentalists' demands for a healthy environment, or the working poor's demands for a living wage (Korten, 1995). However, the idea of free trade hinges around the notion of comparative advantage; and as is recognized even in the pages of the *Economist*, for poor countries, this comparative advantage is poverty:

> The benefits of international trade come from allowing countries to exploit their comparative advantage . . . And much of the Third World's comparative advantage lies, in one way or another, in the fact of its poverty, in particular, cheap labour and a greater tolerance of pollution. (Woodall, 1994:42)

Free trade is both, if we are to believe neoliberalism, the way out of poverty, and feeding on poverty. So the poor will only benefit from free trade to the extent that they remain poor.

Unfortunately, we cannot take comfort in the contradictory nature of the neoliberal mantra, nor dismiss it as the preposterous and impossible dream of economists. However contradictory the neoliberal rhetoric may be in terms of what it promises to deliver, it has not stopped it from becoming a dangerous consensus (Derrida,1994) informing the programmes of 'economic development' promoted by world powers and international institutions. Whilst economists may not be renown for their concerns with 'reality', they have demonstrated remarkable prowess in bringing the real world in line with their neoliberal economic ideas[6] (George, 2000; Polanyi, 1957). Thus these neoliberal ideas have fed and underpinned the structural adjustment programmes of the WB and the IMF, which in the name of liberalization, have provided third world countries with an enormous 'comparative advantage', if that is to be understood in terms of their poverty. There is plenty of evidence suggesting that developmental programmes designed to bring the benefit of global capitalism to the poor by extending free trade and deregulating global markets have mainly benefited Northern multinational corporations (Bello, 2000; *The Ecologist*, 2000; Korten, 1995).[7] In the name of liberalization, corporations have been given free reign to rewrite the constitution of some countries, despoil their environment and take away local population's means of survival.[8]

As the example of PASAR outlined above suggested, corporate actions 'dictated' by the 'force of the market' have 'real effects' on local material conditions, they do so by appropriating or wrecking the means of livelihood of distant communities. Since these effects are often inscribed in and distributed through the environment (eg through the appropriation of land, of life forms as in biopiracy, the degradation of soil, water or air and the depletion of natural resources), it is maybe not surprising that many grassroots movements against global capitalism have tended to articulate their protest around environmental concerns, or land reform. Environmental concerns here are not about aesthetic sensibilities but material conditions for meeting basic subsistence needs, they are matters of survival (Korten, 1995; Thomas-Slayter *et al.*, 1996). As many have noted, the environment acts as a powerful material for critique for it bears the scars of corporate capitalism, of its social injustice and devastation (Bookchin, 1990; Dickens, 1996; Korten, 1995). It is the poor and the marginalized who often bear the brunt of pollution, natural resource degradation, or the appropriation of land (Miller *et al.*, 1996; Pulido, 1996), and who are therefore most likely to know the impact, the devastating effects of corporate capitalism, for, to put it bluntly, they carry these effects on their bodies. It is the location of grassroots protest movements at the points where the devastating effects of corporate capitalism are most likely to be felt, that makes them powerful starting points for critique, for exposing the outrageous effects of corporate actions.

This understanding of the environment, as a set of local, material conditions for survival, has been a central point of critique of global capitalism for many women's environmentalist movements. Through their material positions as carers and main providers of food, women are often the first to know and bear the brunt of environmental degradation; and they have used this 'mundane', everyday knowledge to resist the dumping of toxic waste by corporations (Miller *et al.*, 1996; Seager, 1996), or the so called 'green revolution' promoted by programmes of structural adjustment in developing countries (Agarwal, 1992; Mehta, 1996; Sweetman, 2000). These programmes have encouraged the restructuring of agriculture away from subsistence towards cash crop oriented systems, fed by privatization and the use of expensive technology and pesticides. As many have illustrated, these programmes have had dire effects on women's material conditions and ability to provide for domestic food, water and health needs[9]. The Chipko movement, in the Himalayan valley, was among the first to organize against these programmes of agricultural restructuring (eg Agarwal, 1992; Mehta, 1996); but similar protests have been raised by grassroots women movements in other developing countries (see Campbell, 1996; Sweetman, 1999; Wangari *et al.*, 1996).

Arguing that women may be the first to notice and suffer the effects of corporate capitalism is not to assume that they have some inherent and privileged connections with nature which give them a unique knowledge of or sensitivity to the environment (the 'ecofeminist argument' – eg Merchant, 1980; Plant, 1989). It is not their 'womanhood' that gives them this 'privileged access' to devastation, but their location in certain material conditions (the gendered division of labour, the customs and practices that govern their access to land, market, knowledge and financial resources) (Agarwal, 1992; Rocheleau *et al.*, 1996). And it is obviously not just women who are affected by the environmental and material wreckage created by corporate capitalism; nor are they the only ones to protest (Bennholdt-Thomsen and Mies, 1999; Rocheleau *et al.*, 1996). Indeed, as many recent publications have been at pain to show, grassroots movements against global capitalism are emerging in many different places, and are articulated around a range of concerns from local movements reclaiming the use of the 'commons' (Donahue, 1999; *The Ecologist*, 1993), the related Zapatista movement for self-determination by local people (Holloway and Pelaez, 1998), to protests against acts of 'biopiracy' (Shiva, 1997) sanctioned by GATT regulations on Trade Related Intellectual property Rights (TRIPS)[10]. The point here is not to privilege one group or concern over another, but simply to stress that if the devastating effects of global capitalism are inscribed in the local material conditions of those on the margins, it is at this local, grassroots level that the outrageous nature of these effects can be most powerfully exposed, and that demands for alternatives can be most forcibly made.

But exposing the blatant injustice and insanity of market liberalism is not enough to get us to move away from it. As the 'third way' concocted by world leaders at Davos suggested, the response to mounting evidence of human and environmental devastation is to re-affirm the promise of market liberalism and ensure that no one is spared from its benevolent and irresistible force.

Putting a face to the 'inevitable force of the market'

If utopianism is about opening up a space for alternatives, it has to shatter any notion of 'inevitable' or 'natural' forces, and in particular the commonly accepted notion that the forces of capitalism and neoliberalism are inescapable (Korten, 1995). 'There is no alternative' is a common response to any criticism of neoliberalism and capitalism; neoliberalism may take time to bear its fruits to the disenfranchised, it may even create its victims in the short term, but it is the best of all alternatives, and it is simply not within anyone's power to resist its 'force'.

Thus in response to the problems outlined above, all politicians can do is offer more of the ineffectual solutions that created the problem in the first place.

Encouraging economic growth through deregulation, removing trade barriers, unleashing the 'free forces of the market' are to be the solution to all ills, from poverty, to crime, the provision of better public services, or environmental degradation (Korten, 1995). We indeed seem to have become 'unable to conceive of anything different'. And as Blaug (1998) notes, this sense of closure about the way we organize the economy extends to the type of organization we can conceive of. We, or at least some of us, are unable to break away from the mould of modern capitalist organizations and the principle of 'hierarchism'. For Blaug (1998), 'hierarchism' refers not only to the hierarchy of command typical of modern organizations, but also the division of labour, the centralization of control and the privileging of expert knowledge[11].

Hierarchism and neoliberalism have become like a new religious faith, a form of evangelism (George, 2000; Korten, 1995), and as such are self-confirming prophecies, 'a perceptual aberration, immunized against revelation' (Blaug, 1998:46). The faith goes on, unabated by (more) empirical investigation of its tyranny and devastation, or its blatant failure to reduce poverty (Bennholdt-Thomsen and Mies, 1999; Blaug, 1998; George, 2000; Derrida, 1994)[12].

In order to resist the apparent inevitability of the force of the market, of neoliberalism and capitalism, it is important to understand the mechanisms that serve to sustain it. One of the key mechanisms here is that of distancing, of disconnecting organizational actions and decisions on the one hand, from their effects on the other. These disconnections serve to place organizational effects out of our sight, or at least 'out of our control'. Marx and Bauman have provided useful accounts of the ways these distancing mechanisms create 'perceptual failure', the failure to see that effects are the products of choices and decisions (Blaug, 1998). As Marx understood, capitalism relies on fragmentation on a global scale: the geographical and social distances separating capital, production, and consumption serve to blur the connections between actions and consequences. Capitalism is a global and macro-system that can effectively hide its environmental and social costs behind geographical distance and social divisions; by scattering its effects around the globe it 'prevents us from seeing the aggregate of our actions, the big picture' (Blaug, 1998:39). And modern organizations are built on the same principle of fragmentation and distancing. Bauman (1989) has powerfully demonstrated how the bureaucratic principles of modern organizations, such as the division of labour, hierarchy, the privileging of impersonal rules, expert knowledge and instrumental rationality, translate organizational action into a series of fragmented technical issues, free of questions about moral choice. Modern organizations efface moral responsibility by distancing actions from effects, and effacing the 'face' of those who are made to suffer from these consequences (Desmond, 1998). These distancing mechanisms keep the effects and suffering created by organizations invisible; even when we do see suffering we don't see the connections to our actions, we don't know what lever to pull, or we don't feel that any lever is within our reach. These distancing mechanisms create the impression that the 'system' is unrolling, independently of our action, and there is nothing to stop it.

Yet some are 'saying no' (Korten, 1995) and refusing to take their suffering as the products of 'inevitable forces'. Grassroots protest movements, by retracing the connections between their suffering and corporate or government actions, choices and decisions, are challenging the blind faith in the 'unstoppable' force of neoliberalism and hierarchism. Through their direct actions, they are demonstrating that whilst global capitalism may run according to a certain logic that drives capital where it can attracts most profit and that relies on and reproduces pockets of poverty and devastation, this logic itself does not impose itself on us of its own volition, without some of us letting it do so.

The power of grassroots protest movements extends beyond revealing the devastating consequences of corporate capitalism, it is also about exposing these consequences as the products of actions and decisions rather than the inevitable force of the market. By putting points of resistance, they are forcing those behind neoliberalism to step up their *actions*, to show the faces and decisions behind the faceless and distant 'inevitable force of the market', and to reveal these 'decisions' as, by definition, possibly otherwise. Thus grassroots movements against biopiracy find that their protest don't take them against some faceless force of the market, but into some complex legal regulations formulated by world leaders behind GATT, and that such acts of piracy only become 'legalized free trade' if the WTO, backed up by multi-national corporations and governments, decides so (Shiva, 1997)[13]. And if such acts of appropriation can be exposed as the products of decisions rather than the 'inevitable force of the market', they can also be overturned, as was successfully demonstrated in the case of the lawsuits launched against the patenting of the nem tree by the Grace corporation (BIJA, 1996). When small farmers, consumers or some national governments want to exercise their 'market rights' not to purchase GM food or seeds, it is not the market that threatens disciplinary action, but the combined effort of the US government, biotech corporations and the WTO (Monbiot, 2001)[14]. Nor it is some inevitable market force that appropriates common land or land owned by small farmers, it is sold away to multinational corporations by governments, under pressures from international institutions such as the WB and IMF (Korten, 1995). When people in Papua New Guinea defended their communal rights over the use of land against the 'Land Mobilization programme', it was not the forces of the market that they resisted but their 'government and big companies' decisions' to transform their traditional means of livelihood into profit making palm oil plantations (Bennholdt-Thomsen and Mies, 1999:148). And it is not the market that shoots down or jails landless farmers trying to re-appropriate access to some common land to meet their subsistence needs, 'democratic governments' do so, as the Zapatista movement, found out (De Angelis, 1999; Holloway and Pelaez, 1998). Furthermore, as many women environmentalist movements have suggested, it is not some inescapable logic of the market that dumps toxic waste and builds polluting factories; such dumping and polluting can only be seen as the product of 'economic imperatives', or as contributing to 'economic development' (providing 'needed economic opportunities', as *The Economist* put it), if we have made certain deci-

199

sions about what sort of economy we want, if we have decided that meeting subsistence needs does not count as 'economic development' whilst producing pollution to be cleaned up or sports equipment from logged forests, does (Rocheleau *et al.*, 1996). The privileging and constitution of 'economic growth' as the ultimate value is not dictated by 'the market' but is the result of arbitrary and bizarre accounting practices that count, for example, the cost of cleaning up the environmental disasters as contributions to economic growth (Chomsky, 2000; Korten, 1995).

What all these examples suggest is that the 'forces' of the market appear rather weak without the combined support of laws, the police force, armies, Western governments, multinational corporations, the WTO . . . ; and that these supposedly inevitable, natural forces are constructed and sustained by countless decisions, policies (Bello *et al.*, 2000), and conscious choices (Korten, 1995)[15]. Through their acts of resistance, grassroots movements expose the 'irresistible forces of capitalism' as being the products of decisions and choices; and as such, as being, possibly resistible and reversible. Decisions, by definition, could be otherwise.

Grassroots protest movements remind us that nothing is the product of autonomous, inevitable, faceless 'forces', everything has to be decided, for as Derrida (1999) put it, the world is undecidable. Derrida's notion of undecidability is useful to free social reality from the straight jacket of inescapability within which it is held by triumphalist neo-liberalism, and to open up choice and possibilities. It suggests that reality is always incomplete, containing many latent potentialities; it follows no imperatives, is dictated by no 'force' or programme. And it is precisely because of this condition of undecidability that we have to exercise choice, to make decisions. If everything followed some inevitable logic and imperatives, there would be no choice. Thus history does not reach its end, organizations do not organize, capitalism does not capitalize without some active participation and complicity on our part.

Undecidability means that *we have to decide*; if the world follows no inevitable logic, we have to make choices, and to do so without ever being able to resort to absolute standards by which to judge them, we also chose the standards by which we evaluate our choice. But with undecidability and choice also comes responsibility (Derrida, 1999; Jones, forthcoming). If organizing the economy follows no imperatives but is the product of (however complex, multiple, dispersed) decisions we take, we cannot hide our responsibility for the devastating effects such organizing creates behind some faceless 'programme', some inevitable logic, of the market or otherwise. Undecidability, facing double-binds, deciding between different demands when there is nothing to tell us which way to go, creates the possibility for decision and responsibility, but also for alternatives. It opens up a conceptual space for rethinking the possible and to help us going beyond critique.

Of course undecidability also means that we cannot know for sure that alternatives will be better, we can only hope, take the risk (Young, 1996). Utopianism is about grabbing these moments of hope and risk and running with them,

200

it is about embracing undecidability, and the choices and responsibilities that go with it.

Inventing alternative moral economies

So what alternatives do these grassroots movements practice? Having emphasized the notion of undecidability, and its corollaries of choice and responsibility, it would seem paradoxical to answer this question by heralding a new organizational blueprint. If utopianism is about grabbing moments of choice and responsibility inherent in undecidability, and running with them, it won't do to decide in advance where we should run. However, this is not to say that anything goes. For if, as I suggested earlier, neoliberalism and capitalism have, through various distancing mechanisms, effaced choice and responsibility behind some faceless 'force of the market', any utopian alternative would have to create conditions under which choices were within our reach, and responsibilities for the consequences of our choices were put in our face. This emphasis on choice and responsibility has far reaching organizational implications that I will discuss here under the notion of self-governance. The idea of self-governance, or self-management and self-determination, is a central principle in articulating the alternative 'moral economies' (Bennholdt-Thomsen and Mies, 1999) embodied by grassroots movements, from explicitly anti-corporate movements, to environmental movements, women's movements, land reforms and small farmers' movements.

This principle is also of course central to anarchist ideas and practices on organizing (eg Bookchin, 1971; Malatesta, 1995; *An Anarchist FAQ Webpage*, 2001, Reedy, this volume). Indeed, many of the organizational principles I outline in this section come very close to anarchism. If anarchism is about the freedom to decide how we conduct and organize our lives (Guerin, 1998), then it is closely aligned with the utopian cultivation of possibilities; we can only cultivate possibilities if we (re) appropriate the choices and decisions affecting our lives. Utopianism and anarchism share an emphasis on processes over blueprints, on creating the conditions under which people can organize themselves without submitting to authority or 'force' (Kropotkin, 1970; Ward, 1982).

And grassroots movements seeking to resist the 'force' of neoliberalism are precisely about highlighting and re-appropriating these moments of choice and decisions. There are already numerous publications listing and illustrating these various grassroots movements and their alternative 'moral economies'[16]. As I have already suggested, my aim here is not to provide an overview of these alternatives, but rather to explore the organizational conditions they create to exercise self-governance, to reclaim the choice and responsibility for organizing their lives.

I am of course well aware that such terms as choice, responsibility and even self-governance may appear tame and nauseously reminiscent of both managerial discourse and politicians' manifestos (see Knights and Willmott, this volume). However, there is no reason why managers and politicians should have a monopoly over what these terms means or how they can be practised[17]. Furthermore, creating the conditions for the exercise of self-governance may take us towards more radical alternatives than managers and politicians may want to envisage.

The main idea about self-governance is that decisions are taken by those who will live with the consequences, it foregrounds the ability to make choice about the conditions affecting our lives, but also (re) connects these choices with responsibility and consequences. True, we cannot know in advance all the consequences of our actions, but some things we know. For example we know that if we dump toxic waste somewhere it will in all likelihood impair the health of local people, we know that if we pay people less than a living wage, they will find it difficult to survive. Furthermore, we can also create conditions that may bring the consequences of our action closer to our face. This would involve eliminating as much as possible the distancing mechanisms between actions and effects characteristics of modern capitalist organizations – from the division of labour, to the division between capital and labour, consumption and production, to geographical distance and large organizations. This has far reaching organizational implications, which I sketch out very briefly below.

Implications of scale and localization

If it is, at least partly, through its global and massive scale that capitalism can hide its effects, then any alternative moral economy would have to address the issue of size and localization (Starr, 2000). In order to create the conditions of possibility for self-governance, economic activity should be organized at the smallest, most local level possible (Bello *et al.*, 2000; Bookchin, 1990; Korten, 1995). For example, Bookchin maps his visions of alternative on the 'village republics' which would have to be large enough so that citizens could meet most of their material needs, yet not so large that they were unable to make policy decision in open, face to face public discourse.

But self-governance also has implications for (re) localization (Bello, 2000; Bennholdt-Thomsen and Mies, 1999; Bookchin, 1990; Korten, 1995; Starr, 2000). As I argued earlier, the global nature of capitalism masks the consequences and costs of our actions behind spatial distance. If we are to face the consequences of our choices, we may need to bring them closer to our face. There may be other ways of bringing the consequences of our actions to our face than to bring them physically closer. However, considering that at least some of the consequences of our ways of organizing are distributed through the environment, through polluting, despoiling or appropriating distant land, bringing the environment we 'use' closer to home is a significant way of taking responsibility for our action (Bennholdt-Thomsen and Mies, 1999; Korten, 1995).

Small local self-organizing groups have been the cornerstones of many grassroots alternatives (eg Bennholdt-Thomsen and Mies, 1999; Starr, 2000).

However, privileging small, local organizations is not to say that we should all live in autarky, isolated from other communities. Thus in many alternative visions and grassroots movements, these small units are connected through the creation of federations or 'municipalities' (Bookchin, 1990) that act as networks of exchange. For example, in the Zapatista movement, self-organizing communities can choose to join municipalities which co-ordinate exchange between them to ensure that basic needs are met. A municipality may include between 50 and 100 communities, each delegating one of their members to speak for them in the municipality assemblies, and to report back to them. This system of delegation from below allows decision-making power to remain as close to the grassroots as possible (decisions about the organization of the community remain at that level), and ensures that lines of accountability run from the top down. Thus delegates are given a mandate to represent the views of the group that selected them, and can be recalled (*Chiapas Revealed*, 2001).

Division between capital and labour: reclaiming or protecting the commons

Self-governance requires free access to, and control over, the means of production, and therefore the elimination of the division between owners of capital (be it land, tools or raw material) and labour. This is a point that anarchists have long made to defend their visions of workers' co-operatives (Ward, 1982). As Kropotkin (1985a:145) argued 'the only guarantee not to be robbed of the fruits of your labour is to possess the instruments of labour'. This would involve the abolition of waged labour, and a reconceptualization of property rights over capital. For example, Bookchin (1991) suggests that the notion of property be replaced by usufruct: 'the freedom of individuals in a community to appropriate resources merely by the virtue of the fact that they are using them [. . .] resources belong to the users as long as they are being used. Function, in effect replaces our hallowed concept of property' (ibid:50).

The eradication of the division between labour and capital can take several forms, from the more modest private ownership by either a group of associated workers (worker co-operatives), or small family / individual enterprise who do not own more capital than the owners can work with, to a more radical vision of communal ownership where means of production belong (in the sense of usufruct) to those who work with them (*An Anarchist FAQ Webpage*, 2001). This more radical alternative is illustrated by the various grassroots movements seeking to reclaim or protect the 'commons' (*The Ecologist*, 1993), be it common land (see Bennholdt-Thomsen and Mies, 1999 for examples of various local grassroots movements and initiatives reclaiming use over common land; or Holloway and Pelaez, 1998, on the Zapatista movement), or common knowledge of biological life (eg Shiva, 1997). For example, people of Papua New Guinea have so far been successful in protecting their customary traditions of communal land, as the property of clans rather than state or individuals, against mounting pressures from their government, the IMF and the WB to sell off their land for 'development programmes' (Bennholdt-Thomsen and Mies, 1999).

Subsistence and alternative forms of exchange

The separation between consumption and production is one of the distancing mechanisms that enables consumers either not to know or not to care for the effects of their consumption (eg on those who are slaving away to produce it, or on the environment), and reciprocally, for producers to dump harmful products on unsuspecting consumers[18].

Attempts to break down these distancing mechanisms by drawing towards a subsistence economy (Bennholdt-Thomsen and Mies, 1999), or a greater level of 'self-reliance' (Bello *et al.*, 2000; Bookchin, 1990; Korten, 1995) do not have to involve autarky. Rather these attempts are about opening up the ways in which 'exchange' can be conceptualized and practised. And there have been many attempts to take exchange out of 'the market', as understood by neoliberalism (Bennholdt-Thomsen and Mies, 1999; Norberg-Hodge, 1996). The municipalities in the Zapatista movement provide an alternative co-ordinating mechanism through which independent communities can exchange goods and services (*Chiapas Revealed*, 2001; Holloway and Pelaez, 1998). Indeed, this idea of the municipality, or federation, as a co-ordinating mechanism (controlled from below) for exchanging labour, food, goods or services is a central pillar of anarchists' visions of the economy (Bookchin, 1990). And throughout the world there are many other, maybe less radical, attempts to develop exchange systems that tie consumers and producers more closely together, attaching them to the mutual consequences of their acts of production and consumption. Schemes for developing local exchange such as LETS and Community Supported Agriculture (CSA) are examples of increasingly popular modern alternative exchange systems to the capitalist market that seek to bind consumers and producers together through promise of future labour, products or services (Bennholdt-Thomsen and Mies, 1999; Bond, 2000; Mander and Godlsmith, 1996)[19].

The organisation and division of labour

The division of labour, including hierarchy and the compartmentalization of knowledge, is a prime target of criticism in both practice and theories of alternative moral economies (eg Bookchin, 1990; Dickens, 1996; Kropotkin, 1985b). Indeed, the division of labour and the principle of hierarchy make mockery of any notions of self-governance, autonomy or responsibility. As Bauman (1989) illustrated, it effaces the choices made in organizing, as well as the consequences of these choices. To create the conditions that would enable the functioning of self-governance, people need to have the means both to exercise choice and to know the consequences of their choices (Bookchin, 1991). This again has far reaching implications for the organization of work: firstly to replace hierarchy of command by self-management where decisions about what / how to produce are taken by those affected; secondly, to re-assemble the tasks and functions where possible, and where not, to ensure that these tasks and functions are rotated. To go back to the example of the Zapatista movement, those who are delegated to represent their communities at municipalities' assemblies can only do so for a limited period of time and still have to carry out some of their normal work at the community level (*Chiapas Revealed*, 2001; Holloway and Pelaez, 1998).

The implications of self-management for the organization of work extend far beyond empowering employees to decide how to reach their targets. It means that those who labour can also decide to what end they will deploy their labour and means of production: what they should produce, for whom, and at what cost to themselves. For example, as some rural women's movements have demonstrated, it is about the power to decide that what could be gained by producing crops for the export market would not be worth the loss of domestic crops covering subsistence needs, or the extended journey women would have to make to collect water or firewood (Agarwal, 1992).

Self-governance also means challenging the constitution and distribution of knowledge, and in particular the privileging and sequestrating of 'professional knowledge'. Privileging 'expert' knowledge has been a powerful device to exclude 'ordinary citizens' from decisions, and dismiss their protest (Bookchin, 1990; Dickens, 1996). This is of course a point that has long been made by feminists in relation to medical, environmental, or agricultural knowledge (Agarwal, 1992; Ehrenreich and English, 1979; Inhetveen, 1998). For example, challenging what counts as 'environmental knowledge' has been a key aspect of women environmentalist activists dismissed by government representatives and scientists as 'hysterical housewives' (Seager, 1996):

> . . . environmental degradation is typically mundane: it occurs in small measures, drop by drop, well by well, tree by tree. [. . .] not in big flashy, or global ways. This might suggest the necessity for a reassessment of the conduct and priorities of environmental research which has, in the United Sates, always favoured 'big science'. The notion that local people (and, often, especially local women) who are close observers of their local environment may be the most reliable narrators about environmental problems is discomfiting to big scientific and environmental organisations whose prestige depends on solving 'big' problems in heroic ways (ibid: 280–281)

This is not to say that 'expert', 'professional', 'scientific' knowledge should be dismissed, but that there is no reason why it should be privileged over 'citizen science' (Irwin, 1995), knowledge developed and grounded in civil society (Dickens, 1996), nor why it should be the preserve of a small groups of 'scientists' or professionals.

This has been a rather sketchy and partial account of alternative ways of organizing. My aim, however, was not to provide an exhaustive list of alternative organizational rules (for as anarchists argue, this would undermine the idea of self-governance) but simply to suggest that there are alternative ways of organizing to market liberalism and the principle of hierarchism, and that such alternatives are being practiced by many grassroots movements. To a large extent, the alternative principles I have sketched out here resemble those suggested in anarchist theory. And certainly, the anarchist minimalist idea about the purpose of the economy would be fitting for the alternative moral economies I have talked about: 'to create favourable conditions for giving society the greatest amount of useful products with the least waste of human energy' (Kropotkin, 1985a:175). This hardly provides us with a blueprint for organizing. Indeed, it opens endless questions: what counts as 'useful product', or 'waste in human energy', how much of such waste should we tolerate, how should it be distributed . . . ? And this is precisely the point, to open these questions and endless possibilities to public debate, so that we can decide.

But as this section has demonstrated, leaving people the freedom and responsibility to choose how they organize their lives and economic affairs is not to say that 'anything goes'; creating the conditions for self-governance has important organizational implications. These conditions point towards small, local, self-governing, self-reliant communes as the building blocks for alternative moral economies. But here I feel the need to add a caveat. There is a worrying tendency in writing about these alternative grassroots movements to align small self-reliant communes with some spiritual revival (Bahro, 1984; Bookchin, 1990; Korten, 1995). My argument is not about spiritual healing, nor the recovery of some long lost moral order, but essentially about creating the material conditions for the cultivation of possibilities, for (re) claiming control over the ways in which we organize our lives. Self-governance and small self-reliant communes are not an end in themselves, not the answer to all problems, they are only the material conditions under which we can start to open up alternative possibilities to neoliberalism and its devastation.

Permanent disruption

Indeed, simply flagging up terms such as self governance, responsibility, small scale community, or even revolution and anarchy does not in itself produce the promise of a better or even different future; for these terms can be incorporated into forms of oppressive orders and they have been embraced by all sides of the political spectrum (eg Frankel, 1987). And as I have argued in introduction, echoing many of the contributions to this book, many of the terms that have traditionally fed the radical imagination have been assimilated into tame and docile visions of a third way or Starbuckstopia. Of course there is no escaping the danger of assimilation, but instead of responding with 'resigned silence' we could maybe see such danger as providing the foundation for a permanent revolution (Sargisson, 1996), and the endless cultivation of possibilities.

If utopianism is about the opening up of possibilities, it requires some mechanisms that will stop it hardening into utopia, some arrested vision of a better society that becomes 'the only alternative'. Utopianism, if it is to be kept moving and opening up possibilities, needs to bump across tension zones (Marin, 1984), to be disrupted. In this section, I suggest that the grassroots nature of the alternative movements I have been concerned with here provides powerful disruptive mechanisms that make such movements utopian and stop them degenerating into some tame vision of a third way. I discuss these disruptive mechanisms by addressing one of the main criticisms of grassroots attempts to develop alternative forms of organising. Briefly put, the criticism goes as follows: grass roots alternatives are too small, too local, too disjointed to pose a real threat to global capitalism and neoliberalism (Blaug, 1998). Big problems require big solutions. In answer to this criticism, I want to argue that it is precisely the small, decentralized and multiple, or disjointed, nature of these grassroots movements that make them effective vehicles for utopianism, that keeps them from cohering, or being assimilated, into another dogmatic vision.

Recounting a visit of Hilary Clinton to rural women in Bangladesh targeted by a 'development programme', Bennholdt-Thomsen and Mies (1999) evoke the hostility with which she was met as follows:

> Rural women in Bangladesh and in other countries of the South do not need any empowerment from the White House of from other sections of the rich world. They are strong women. What they really need is that various kinds of oppressors get off their backs: patriarchal men in their own country, TNCs, the World bank and the IMF with their structural re-adjustment programmes, national bureaucracies who follow the orders of these guardians of international capital. (Bennholdt-Thomsen and Mies, 1999:5)

True, some institutional measures could be taken by governments and international institutions to 'get encroachers off people's back', to create 'enabling conditions from above' (Dickens, 1996). And there is no lack of sound advice as to the type of fiscal regime or legislation that could be implemented by states and international institutions to break down the power of global corporations and create from above the conditions that would enable people to have more control over their lives (see Bello *et al.*, 2000; Korten, 1995 for the most careful and detailed proposals). However, there are at least four problems with this 'enabling from above view'.

Firstly, the institutions that would have to implement this 'enabling from above' (eg national states, international institutions) are precisely those who are implicated in the encroachment in the first place. There seems to be some contradiction between, on the one hand, arguing that the encroachment of the material conditions of existence by corporate rule has been helped by national and international institutions, and on the other, arguing that these same institutions can be used to make corporations back off. This contradiction is illustrated in Korten's (1995) analysis. He starts by arguing that national governments and international institutions have either become impotent in the face of corporate colonialism, or have actively facilitated it. Yet he ends with a series of proposals for legislative and fiscal changes, that presumably would have to be implemented by some 'official institutions'[20]. This begs the question of who exactly is to implement these changes? Even if we optimistically assume that eventually, through pressure from public opinions and various activist groups, national governments will have to implement some of these reforms, it still raises the question of how long exactly are the poor supposed to wait (Rich, 2000). In the meantime, direct action by grassroots movements seems to be the most effective means of getting 'oppressors off people's back'.

The second argument for privileging direct action by grassroots movements over centralized, institutional solutions has to do with utopianism and the conditions that enables the cultivation of possibility. As I have argued, grassroots movements embody utopianism, not so much in the organizational alternative forms they invent but in the very fact that they dare to invent alternatives. This daring to imagine and practice alternatives itself relies on self-governance: the ability, through collective direct action, to reclaim control over the conditions of our existence. Of course, hope in better futures can feed on some dream of a *'deus ex machina'*; we can hope that some god, the state, mother nature, the 'revolution', liberal democracy or the forces of the market will come to our rescue in some big heroic way. However the hope in the benevolent power of such 'force' has a poor historical record, and represents another form of enslavement into a myth about the inevitability and omnipotence of something beyond ourselves. If utopianism is about establishing the conditions under which we can be free to decide our own affairs, we can develop alternatives, it is simply paradoxical to believe that this freedom can be achieved through centralized means, a gift of empowerment from above. This is a point that has long been made by anarchists: people can only free themselves through their own actions; they cannot be 'set free' by centralized solution (eg *An Anarchist FAQ Webpage*, 2001; Kropotkin, 1970).

The third argument has to do with effectiveness, and this is illustrated with Guattari's (2000) idea about resingularization against the homogenizing effects of what he calls 'Integrated World Capitalism' (IWC). If IWC operates by infiltrating all domains of our lives, from economic to social and cultural, it needs to be confronted in the everyday, in our personal, domestic and social lives. It needs to be opposed at the multiple points where it creates its effects, in all its ramifications, by getting hold of 'little events', 'singular points when they occur' (ibid.: 11). Guattari's argument about singular points is reminiscent of the 'rhizomatic action' he developed with Deleuze (Deleuze and Guattari, 1987)[21]. And as Blaug (1998) argues, such rhizomatic action seen in the spontaneous, self-organized, disparate coordinating attempts of grassroots movements can be very effective in defeating hierarchism, and in meeting local people's social and material needs. True, grassroots movements haven't changed the world; the successful lawsuit against the Grace corporation for biopiracy of the nem tree has not brought GATT, nor Grace, to its knees; the Zapatista movement is still fighting; the refusal of people in Papua New Guinea to sell off their collective land in order to repay the country's debt has not made the World Bank or the IMF crumble. But it has made a difference to those who have resisted, or are still fighting against, the corporate appropriation of their means of survival. And of course, there are also many things grassroots movements can't do: they cannot run states (Blaug, 1998), far less the 'global economy', nor produce standardized hamburgers around the world. But shouldn't this be to their credit? And shouldn't we ensure that grassroots movements remain ineffective at running states; that they remain small, spontaneous, disjointed, and do not congeal into the formation of another 'unified vision of a better future', another truth, policed by another leader?

And this is the fourth point, if utopianism is about avoiding the closing off of possibilities, it needs multiple breaking points for stirring things up, stopping the 'good life' hardening into forms of oppressive habits and totalitarian tendencies. It lives in the tension created by the juxtaposition of multiple possibilities; it lives in dissensus rather than in the search for consensus:

> Rather than looking for some stupefying and infantalizing consensus, it will be a question in the future of cultivating dissensus. (Guattari, 2000:50).

Dissensus, disunity, multiple points, far from diluting the strength of these grassroots movements stand as effective weapons against the seduction of closure, the snugness of comfort. The juxtaposition of disconnected grassroots alternatives serves as a reminder that any form of organizing has to establish itself against others, that there are always alternatives.

Fanciful middle-class dream?

By bringing together utopianism and grassroots movements, my intention has been to highlight the possibilities that tend to be effaced by much of organizational and political discourses and practices, to broaden the imagination of 'organization' (Parker, 2002b). By reading grassroots alternatives in terms of utopianism, I have tried to evoke their movement, the (out)rage and hope that move them to reclaim their history from reaching a 'dead end'. Reading these movements in terms of utopianism suggests that their significance lies well beyond the alternative organizational forms they create or the local situations they seek to transform; they stand as an emblem of possibility. By bringing grassroots alternatives practices within a discussion of utopianism, I also wanted to suggest that utopianism is not about some escapism, some fanciful middle class dream, but is eminently practicable, and in fact, at least for some, a matter of urgency. As Bookchin (1991) suggests, perhaps at no other time has the re-invention of possibilities been so crucial:

> If accounts of the 'poisoning of America' are even modestly accurate, utopian thinking today requires no apologies. Rarely has it been so crucial to stir the imagination into creating radically new alternatives to every aspect of daily life. Now, when imagination itself is becoming atrophied or is being absorbed by the mass media, utopian thinking may well be its most rejuvenating tonic. [. . .] Utopian dialogue in all its existentiality must infuse the abstractions of social theory. My concern is not with utopistic 'blueprints' (which can rigidify thinking as surely as more recent governmental plans) but with the dialogue itself as a public event. (Bookchin, 1991:334).

However, whilst utopianism may be about the possible rather than dreams, and may be practised by grassroots movements emerging from the most marginalized and disenfranchised to reclaim the conditions of their existence, there is no escaping the fact that those who write about them in the columns of *The Guardian*, in books, or academic publications tend to be middle class professionals whose career, if not fame, is built on these stories. This, of course, is not to say that we, middle-class professionals, are not genuinely concerned, but that we cannot avoid the fact that there is something highly hypocritical in denouncing a system of which we are the main beneficiaries, whilst claiming that such system is not inevitable. So I can no longer defer one of the discomforts that has troubled me throughout writing this chapter. If I am that bothered, can't I find more effective ways to express and act out my concerns, to 'cultivate possibilities', than write academic papers?

One answer is that we do our politics outside our jobs, so we may have feeble attempts at shopping at farmers' markets and boycott supermarket chains when we can spare the time, at growing a few vegetables; we may even get involved in some local initiatives for sustainable development. Another answer, not incompatible with the first, is that we bring our politics a bit more into our jobs, and this may mean changing the ways in which we do being 'academics'. Instead of just writing about grassroots alternatives, we could get involved in their development through action research, or by taking a more active role in shaping public discourse about the possibility of alternatives (Bennholdt-Thomsen and Mies, 1999). So writing papers could be seen as simply one of the forums through which we engage in public debate. Another channel for such debate could be through our teaching; we could teach 'organizing' to captive audiences of undergraduate and postgraduate students in a way that would trace the connections between organizational actions and the effects that are often effaced, we could also unsettle the inevitability of hierarchism and neoliberalism and point to organizational alternatives. No doubt some of us do this already.

We could engage in public debate with other audiences, not through parliamentary politics or 'government partnership' but by creating public spaces and channels through which ideas, possibilities and hopes can circulate. 'Intellectuals', if this is the grand label we want to apply to ourselves, have not always been isolated behind the walls of universities and academic conferences. The Left Book Club set up in Britain the 1930s is an interesting, if short-lived, historical example of academics trying, in some sense successfully, to spread ideas through the circulation of cheap books and pamphlets, and the creation of local spaces and clubs where ideas could be open to public debate (Laity, 2001). I am not suggesting that we start going to distribute and discuss our articles in inner-cities, but maybe that we could do more to address the concerns, or lack of concerns, of groups not sitting in lecture theatres.

Of course, all these suggestions about how we could use our academic positions to broaden the collective imagination of organizing constitute a rather convenient way of staying in our secure jobs, with a safe conscience. I could equally (and maybe more convincingly) argue against the value or effectiveness of any of the above. I won't spell out the counter-arguments for they have become all too familiar (something to do with hypocrisy, arrogance, naiveté, and worst of all curses, lack of reflexivity); and in the age of compulsory reflexivity, the counter-arguments are just as self-serving. And of course recognizing this is also self-serving, an additional loop on the loop . . .

But let's get out of this long rehearsed cycle of paralysis and self-indulgent torturing. It may be little comfort, but we have some choice in how we do 'academics', we can decide who we talk to, who we talk for, what we talk about . . . and of course, we could also chose to quit and cultivate other possibilities.

Acknowledgements

I would like to thank Yiannis Gabriel, Mihaela Kelemen, Martin Parker and Edward Wray-Bliss for their thoughtful and supportive comments on an earlier draft of this chapter.

Notes

1 The eclectic nature of grassroots movements and the impossibility to identify them with a single, unifying set of interests, has been stressed by many. For example Bennholdt-Thomsen and Mies (1999) argue that whilst the subsistence approach they want to advocate as an alternative to corporate liberalism has originated in women movements, it has come to embrace a wide range of groups and interests, from anarchist groups, ecological movements, organic farmers, consumer-producer associations, developmental movements, anti-nuclear movements. Similarly, Bond (2000) describes these movements under the label of 'new social movements', recognizing that such a label is used more for convenience than to indicate a particular political-ideological agenda. Starr (2000), in a sort of inventory of grassroots alternatives, is also at pain to show the wide ranging concerns, organizational forms and political agendas these movements represent.

2 There are already numerous publications documenting some of these grass roots movements (Bennholdt-Thomsen and Mies, 1999; Bond, 2000; Ekins, 1992, 1999; Rocheleau *et al.*, 1996) or attempting to map them out (Starr, 2000).

3 See for example Marge Piercy's (1979) *Women on the Edge of Time* in which the inhabitants of Mattapoisett, a utopian futuristic society, expose to Connie, a disenfranchised Mexican-American woman embodying all possible forms of abuse in contemporary society, the insanity of her time; for a more general discussion of the technique of estrangement in utopian science fiction, see Moylan, 1986.

4 This is not to say that theory, or the work of these 'intellectuals', is not of use in understanding how these devastating effects come about, or get effaced from view, as I will argue in the next section, but simply that invoking Marx, Foucault or Derrida adds little to the immediacy, urgency or horror of the scenes of human and environmental devastation described in the PASAR example.

5 'At a time when some have the audacity to neo-evangelise in the name of the ideal of a liberal democracy that has finally realized itself as the ideal of human history: never have violence, inequality, exclusion, famine, and thus economic oppression affected as many human beings in the history of the earth and of humanity. Instead of singing the advent of the ideal of liberal

democracy and of the capitalist market in the euphoria of the end of history, culminating in the 'end of ideologies' and of the end of the great emancipatory discourse, let us never neglect this obvious macroscopic fact, made up of numerable sites of suffering: no degree of progress allows one to ignore that never before, on absolute figures, never have so many men, women and children been subjugated, starved or exterminated on earth' (Derrida, 1994:85).

6 As will be discussed in the next section, the neoliberal economic school has invested enormous resources in ensuring that the world runs according to its rubric (George, 2000).

7 The World Bank itself reported that programmes of structural adjustments led to the increase in the number of people living in poverty (that is on less than $1 a day): from 1.1. billion in 1985 to 1.2 billion in 1998 and expected to raise to 1.3 million in 2000 (Bello, 2000).

8 The vicious circle of poverty and increasing dependence on corporations created by WB and IMF programmes of structural adjustment is may be best illustrated with reference to the agricultural sector and the so-called 'Green Revolution'. The 'Green revolution' was to transform agriculture from a subsistence to a cash earning, export oriented system, sustained by pesticides and high capital investment; However, it often amounted to little more than a market expansion programme for Northern agribusiness corporations further impoverishing small farmers (eg Khor, 1996; Ishii-Eiteman *et al.*, 2000):

'. . . the economic, social and cultural impacts of WB agricultural projects are often ruinous to the poorest farmers. Living on marginal lands, peasant farmers are rarely able to compete for long in the export or cash crop market. Unable to repay the costs of inputs provided by the WB, many fall deeper into debt or are forced to sell their land [. . .] The Bank financed over US$250 million in pesticide purchases between 1988 and 1995; all contracts signed between 1993 and 1995 went directly to foreign-owned pesticide companies in France, Germany, the United States, the United Kingdom and Japan. Meanwhile, farmers participating in these projects jeopardize their health and the ecological stability of their farming systems by using more pesticides.' (Ishii-Eiteman *et al.*, 2000:1–2)

9 As Agarwal (1992) reports in the case of India, the privatization and commercialization of common land and forest has meant that rural women have to travel further and further afield, as well as spend more and more of their day to collect the firewood on which domestic energy depends; the logging of privatized forests (to produce sports equipment for Western markets, for example) has also deprived these women of vital resources (such as medicinal or nutritional plants, trees and roots, common land for grazing, or growing crops); the drying up or pollution of water tables due to the increasing use of pesticides on 'cash crops' has produced a shortage of drinking water; the considerable displacement of rural population to make way for the construction of irrigation projects, dams or large scale deforestation has also severely disrupted the social support networks on which poor rural households depended for labour-sharing arrangements, or the exchange of food and other resources.

10 TRIPS allow corporations to patent knowledge on biological life forms, and monopolize the commercialization of such knowledge. For example, local farmers and population in India were dispossessed of their knowledge of the properties of nem tree, used for thousands of years by local population as a disinfectant and pesticide, by Tony Larson, an American 'researcher', who acquired the patent for all nem products and sold it to the W.R. Grace corporation. After this, Indians who wished to produce anything from nem had to pay a license fee to Larson and W.R. Grace. Whilst this case was fought successfully before the US patent office (BIJA, 1996; Shiva and Holla-Bhar, 1996), many other such acts of 'biopiracy' legalized by 'free trade regulations' have dispossessed small farmers from knowledge and means of survival (eg Bond, 2000; Shiva, 1997).

11 And, despite talk about decentralization, empowerment, network, flat organizations, and 'sharing knowledge' in contemporary management discourse, none of these supposedly 'revolutionary' organizational principles do much to undermine the hierarchism principle: thus whatever decentralization, empowerment, flattening may occur, it is only on terms decided from above.

12 As Derrida (1994) comments in relation of Fukuyama's thesis, there is a convenient slippage between empirical reality and regulatory ideal in the neo-liberal camp that is indeed self-

fulfilling and allows 'believers' to keep their faith. Switching to neoliberalism as a 'force', a regulatory ideal, that will take us to the yet-to-be-realized promised land acts as a convenient mechanism for absolving it from any responsibility for the atrocities committed in its name in the present:

'As he [Fukuyama] can't deny without ridicule all the violence, the injustice, the tyrannical or dictatorial manifestations of what he calls 'megalothymia' [. . .] as he must concede that they're raging in the capitalist world of imperfect liberal democracy [. . .] Fukuyama doesn't hesitate to slide one discourse under another – to the announcement of the 'good news' as fact [. . .] he substitutes the announcement of the good news as ideal.' (Derrida, 1994: 109).

13 For a list of the corporations behind the '20 worst cases of biopiracy', see the excellent website of the Rural Advancement Foundation International at *http://www.rafi.org/web/docus*.

14 It is difficult to sustain belief in the 'natural or inevitable' force of the market when we consider that the international organizations such as the IMF, the WTO and the WB which serve to shape and sustain the 'global market' have taken years of planning and efforts from the world major corporate and state powers (Korten, 1995; Starr, 2000). Indeed, if the WTO were about free trade and unleashing the 'natural forces of the market', it would not need 900 pages of rules (Starr, 2000); and if the World bank was about responding to the market, it wouldn't need to invest large amounts of effort in creating demands for its products in developing countries through various training programmes on the preparation of loans application (Korten, 1995).

15 Polanyi (1957) argued that 'the market' as understood in neoliberal economic theory is not a natural force imposing itself through 'inevitable laws' but is constructed, partly through economic theory itself. George (2000) documents how neoliberalism, from being a small and unpopular sect in post war period has grown into a 'major world religion'. Central to this increasing popularity is the vast resources and ideological work that neoliberal economists themselves have invested in selling their ideas, by 'creating a huge international network of foundations, institutes, research centres, publications, scholars, writers and public relations hacks to develop, package and push their doctrine relentlessly' (ibid: 29).

16 For illustrations of alternative ways of organizing practiced by grassroots movements, see for example Bennholdt-Thomsen and Mies (1999); Bond (2000), Ekins (1992); Mander and Goldsmith (1996), Starr (2000).

17 Indeed, as some anarchists have noted (eg Ward, 1990), it is ironic that terms such as 'self-help' or 'mutual aid' have so easily slipped into New Right (and New Left) vocabulary when they were once the cornerstones of radical political projects (eg the Spanish collectives, the Gandhian village republics, the Paris Commune).

18 The distancing involved in capitalist market exchange is well illustrated with the example of food. The food on a dinner place in the US will have travelled an average of 2000 miles and is 95% controlled by a few multinational corporations (Lehman and Krebs, 1996).

19 For example, in CSA, consumers provide advance yearly payment to farmers who can use such advance as investment to grow crops and provide consumers with a guaranteed share of the farm products over the year (Bennholdt-Thomsen and Mies, 1999; Imhoff, 1996; Norberg-Hodge, 1996). LETS schemes are another example of local exchange systems based on local 'currency' that can be used to exchange services between members (Dobson, 1993). And small businesses are setting up local bartering systems allowing them to trade their goods and services in exchange for products offered by other businesses in the bartering scheme (Jones, 2001).

20 Lucas (2001), a Green MEP trying to implement reform 'from the inside' of European Parliament, made a similar paradoxical move in a recent article in the *Guardian*. After providing a critique of the ways in which European policies are dictated by corporate interests lobbying in the corridors of Brussels, she ended with a manifesto for change through European parliamentary politics.

21 Here we have to bear in mind that although *Three Ecologies* was only translated into English in 2000, it was originally written in 1989.

References

Alvesson, M. and Deetz, S. (2000) *Doing Critical Management Research*. London: Sage.

An Anarchist FAQ Webpage (2001) Version 9.0. http://*www.anarchistfaq.org*.

Bahro, R. (1984) *From red to green*. London: Verso.

Bauman, Z. (1989) *Modernity and the Holocaust*. Cambridge: Polity.

Bello, W. (2000) *From Melbourne to Prague: the Struggle for a deglobalized world*. Talk delivered in demonstration against the World Economic Forum, Melbourne, 6–10 September (available at http://www.zmag.org/melbourne_to_prague.htm).

Bello, W. (1993) Global economic counter-revolution: the dynamics of impoverishment and marginalisation, in R. Hofrichter (ed) *Toxic Struggles: The Theory and Practice of Environmental Justice*: 197–298. Philadelphia: New Society.

Bello, W., Bullard, N. and Malhotra, K. (eds) (2000) *Global Finance: New Thinking on Regulating Speculative capital Markets*. London: Zed Books.

Bennholdt-Thomsen, V. and Mies, M. (1999) *The Subsistence Perspective: beyond the globalised economy*. London: Zed Books.

Blaug, R. (1998) The tyranny of the visible: Problems in the evaluation of anti-institutional radicalism, *Organization* 6(1): 33–56.

BIJA (1996) Intellectual Property Rights, Community rights and biodiversity, 15/16: 25.

Bond, P. (2000) Their Reforms and Ours, in W. Bello, N. Bullard and K. Malhotra (eds) *Global Finance: New Thinking on Regulating Speculative capital Markets*. 61–81. London: Zed Books.

Bookchin, M. (1991) *The Ecology of Freedom*. Montreal: Black Rose Books.

Bookchin, M. (1990) *Remaking society: Pathways to a green future*. Boston: South End Press.

Bookchin, M. (1971) *Post Scarcity Anarchism*. London: Wildwood House.

Burkeman, O. (2000) Howard's Way. *The Guardian, G2*, Friday October 20: 4–5.

Campbell, C. (1996) Out on the front line but still struggling for voice: women in rubber tappers' defence of the forest in Xapuri, Brazil, in D. Rocheleau, B. Thomas-Slayter and E. Wangari (eds) *Feminist Political Ecology: Global issues and local experiences*. London: Routledge.

Chiapas Revealed (2001) 'What is it that is different about the Zapatistas?' Issue 1: 1–24. http://flag.blackened.net/revolt/mexico/comment/andrew_diff_feb01.html.

Chomsky, N. (2000) Unsustainable non development. Znet, 30 May, *http://zmag.org/ZSustainers/Zdaily/2000-05/30chomsky.htm*.

De Angelis, M. (1999) Globalization, New Internationalism and the Zapatistas, *Capital and Class*, 70: 9–37.

Deleuze, G. and Guattari, F. (1987) *A Thousand Plateaus: Capitalism and Schizophrenia*, trans. B Massumi. Minneapolis: University of Minnesota Press.

Derrida, J. (1994) *Specters of Marx: the State of the Debt the Work of mourning and the New International*, trans. Peggy Kamuf. New York: Routledge.

Derrida, J. (1999) Hospitality, Justice and Responsibility, in R. Kearney and M. Dooley (eds) *Questioning Ethics*. London: Routledge.

Desmond, J. (1998) Marketing and moral indifference, in M. Parker (ed) *Ethics and Organizations*. 173–196. London: Sage.

Dickens, P. (1996) *Reconstructing Nature: Alienation, Emancipation and the Division of Labour*. London: Routledge.

Dobson, V.G. (1993) *Bringing the Economy Home from the Market*. Montreal: Black Rose Books.

Donahue, B. (1999) *Reclaiming the commons: community farms and forests in a New England town*. New Haven, Conn.: Yale University Press.

The Ecologist (2000) Special issue on 'Globalising Poverty', November.

The Ecologist (1993) Whose Common Future? Reclaiming the commons. London: Earthscan.

Ekins, P. (1992) *A New World Order: Grassroots Movements for Global Change*. London: Routledge.

Ehrenreich, B. and English, D. (1979) *For Her Own Good: 150 Years of the Experts' Advice to Women*. New York: Double Day.

Fournier, V. and Grey, C. (2000) At the critical moment: Conditions and prospects for critical management studies, *Human Relations*, 53 (10): 7–32.

Frankel, B. (1987) *The Post-Industrial Utopians*. Oxford: Blackwell.

Fukuyama, (1992) *The End of History and the Last Man*. New York: The Free Press.

Gabriel, Y. (2001) The state of critique in organizational theory, *Human Relations*, 54 (1): 23–29.

George, S. (2000) A short history of neoliberalism, in W. Bello, N. Bullard and K. Malhotra (eds) *Global Finance: New Thinking on Regulating Speculative capital Markets*: 27–35. London: Zed Books.

Goldsmith, E. (1996) The last word: family, community, democracy, in J. Mander and E. Goldsmith (eds) *The case against the global economy and for a return to the local*: 501–514. San Francisco: Sierra Club.

Guattari, F. (2000/1989) *Three ecologies*, trans. I. Pindar and P. Sutton. London: The Athlone Press.

Guerin, D. (ed) (1998) *No Gods, No Masters: An Anthology of Anarchism*. Edinburgh: AK Press.

Guttenplan D. (2001) The lessons we can learn from the 60s. *The Guardian Society*, Wednesday 29 August: 5.

Harvey, D. (2000) *Spaces of Hope*. Edinburgh: Edinburgh University Press.

Holloway, J. and Pelaez, E. (eds) (1998) *Zapatista! Re-inventing revolution in Mexico*. London: Pluto Press.

Imhof, D. (1996) Community Supported Agriculture: Farming with a Face on it, in J. Mander and E. Goldsmith (eds) *The Case against the global economy*: 425–433. San Fransicso: Sierra Book Club.

Inhetveen, H. (1998) Women Pioneers in Farming: A Gendered history of agricultural progress, *Sociologia Ruralis*, 38 (3): 265–284.

Irwin, A. (1995) *Citizen science: a study of people, expertise and sustainable development*. London: Routledge.

Ishii-Eiteman, M., Hamburger, J. and Tozun, N. (2000) Prague 2000 Issue Briefing, *Pesticide Action Network North America*, August (available at *www.bicusa.org*).

Jacques, R. (1996) *Manufacturing the Employee: Management knowledge from the 19th to the 21st centuries*. London: Sage.

Jones, C. (forthcoming) Jacques Derrida: Possibilities of deconstruction, in S. Linstead (ed) *Postmodern Organisation Theory*. London: Sage.

Jones, R. (2001) Coming up with the goods, *The Guardian*, Jobs and Money Section, Saturday 30th of June: 4.

Khor, M. (1996) Global economy and the third world, in J. Mander and E. Goldsmith (eds) *The case against the global economy and for a return to the local*: 47–59. San Francisco: Sierra Club.

Klein, N. (2000) *No Logo*. London: Harper Collins.

Korten, D. (1995) *When Corporations Rule the World*. West Hartford, CT: Kumarian Press.

Kropotkin, P. (1985a) *The Conquest of Bread*. Catania: Elephant Editions.

Kropotkin, P. (1985b) *Fields, Factories and Workshops Tomorrow*, ed. by C. Ward. London: Freedom Press.

Kropotkin, P. (1970) *Kropotkin's Revolutionary Pamphlets*, ed. By R.N. Baldwin. New York: Dover Press.

Kumar, K. (1993) The End of Socialism? The End of Utopia? The End of History?, in K. Kumar and S. Bann (eds) *Utopias and the New Millennium*: 63–80. London: Reaktion Books.

Laity, P. (2001) The left's ace of club, *The Guardian Saturday Review*, 7 July: 1–3.

Lefebvre, H. (1971) La commune: Derniere fete populaire. In J.A. Leith (ed) *Images de la Commune*: 33–45. Montreal: McGill-Queen's University Press.

Lehman, K. and Krebs, A. (1996) Control of the world's food supply, in J. Mander and E. Goldsmith (eds) *The case against the global economy and for a return to the local*: 122–130. San Francisco: Sierra Club.

Levitas, Ruth (1990) *The Concept of Utopia*. Hemel Hempstead: Allan.

Lucas, C. (2001) The heart bleeds. *The Guardian Society*, Wednesday 27 June: 8.

Malatesta, E. (1995) *The Anarchist Revolution*, ed. By R. Vernon Richards. London: Freedom Press.

Mander, J. and Goldsmith, E. (eds) (1996) *The case against the global economy and for a return to the local.* San Francisco: Sierra Club.

Marin, L. (1984) *Utopics: Spatial Play.* London: Macmillan.

Mehta, M. (1996) Our lives are no different from that of our buffaloes: agricultural change and gendered spaces in a central Himalayan valley, in D. Rocheleau, B. Thomas-Slayter and E. Wangari (eds) *Feminist Political Ecology: Global issues and local experiences.* London: Routledge.

Merchant, C. (1980) *The Death of Nature: Women, Ecology and the Scientific Revolution.* San Francisco: Harper and Row.

Mihevc, J. (1995) *The Market Tells them so: The World Bank and Economic Fundamentalism in Africa.* London: Zed Books.

Miller, V. *et al.* (1996) Feminist political and environmental justice: women's community activism in West Harlem, New York, in D. Rocheleau, B. Thomas-Slayter and E. Wangari (eds) *Feminist Political Ecology: Global issues and local experiences.* London: Routledge.

Monbiot, G. (2000) *Captive State: the corporate takeover of Britain.* London: Macmillan.

Monbiot, G. (2001) Market Enforcers, *The Guardian*, Tuesday 21 August: 15.

More, T. (1516/1965) *Utopia*, trans. P. Turner. Harmondsworth: Penguin Classics.

Moylan, P. (1986) *Demand the Impossible.* London: Methuen.

Norberg-Hodge, H. (1996) Shifting direction: from global dependence to local interdependence, in J. Mander and E. Goldsmith (eds) *The Case against the Global Economy.* San Francisco: Sierra Club.

Parker, M. (2002a) NoTheory: Review of N. Klein, No Logo, *Organization*, 9 (2).

Parker, M. (2002b) *Against Management.* Oxford: Polity.

Piercy, M. (1979) *Women on the Edge of Time.* London: The Women's Press.

Plant, J. (ed) (1989) *Healing the Wounds: The Promise of Ecofeminism.* Philadelphia: New Soc Publishers.

Polanyi, K. (1957) *The great transformation the political and economic origins of our time.* Boston: Beacon Press.

Pulido, L. (1996) *Environmentalism and Economic Justice.* Tucson: University of Arizona Press.

Rich, B. (2000) Still Waiting: the failure of reform at the World Bank, *The Ecologist*, November: 4–10.

Rocheleau, D., Thomas-Slayter, B. and Wangari, E. (eds) (1996) *Feminist Political Ecology: Global issues and local experiences.* London: Routledge.

Sargisson, L. (1996) *Contemporary Feminist Utopianism.* London: Routledge.

Seager, J. (1996) Hysterical housewives and other mad women: Grassroots environmental orginizing in the United States, in D. Rocheleau, B. Thomas-Slayter and E. Wangari (eds) *Feminist Political Ecology: Global issues and local experiences.* London: Routledge.

Shiva, V. (1997) *The Plunder of Nature and Knowledge.* South End Press.

Shiva, V. and Holla-Bhar, R. (1996) Piracy by patent: The case of the Neem Tree, in J. Mander and E. Goldsmith (eds) *The Case against the Global Economy.* San Francisco: Sierra Club.

Starr, A. (2000) *Naming the Enemy: Anti-Corporate Movements confront globalization.* London: Zed Books.

Sweetman, C. (1999) *Women, Land and Agriculture.* Oxford: Oxfam Publishing.

Thomas-Slayter B., Wangari, E. and Rocheleau D. (1996) Feminist Political Ecology, in D. Rocheleau, B. Thomas-Slayter and E. Wangari (eds) *Feminist Political Ecology: Global issues and local experiences.* London: Routledge.

Wangari, E. *et al.* (1996) Gendered visions for survival: semi-arid regions in Kenya, in D. Rocheleau, B. Thomas-Slayter and E. Wangari (eds) *Feminist Political Ecology: Global issues and local experiences.* London: Routledge.

Ward, C. (1990) *Talking Houses*, London: Freedom Press.

Ward, C. (1982) *Anarchy in Action*, 2nd ed. London: Freedom Press.

Woodall, P. (1994) The Global Economy, *The Economist*, 1 October.

Young, R. (1996) *Intercultural communication: Pragmatics, genealogy and deconstruction.* Clevedon: Multilingual Matters Ltd.

Utopia and the organizational imagination: eutopia

Martin Parker

When I was half way through the opening chapter in this book[1], I realized I was stuck. I had begun with pessimism, with a deep sense of despair at what was currently happening around me. Utopia was nowhere. The ruins of the World Trade Centre and then the ruins of Afghanistan provided the backdrop, but even in my sheltered world there was little to provide optimism. Novelists and film makers prefer dystopia and conspiracy. Market managerialism, not sky-scraping ambition, dominates everyday life and, simultaneously, the intellectual credibility of radical utopian thinking is deeply compromised by the ever-growing piles of pro-managerial futurology. Even the contemporary currents of social theory seem to be moving in more cautious directions. As much of this book testifies, small stories and tactical engagements are preferred to grand visions. Whether in the realms of theoretical abstraction or grant-driven policy application, the commonality is a withdrawal from vainglorious claims to be able to change the world. Hubris has had its nemesis, and we live after utopia.

But half way through that opening chapter, I wanted to change tone. I wanted to gradually convince the reader that all these reasons really made utopianism even more urgent than before. Thomas More's pun (whether intentional or not) was that utopia is both 'no-place' (*outopia*) and 'good-place' (*eutopia*). However, in order to turn the former into the latter I needed to find a way of convincing the reader, and myself, that this multitude of objections could be set aside. Normally, in essays of this kind, the technique would be to persuade with reason and rhetoric, backed up with supporting references. The objections would be taken one by one, and exposed as based on inadequate evidence or questionable assumptions. There would be some form of reasoning that would carefully lead the reader from one position to the other. That, after all, is what intellectual work is supposed to involve. However, at the point where I needed such arguments, I found myself unable to make that leap based on anything recognizably like academic logic. On the one hand, the grim realities of the present age demand to be thought about seriously, and do not invite easy solutions. On the other . . . On the other . . . So I had to start again, in a different way.

Utopianism, *eutopianism*, is a systematic investigation of alternative principles of organization. Most, if not all, fictional and actual utopias rely on a re-formulation of the principles of social order. They are in that sense organized, though often on different principles to the market managerial hegemony. Hence social experiments like New Lanark, the Oneida community, workplace and feminist co-operatives, religious orders and so on must re-articulate what it means to be a member of a particular organization (see, for example Lockwood, 1973; Sargisson, 1996). Explicit and implicit rules must be re-articulated, principles of management and hierarchy must be re-thought, the penalties and rewards for deviance and compliance need to be re-formulated and so on. It seems to me that we do not need metaphysics, statements about the eternal truths of human nature, inspiring but empty claims about freedom and autonomy, the principle of hope or the utopian horizon, to understand such matters. All that is required is that we are unhappy with the present state of affairs and prepared to acknowledge that there are always alternatives. History has not ended.

To put it simply, I do not believe that there is only one best way for human beings to do organization[2]. That sense of fate, of there being no reasonable alternative, is probably the most disabling assumption of all in terms of utopian experimentation. When organizing, as an open-ended and polymorphous collective project, gets reduced to market managerialism, then it might seem that there is nowhere else to turn. But I, and some others, do not believe that this is the case. Recognizing the historical and social specificity of contemporary forms of organizing is very important in this respect. For most of human history and in most cultures, organizing has been done without managers and markets as we now understand those terms. Why, then, should we assume that all these other organizational forms are now redundant or that the organizational assumptions that permeate contemporary life cannot be altered in ways that we have not yet imagined? In Yevgeny Zamyatin's scientifically managed dystopia *We* (composed in the Soviet Union of the 1920s) the ultimate victory of OneState is to be guaranteed by the Great Operation that eradicates the imagination. This operation will finally cure human beings of:

> . . . the worm that eats out black wrinkles on the brow. This is the fever that drives you to run farther and farther, even though that 'farther' begins in the place where happiness ends. This is the last barrier on the path to happiness. (1993:172)

In Zamyatin's Soviet Union, imagination was under threat from one best way Taylorism combined with the central planning of freedom. Now it is under threat from the conservative utopianism of market managerialism.

I need to expand on this a little, though. It is all very well to claim that more imagination is needed, but what kinds of organizing am I suggesting as alternatives? Following the line suggested by both Reedy and Fournier in this volume, I want to make some proposals, however unfashionably practical this may seem. Treat them, if you will, as beginnings and not endings, in Lightfoot and Lilley's sense of those terms (this volume). The first point to make here is something about scale. From Weber to contemporary anti-globalization protests, one of the common complaints has been that organizing is getting too big to be human (Korten, 1995, Monbiot, 2000). The gigantic size of administrative and corporate organization has several important consequences. First, such institutions have a great deal of power and influence which allows them to effectively side-step many formal and informal constraints on their activities. Second, their spatial dispersion and levels of hierarchy means that people who make decisions will rarely be confronted by their effects. Further, assumptions about economies of scale and the accelerating mobility of capital result in the destruction of smaller organizations and an increasingly homogenized set of choices.

For these reasons, opposing giganticism seems an obvious first step. Creating and protecting a range of small, local organizations might then provide meaningful alternatives. If organizing were performed on a smaller scale, local forms of formal and informal regulation and pressure would be more likely to have an effect on changing forms of behaviour which are deemed to be unde-sirable. In economic terms, it is more difficult to externalize your costs if this involves local firms doing damage to local resources, labour markets or reputa-tion. At the same time, if the regulatory power of gigantic states is no longer needed to counter the predatory instincts of big corporations, then state level forms of governance can themselves shrink and become more local. Genuine forms of regional autonomy, of subsidiarity, might then be a practical alterna-tive. This would, of course, entail some form of protectionism – a word that is now usually deployed to mean selfish insularity rather than defending people and practices that a particular community happens to care about. Protection of jobs, local organizations and markets, the built and natural environment and so on, would have to be re-legitimized as credible. The mythic naturalism of a market-led managerialism, that sweeps away inefficiencies in the name of con-sumers, needs to be exposed as a practice that effectively hollows out localities and benefits the powerful in the corporate centres.

But scale is not the only issue here, simply because there are also many other dimensions upon which organizing might be re-imagined. The most obvious example of this is the co-operative, which could potentially be a fairly large organizational form. Indeed, feminist and worker co-operatives are a small but significant feature of contemporary industrial capitalism. In an ideal co-op, all members would share in the profits and the risks, but no-one outside the co-op would be allowed to have shares. In its literal meaning, this means that the organization is a venture that must rely on the co-operation of all its members for its success. Co-operatives might have extended managerial hierarchies, elaborated divisions of labour, and engage in forms of production that other constituencies might find objectionable. Or they might be feminist, egalitarian and driven by a concern to avoid forms of exploitation. But this is not the point. What co-operatives can achieve is a collective organization that is ultimately responsible to its members, not to a faceless group of investors spread across the globe. This might make co-operatives locally responsible but it will certainly make them more democratic than present forms of managerialism.

This brings me on to potentially the most underdeveloped set of ideas. When organizational structure is discussed in the context of management, it is usually framed as a set of immutable imperatives or contingencies dependent on environmental constraints. So, as Grey and Garsten's chapter nicely illustrates, stable markets support machinic structures, whilst turbulent markets require organic structures, or some version of that argument. But this is to reduce the engineering of organizations to a remarkably narrow set of choices. It is simply assumed that managers will occupy the top of some form of hierarchy with significant diversities of status and reward, that there will be top-down communication, specific role definition, the separation of public and private domains and so on. But this is a very particular solution that reflects certain narrow assumptions about control, skill and rationality when there may be other solutions to organizing that have quite different consequences for the members of the organization. It might instead be proposed that we could understand, for example, Weber's 'ideal type' bureaucracy as a formulation of general problems that all complex organizations need to negotiate. Thus there needs to be some rules, some internal differentiation, some way of making decisions and so on. However, the practical way that these problems are negotiated is contingent on various circumstances and choices. These are best conceived of as problems that any organizer needs to address and not ready made solutions that any organization must adopt. There are alternatives but they are alternatives within limits of possibility.

One way of illustrating this is to argue that Weber has pointed to the importance of any organization having some kind of co-ordination mechanism. For any complex organization to function, it requires that one part of the organization ensures that the other parts are functioning in a way that is mutually supportive and meet the explicit goals of the organization. However, the usual resolution of this problem is the formulation of a hierarchy with the co-ordination mechanism at the apex. Yet there is no necessary structural reason why the co-ordinators should be given a higher status and reward position within the organization. Indeed, they could simply be seen as another part of the organization, no more or less functional or central than other parts. The same argument can be used for other parts of the bureaucratic model too. Specialization is undoubtedly a functional result of complexity, if an organization did not have specialized roles it would not be able to perform complex tasks. Yet the permanent association of particular persons to particular roles is not a logical consequence of this and neither is the assumption that some specialisms are more important than others. In addition, the assumptions that particular roles have to be carried out by one person, rather than a group, and that such roles are fixed and not negotiable, may also be unjustified. With regard to rules it is again taken as read that organizations need rules in order that they be constituted as 'organized'. Yet it does not follow from this that the rules are not periodically re-negotiable and contingent on the members' perceptions of the organization's central task.

So this still leaves a great many choices for imagining organizations that are not based on a market managerial model. These would be organizations that would recognize the 'functional imperatives' of complex organizing whilst refusing the definitions of the solution that have now become hegemonic. Thus there might be a form of limited task specialization that acknowledged areas of expertise but would not imply that only experts, professionals or managers have power over particular areas of the organization's activity. Specified roles could be replaced by negotiated allocations of personnel to cope with particular problems or opportunities. There would probably still need to be a centre which was responsible for strategic decision making and co-ordination but its power may be continually re-negotiated by the members of the organization. Promotion might be replaced by an agreement that a particular individual or group had certain skills that required them to take a certain position within the organization for a determined period. Any organization must depend on certain rules, such as the circulation of decision makers, but its members may choose to treat these as guides and not determinations – there might be no final appeal to the 'rulebook'. Debate about the organization's means could be just as important as debate over the organization's ends, with individual members having a genuine chance to influence the overall direction in ways that they felt were desirable. The continual encouragement of public debate about the nature of the organizing being done would therefore be necessary to ensure that members felt committed to all or part of its activities. In sum, and as I suggested in the opening chapter, it might be possible to treat organization as a verb rather than a noun, one in which assumptions about both means and ends are continually being renegotiated. This might help to prevent organizing from becoming too stratified, too reified, and hence work against the possibility that any one group might become dominant within a given organizational context. Playing with these structural descriptions seems both theoretically possible and, to my mind, politically attractive. The structural arrangements that pertain within a given organization could then be treated as ways of doing politics, and not merely attempts to re-engineer managerialism.

One of the interesting consequences of these experiments in organizational size, ownership and structure is that the clarity of the boundaries between work and leisure, the public and the private, production and consumption and so on, begins to look increasingly vague. If work is conceptualized as wage labour, and often labour that is fairly meaningless for those people who engage in it, then alternative organizational forms such as those I have described here can be seen as attempts to make work more meaningful. But, in case this sounds like another version of managerial humanism, we might need to expand what the word 'work' could mean. Work, however badly paid, alienating or destructive has often been articulated as a virtue in itself and has been counterposed to the dangers of idleness and sloth. But this is to strangle the meaning of the word to an unacceptable degree. If, along with the young Marx, work is instead seen as one of the ways in which human beings can be creative, and perhaps is an element of being part of co-operative organization, then it might be rescued from market managerialism. This might involve remembering and revitalizing older conjunctions of work and leisure. After all, there have been other times and places where work was part of a productive, creative, informal and perhaps even familial setting. Work, in other words, could be one of the ways in which we become human, and not just a job performed for money.

Finally then, what of management? Is this a word and associated set of concepts that can also be re-imagined and expanded in more emancipatory directions? This, it seems to me, is more difficult. As it is presently constituted, management is premised on separation of intellectual and practical labour. It is intimately tied up with a particular professionalization project, with certain ideas about expertise and personhood, as well as the huge legitimation industry associated with the business school, training centres, consultancy firms, magazine and book publishers and so on. Yet it is presented as if it were a neutral technology of organizing, often by borrowing its legitimacy from a version of science aimed at the systematic improvement of the human condition. But can management become simply another term for co-ordination? This would mean that those who engaged in co-ordination, a necessary function in complex organizing, did not recognize themselves (and were not recognized by others) as being in some way different in status from those that do other things. To be clear though, this is not a question of doing away with co-ordination, merely ridding ourselves of the assumption that managerialism is constitutive of organizing. It is not a question of who manages, of substituting bad management for good management, but a question of the construction of historically particular organizational forms. Organization, in the most general sense of patterning and arranging, is not necessarily managerial.

The point of these speculations (which I hope are not 'presumptions', as Grey and Garsten might have it, this volume) is simply to demonstrate that there are other ways of thinking about how human beings might organize themselves, and that these alternatives are all prefigured in utopian speculation. Indeed, it might be argued that it has been the marginalization of utopian fiction to a kind of genre study within literature that has effaced the very practical and organizational elements of this body of writing. All the utopias mentioned in the essays in this book are thought experiments which alter key organizational variables. Thomas More, for example, writes of alternative forms of democracy, the division of labour, social mobility, economics and exchange, law and morality, education, and surveillance – amongst many other matters[3] . Similar lists could be produced for Plato, Campanella, Bacon, Owen, Fourier, Cabet and so on. These are, amongst other things, books about organization. These are works that demonstrate – though trips to undiscovered islands, the moon, the centre of the earth, the past, the future and dreams – that there are many, many different ways in which organization can be imagined.

However, I can imagine that some readers might feel that I am reducing these texts to sets of principles in organizational design, and that this is far too limited an understanding. But this is only an important objection if matters of organizational design are seen as somehow outside the province of politics. Rather, I would argue that matters of organizational structure are politics made durable, a suggestion implicit in Law and Mol's chapter. The size and shape of the patterns and processes that constitute human beings in particular contexts are precisely the stuff of politics. That is why, all too often, early utopias took the fantastic form that they did. More's condemnation of, say, the poverty that resulted from the acts of enclosure had to be ventriloquized through his fictional travellers and prefaced with careful dissembling about the light hearted intentions of this trifling buffoonery[4]. The radicalism of the eutopia lies in its pointed alternatives to the present, and what else can these be but matters of organization?

Now this is not to say that this means that all utopias, or all the organizational alternatives that they present, are viable and valuable for the present times. Aspects of More's utopia now look very authoritarian – its attitude towards women, its penal code, its lack of personal liberty (Berneri, 1971:82). What might have seemed progressive in the England of Henry VIII now seems ascetic and violent. But this is to say no more than that utopias are written in a particular time and that they may not have travelled well. The possibility also exists, however, that they may bear some very serious examination and might be arguing the case for forms of organization that would be more desirable than those we experience at present. Not always, but sometimes, and sometimes is surely better than never.

In summary then, my argument here is one that is based on nothing else than impatience with the present[5]. Notwithstanding the images on my TV screen, the popularity of dystopianism, the hegemonic ideology of market managerialism, the pseudo-utopias of turbo-capitalism and the well intentioned caveats of the policy makers and social theorists, it still seems to me that there are many different ways of thinking about how human beings might organize themselves. These are, I suggest, matters that can be imagined and there are few better ways to see this imagination at work than in utopian fiction and (to a more limited extent) in utopian practice. Making this kind of argument does not involve any particular committment to a final utopian blueprint, to a solution that will result in a genuine end of history. I assume, along with everybody else in this volume, that such a position is neither likely nor desirable. Even the inhabitants of More's utopia were quite prepared to change their ideas if better ones came along, or so they claimed in their prayer (1965:128).

I began this book with the image of the burning ruins of the World Trade Centre, and the despair that seemed to follow. Given that starting point and along with Roy Stager Jacques, a principled and sensible pessimism seemed to set the tone for the opening chapter. In this chapter and in the way I have organized the essays in this book, I have attempted to put forward what I hope is a principled and sensible optimism. But there is no way of adjudicating between these two. They are, in a sense, no more than matters of temper. There is no compelling evidence that could persuade someone to hold to one position rather than another. The variety of positions and tempers found in this book will probably have attracted and repelled you in fairly equal measure. But that seems to indicate just how important these issues are, and the central tension which is constitutive of the concept of utopia. So the principal moral of my beginning and ending to this book is that we should not let this word become a historical curio, another term for futile speculations and idealistic dreaming. This is to let one particular ideology substitute itself for thought, and for matters of organization to be treated as settled. If utopia is nowhere, it is not dangerous, but if it is somewhere, it is potentially very dangerous indeed. Particularly to those people who would rather that it stayed in books.

Notes

1 An introductory essay which was going to be my only contribution to this volume.
2 The arguments below are expanded upon in Parker (2002).
3 In the 1965 edition of *Utopia* – democracy on pages 74 and 123, the division of labour on 75, 82, 106, mobility 78, economics 80, 85, surveillance 84, education 75, 77, 89,124, law and morality 106.
4 Though I accept Ackroyd's point in his chapter that More *may* have intended to satirise alternatives, and not to sponsor them, *Utopia* (as Ackroyd acknowledges) can now be read very differently. But then evaluating More's intentions is a matter that neither critics or dramatists can ever solve (see Paul Turner's introduction to the 1965 edition, or Robert Bolt's play *A Man for All Seasons*, 1995). In any case, it is not that important to my argument.
5 Which was also my motivation for putting this collection together, as well an earlier collection on *Ethics and Organizations* (1998) to which this is a kind of sequel.

References

Berneri, M. (1971) *Journey Through Utopia*. New York: Schocken.
Bolt, R. (1995) *A Man for All Seasons*. London: Methuen.
Korten, D. (1995) *When Corporations Rule the World*. West Hartford, CT: Kumarian Press.
Lockwood, M. (1973) 'The Experimental Utopia in America'. In F. Manuel (ed.) *Utopias and Utopian Thought*. Souvenir Press: London, 183–200.
Monbiot, G. (2000) *Captive State: The Corporate Takeover of Britain*. London: Macmillan.
More, T. (1965) *Utopia*. London: Penguin.
Parker, M. (ed.) (1998) *Ethics and Organizations*. London: Sage.
Parker, M. (2002) *Against Management*. Oxford: Polity.
Sargisson, L. (1996) *Contemporary Feminist Utopianism*. London: Routledge.
Zamyatin, Y. (1993) *We*. London: Penguin.

Notes on contributors

Stephen Ackroyd is Professor of organizational analysis in the Lancaster University School of Management. His main research interest, at the moment, is in change in the organization of the largest British firms, especially the sixty or more still involved in manufacture with a market capitalisation of more than a billion pounds. In the recent past he has researched small IT companies and business consultancies, as well as the changing organization of the public sector. However, he has also a long-standing interest in the philosophy, history and sociology of social science. His recent books include *Organizational Misbehaviour* (with Paul Thompson), *Realist Perspectives on Management and Organization* (edited with Steve Fleetwood) and *The Organization of Business*.

Gibson Burrell is Professor of Organizational Behaviour at the University of Warwick where he has been for 14 long, long years. Despite the subject matter of the chapter and occasional letters from the Vice Chancellor, the prospect of part-time gardening, early retirement or even a leaving gift of a sharp set of secateurs holds very little attraction for him.

Karen Dale is a Lecturer in Organizational Behaviour and Industrial Relations at Warwick University. She has published a number of articles in the areas of gender and equality, and the body and organization. Her book, *Anatomizing Embodiment and Organization Theory*, was published by Palgrave in 2001. Currently she is working with Gibson Burrell on a book on architecture, space and organization.

Valérie Fournier is Senior Lecturer in Organization Studies at Keele University. Her writing so far has been concerned with disciplinary practices, subjectivity and embodiment in organizations, and has been published in a range of sociological and organizational journals such as *Body & Society, Gender, Work & Organization, Organization* and *The Sociological Review*. Her growing commitment to exploring alternative forms of organizing has directed her interests towards anarchist theory, anti-capitalist protest movements, alternative medicine and women farmers' cooperatives.

Christina Garsten is Director of the Stockholm Centre for Organizational Research and Associate Professor of Social Anthropology at Stockholm University. She has been a Visiting Fellow at Stanford University, European University Institute, Leeds University and the Swedish Collegium for the Advanced Study of Social Sciences. Her research interests are in the anthropology of organizations and markets, with a particular eye on processes of globalization and the many facets of management of culture in organizations. She is the Chair of the Information Technology programme committee in the Humanities and Social Sciences section of the Swedish Research Council and a member of the editorial board of *Nordiske Organisasjonsstudier*.

Christopher Grey is Senior Lecturer in Organization Theory at the Judge Institute of Management, University of Cambridge. He has previously held posts at UMIST and Leeds University and is a Visiting Fellow at the Stockholm Centre for Organizational Research. He writes on professional socialization and identity; the sociology of management and management education and an alarming array of esoterica, this chapter being the latest example. He is Editor-in-Chief of *Management Learning*, a member of the DfES National Educational Research Forum, a member of the editorial board of *Reason in Practice* and a member of the Executive Committee of the American Academy of Management, MED Division.

Roy Stager Jacques (Roy Jacques in works authored prior to January, 2001), MBA. PhD, received his graduate degrees in Management at the University of Massachusetts, Amherst, MA, USA. He has taught undergraduate and postgraduate courses in the US and at the University of Otago, Dunedin, New Zealand. The main threads of his intellectual interests have been gender studies and the socio-historical origins of the discursive boundaries shaping the institutional relations that have coalesced as 'management.' He presently runs Ravenheart of Sedona, a coffee house he and his wife created in Sedona Arizona.

David Knights is Professor of Organizational Analysis and Head of the School of Management at Keele University. He is the editor of the journal *Gender, Work and Organization* and his most recent publications include: 'Autonomy-retentiveness! Problems and prospects for a post-humanist feminism' *Journal of Management Inquiry*, 9/2, 2000; 'Ain't Misbehavin'?: Opportunities for Resistance within Bureaucratic and Quality Management Innovations', *Sociology*, July, Vol. 34 No. 3, 2000 (with D. McCabe); Knights, D., Noble, F., Vurdubakis, T. and Willmott, H. (2001) 'Chasing Shadows: Control, Virtuality and the Production of Trust', *Organization Studies*, Volume 22. No. 2, pp. 311–336; *Management Lives; Power and Identity in Work Organization*, Sage Publications (with H. Willmott) and *The Re engineering Revolution: Critical Studies of Corporate Change*, Sage Publications (edited with H. Willmott). His recent research has focused on ICT and virtuality, call centres, and financial services education and social exclusion.

John Law is Professor of Sociology and Science Studies at Lancaster University. He works on technologies, materialities, spatialities, organizations, subjectivities and methods. His books include *The Method Assemblage* (Continuum, 2003), *Aircraft Stories* (Duke, 2002), and *Organizing Modernity* (Blackwell, 1994), and his co-edited books include *Complexities: Social Studies of Knowledge Practices* (Duke, 2002), *Actor Network Theory and After* (Blackwell, 1999), and *Machines, Agency and Desire* (TMV, 1998)

Geoff Lightfoot is Visiting Lecturer in Accounting and Enterprise in the Management Department at the University of Keele. His research interests include the use of Darwinist metaphors in management and accounting, as well as futures trading on capital markets. He recently co-edited *Science Fiction and Organization* (Routledge, 2001).

Simon Lilley is Senior Lecturer in Management Information and Organization in the Department of Management, Keele University. Simon previously taught at the Universities of Edinburgh, Glasgow and Lancaster and at the Manchester School of Management, UMIST. His research interests turn around the relationships between (human) agency, technology and performance, particularly with respect to a post-structural understanding of these terms. These concerns are reflected in his continuing focus on the use of information technologies in organizations and he currently researching the regulation and conduct of financial and commodity derivatives trading.

Annemarie Mol is Socrates Professor of Political Philosophy at the University of Twente. Her recent publications include *Differences in Medicine. Unraveling Practices, Techniques and Bodies* (edited with Marc Berg, Duke University Press, 1998) and *The Body Multiple. Ontology in Medical Practice* (Duke University Press, 2002). She is currently exploring the figure of the 'active patient' and developing the project of 'empirical philosophy'.

Rolland Munro is Professor of Organisation Theory and Director of the Centre for Social Theory and Technology at the University of Keele. He is currently writing a book on the Euro-American's social and cultural entanglement with technology, provisionally entitled *The Demanding Relationship*, to clarify ideas like motility, disposal, discretion and punctualising. His recent books include *Ideas of Difference*, co-edited with Kevin Hetherington (Blackwell, 1997) and *The Consumption of Mass*, co-edited with Nick Lee (Blackwell, 2001).

Martin Parker is reader in social and organizational theory in the Department of Management at the University of Keele. He holds degrees in anthropology and sociology from the Universities of Sussex, London and Staffordshire and previously taught sociology at Staffordshire. His writing is usually concerned with organizational theory and the sociology of culture but he engages in dilettante dabbling in anything else that catches his eye. His recent books are *Organizational Culture and Identity* (Sage, 2000), and *Against Manage-*

ment (Polity, 2002) as well as the co-edited *Science Fiction and Organization* (Routledge, 2001) and *The Age of Anxiety* (Blackwell, 2001).

Patrick Reedy is a lecturer in management in the Department of Management Studies at the University of York. Before this he spent many years as a manager in the Further Education sector, eventually deciding that teaching managers was a more enjoyable occupation than managing teachers. His research interests include management learning; managerial identity and critical management and organization studies.

Hugh Willmott is Diageo Professor of Management Studies at the University of Cambridge and a Visiting Professor at the Universities of Lund and Cranfield. He is currently working on a number of projects whose common theme is the changing organization and management of work. His books include *Critical Management Studies* (Sage,1992, co-edited), *Making Sense of Management: A Critical Introduction* (Sage, 1996, co-authored) and *Management Lives* (Sage, 1999, co-authored. Hugh has served on the editorial boards of a number of journals including *Administrative Science Quarterly*, *Organization*, *Organization Studies* and *Accounting, Organizations and Society*. Further details can be found on his homepage:
http://dspace.dial.pipex.com/town/close/hr22/hcwhome

Index